M000287045

OPERATION
COLOSSUS

OPERATION
COLOSSUS
THE FIRST
BRITISH AIRBORNE RAID
OF WORLD WAR II

LAWRENCE PATERSON

Foreword by
Major-General Adrian Freer

Greenhill Books

Operation Colossus
First published in 2020 by
Greenhill Books,
c/o Pen & Sword Books Ltd,
47 Church Street, Barnsley,
S. Yorkshire, S70 2AS

www.greenhillbooks.com
contact@greenhillbooks.com

ISBN: 978–1–78438–378–7

All rights reserved.
© Lawrence Paterson, 2020
Foreword by Adrian Freer © Greenhill Books, 2020

The right of Lawrence Paterson to be identified as author of this work
has been asserted in accordance with Section 77 of the
Copyrights Designs and Patents Act 1988.

CIP data records for this title are available from the British Library

Designed and typeset by Donald Sommerville

Printed and bound in the UK by TJ International Ltd, Padstow

Typeset in 10.3/14.7 pt ITC Giovanni

Frontispiece: Full-scale training drop with containers and men at Tatton Park.

Contents

	List of Plates and Maps	vii
	Glossary	ix
	Foreword *by Major-General Adrian Freer, OBE*	xiii
	Introduction and Acknowledgements	xvii
Chapter One	'We ought to have . . . 5,000 parachute troops'	1
Chapter Two	Training	33
Chapter Three	The Target	47
Chapter Four	Malta	75
Chapter Five	The Raid	91
Chapter Six	Manhunt	112
Chapter Seven	Aftermath	150
Chapter Eight	The Reckoning	192
Appendix	X Troop	220
	Notes	222
	Bibliography	230
	Index of X Troop Personnel	233
	General Index	235

Plates and Maps

Plates

A Whitley II over Tatton Park during parachute training.

Soviet paratroopers.

The débâcle of Dunkirk.

Bruce Williams, who crewed as a rear-gunner during Colossus.

Squadron Leader Louis Strange.

Lt.-Col. Charles Jackson, CO of No.2 (Parachute) Commando.

Gen. Dill inspects 11 SAS Battalion, December 1940.

Recruits training for jumping through the hole in a Whitley bomber.

The perch from which the Whitley 'pull off' method was used.

'Going through the hole' on a Whitley for real.

Italian internment on the Isle of Man.

Fortunato Picchi.

Raoul Lucovich, alias Ralph Henry Lucky. *(Dierdre Le Faye)*

'Tag' Pritchard, commanding officer of X Troop.

Wally Lashbrook with his DFC ribbon.

An artist's impression of the capture of Prince Olaf of Norway's car during the manoeuvres at Shrewton.

X Troop with a warrant officer instructor.

Flying Officer Adrian 'Warby' Warburton.

Corporal Ralph Chapman. *(Tony Chapman)*

A Whitley bomber dropping paratroopers.

Men of 11 SAS Battalion in January 1941.

X Troop before they left for Malta. *(Airborne Assault Museum)*

The photograph of the Tragino aqueduct used in planning the mission.

The nearest of the farmhouses to the aqueducts. (*Graham Fielder*)

The aqueduct over the Fosse della Cinestra.

A photo taken from Calitri, showing the Tragino aqueduct, Fosse della Cinestra aqueduct and the small bridge. (*Graham Fielder*)

Campo 78, Sulmona. (*ICRC, V-P-HIST-03491-08*)

X Troop men in their compound in Campo 78.
   (*Airborne Assault Museum*)

Members of X Troop at Campo di Lavoro 102 in 1942.
   (*Airborne Assault Museum*)

Fortunato Picchi's mugshot following capture

Roll call at Campo 78, Sulmona.

Oflag IX-A/Z, where Captain Lea ended the war.
   (*ICRC V-P-HIST-02284-52*)

Private James Parker in his Durham Light Infantry uniform.

Private Nicola Nastri after the war.

Christopher Gerald Lea photographed post-war.

Percy Clements in 1944.

Arthur Lawley in 1944–5.

'Tag' Pritchard and liberating Soviet troops, April 1945.

Anthony Deane-Drummond.

Maps

The Pugliese aqueduct system, 1941	page 49
Italy, with the target location and prisoner of war camps	93
The target area and drop zones	96
Attack force blocking positions	105

Glossary

Bersaglieri – Italian specialist light infantry.

Campo – Italian prisoner of war camp.

Carabinieri – Branch of the Italian armed forces tasked with domestic policing duties and, during the fascist years, suppression of opposition inside Italy.

Combined Operations Headquarters – British War Office department established in 1940 to harass Axis forces on the European continent by raids carried out by use of combined naval and army forces.

DZ – Drop Zone.

Guncotton – Nitrocellulose; highly flammable compound formed by nitrating cellulose (in this case cotton) through exposure to nitric acid. Suitable for blasting as a low order explosive (which does not 'detonate' like high explosive).

MI5 – British Directorate of Military Intelligence Section 5, Britain's domestic counter-intelligence and security agency.

MI9 – British Directorate of Military Intelligence Section 9, department of the War Office tasked with helping available European Resistance networks assist the escape of Allied airmen shot down over Europe.

MSVN – *Milizia Volontaria per la Sicurezza Nazionale*, better known as the 'Blackshirts' due to their uniform. The paramilitary wing of the Italian national Fascist Party.

Mentioned in Despatches – (MiD) a member of the armed forces mentioned in despatches is one whose name appears in an official report, detailing his or her meritorious conduct, written by a superior officer and sent to the high command.

Oflag – *Offizierslager*, German prisoner of war camp for officers, established by the German Army.

RAF – Royal Air Force.

RAFVR – Royal Air Force Volunteer Reserve.

RN – Royal Navy.

RNVR – Royal Navy Volunteer Reserve.

Regia Marina – Italian Navy.

SIM – *Servizio Informazioni Militare*, Italy's primary military intelligence agency.

SOE – Special Operations Executive, a wartime British organisation designed to conduct espionage, sabotage and reconnaissance in occupied Europe.

SIS – British Secret Intelligence Service, also known as MI6.

SS – Frequently used to apply to the *Schutzstaffel*, the Nazi paramilitary force that became a sprawling security apparatus with a separate combat arm. In most case within this book, however, it applies to 'Special Services', Britain's Commando troops.

Stalag – contraction of the German word *Stammlager* which itself is short for *Kriegsgefangenen-Mannschafts-Stammlager*: Prisoner of War Camp. '*Stalag Luft*' designates a camp operated by the Luftwaffe.

Statischute – parachute equipment operated by static line (attached to the aircraft interior) rather than by manually operated ripcord.

Glossary

Comparative Rank Table

British Army	Royal Air Force	Italian Army
Lieutenant-General	Air Marshal	Generale di Divisione
Major-General	Air Vice-Marshal	Generale di Brigata
Brigadier	Air Commodore	–
Colonel	Group Captain	Colonello
Lieutenant-Colonel	Wing Commander	Tenente Colonello
Major	Squadron Leader	Maggiore
Captain	Flight Lieutenant	Capitano
Lieutenant	Flying Officer	Tenente
2nd Lieutenant	Pilot Officer	Sottotenente
Warrant Officer I	Warrant Officer	Aiutante di Battaglia
Warrant Officer II	–	Maresciallo Maggiore
Staff Sergeant	Flight Sergeant	–
Sergeant	Sergeant	Sergente
Corporal	Corporal	Corporale
Lance-Corporal	Senior Aircraftman	–
Private/Sapper	Aircraftman	Soldato

Rank Distinctions

Substantive – fully paid and confirmed rank.

Temporary – usually granted for a specific task or mission with the holder having the authority (but not the pay or benefits) of that rank while occupying the specific position. Despite the name, temporary rank may be held for a considerable period of time.

War substantive – a temporarily confirmed rank held only for the duration of that war.

Foreword

Lawrence Paterson has written a lively and informed account of the earliest British parachute operation of WWII. Conceived during 1940 and executed in February 1941, Operation Colossus provided operational exposure of the parachute arm in its earliest incarnation. At its outset parachuting was considered a means of insertion to support raids against enemy targets, principally on mainland Europe under the auspices of Combined Operations and the fledgling commando forces. Indeed, Number 2 Commando was designated II SAS and those who undertook Operation Colossus were drawn from its ranks.

The book's early chapters provide a vivid account of the trials and tribulations of those charged with turning Churchill's broad direction for a corps of 5,000 parachute troops into reality. Parachuting and developing an airborne arm was not a priority for the RAF as it was perceived to divert resources away from the strategic bombing campaign. However, perseverance by the Army and RAF 'airborne pioneers' at the Central Landing Establishment at Ringway and Tatton Park, coupled with the rigorous field training undertaken at the commando school at Achnacarry and out to Knoydart to the west provided the impetus from which to select a small force to undertake a parachute insertion to attack the Tragino Aqueduct.

Operation Colossus was launched from Malta following pre-positioning of the raiding force from Mildenhall. At the time such a flight was, in itself, no mean feat and the Whitleys arrived in Malta packed to the gunnels with the raiding force and spare aircraft parts. The insertion, on the night of 10 February 1941, was not without its mishaps and a scattered drop mirrored subsequent divisional-size parachute insertions later in the war.

One of the strengths of Paterson's book is the detail with which he describes the level of cooperation between the RAF and the Army at the 'business end' to make the attack work. It is interesting to note, for example, that the senior airman for the insertion was Willie Tait who went on to command 617 (Dambuster) Squadron and finished the war as a highly decorated wing commander.

The effects of the raid itself, whilst it was successful, were soon repaired by the Italians. However, with the use of first-hand accounts, Paterson brings to life the significant challenges that were faced by the raiding party during its attempt to reach the Italian coast for extraction by an RN submarine. As it happened, all of the force were captured and imprisoned as POWs and there was no rendezvous with the RN, unlike a year later during the Bruneval Raid.

Thereafter Paterson concentrates on their experiences and the successful escape of Tony Deane-Drummond who was to be prominent during the Battle of Arnhem where he was, once again, to evade capture through a series of adventures. There is also tragedy and Paterson describes, sympathetically, the recruitment and commitment of an Italian SOE operative who accompanied the raiding force, Fortunato Picchi. Picchi was captured along with the rest of the raiders and his 'French' cover story was exposed under interrogation; he was executed for treason by the fascists.

Whilst the book's title is *Operation Colossus*, its strength is the detail it provides in describing the early days of Britain's airborne forces and in particular the substantial efforts of Major John Rock and Squadron Leader Louis Strange, representing khaki and light blue respectively. They were pioneers, and their efforts in circumventing the vagaries of military bureaucracy set the tone for the development of the UK's main wartime airborne formations, the 1st and 6th Airborne Divisions.

Operation Colossus did what it was supposed to do, albeit that was probably not known at the time. It established it was possible to land parachute troops with their equipment close to a chosen target. Thereafter, the parachute arm moved away from 'raiding' to form parachute battalions and parachute and airlanding (glider) brigades within an all-arms divisional construct.

However, what Colossus had also done was to demonstrate the value of rigorous and demanding training in producing airborne soldiers whose fortitude and resilience was to prove instrumental in setting the tone for airborne operations later in the war.

These same characteristics remain every bit as important today as they were then.

Adrian Freer

Introduction and Acknowledgements

The timing of this book was actually quite fortuitous. I had just recently moved to Puglia, southern Italy, when my publisher Michael Leventhal recommended that I write a book about Operation Colossus; this would be the first time I have written about the Allied forces. Not only is it a fascinating story full of truly interesting individuals, but the culminating events of this often-forgotten mission took place about two hours' drive from where I live. Indeed, I can see part of the aqueduct system that Colossus was designed to disrupt from the roof terrace on my house.

An important note to make is that the anglicised version of 'Puglia' is 'Apulia'. Unless the latter spelling is included within an official title, I have opted to use the Italian form 'Puglia' for this region; also, to Italians, if something is 'of the Puglia region' it is 'Pugliese'.

Operation Colossus remains somewhat legendary within the annals of Britain's airborne forces, though it has been frequently overlooked by all but the most serious aficionados of military history. The raid itself was a remarkable feat, especially considering the distances to be covered, logistical complications and – as we shall see – an almost stunning lack of planning by those not tasked with the attack itself. Its success or failure depended on a group of men using methods and equipment thus far untried by the British Army who were truly therefore 'guinea pigs' for those that would follow in their footsteps. There is already an existing book about this remarkable operation written by Raymond Foxall, published in 1983 and fittingly entitled *The Guinea Pigs*. Foxall, a former journalist and soldier who served during the Second World War, covers the details of the raid itself extremely well and frequently in the first person as he was able to speak with many who had taken part in Colossus, and who are sadly now no longer with us. He has adopted the story-telling method of recreating either actual, or figurative, conversations between the men involved in order to put across information about what occurred. I, on the other hand, have not. I feel that the best way for this book to sit alongside such works as Foxall's is to examine the documentary record, using quotes from the men involved where available (these are sadly quite scarce) and filling in the blanks wherever possible with secondary sources or 'drier' military primary source material. However, this has also resulted in a few discrepancies between what I have discovered from my sources and the particulars of events as written elsewhere. Where possible, I have highlighted these. Sadly, the lack of surviving men of X Troop, and dearth of Italian documentary material – either hard to find or difficult to verify – often does not prove the veracity of either account. So, we have to do the best with what we have available. Probably the most detailed accounts committed to paper were made by Anthony Deane-Drummond, then a humble lieutenant at the time of the raid, later retiring as a major-general. He wrote a book of his experiences called *Return Ticket* (later updated and renamed *Arrows of Fortune*) and I have also quoted several passages from his account as he tells the story as a man that was actually there. I like the immediacy of his writing and feel slightly churlish attempting needlessly to paraphrase his prose. I also thoroughly recommend the book to anybody interested in one of Britain's most accomplished paratroopers of all time.

With that in mind, I decided to approach the topic of Operation Colossus in a slightly wider sense than previously employed. The parachute drop of British troops in February 1941 was the culmination of a remarkable period of inventiveness and ingenuity undertaken by some of the most interesting characters of the British Army and Air Force in 1940. While the use of paratroopers had been solidly undertaken with dazzling success by the Wehrmacht – but would soon reach a crisis in May 1941 with the severe losses of their Cretan invasion – it was little more than an afterthought within the British military to that point. The sudden 'crash course' in learning that followed the decision to create a British parachute force was remarkable both for its highly driven and nonconformist personnel and its unorthodox methods. Many who were on the periphery of the attack itself played important roles in Colossus, and frequently went on to illustrious and remarkable military careers. The complexities of the formation of Britain's Commandos is necessary to the main narrative, as is its extension to the creation of a Special Air Service unit in 1940 which predates the formation of the 'real' Special Air Service as we know it: an unnecessary complication in nomenclature which it is also important to clarify as some names occur in both stories.

Therefore, the story of Operation Colossus extends both before and after the raid itself. Even once the mission itself was over, the fates and activities of many of these remarkable men deserve to be told, at least in overview, though some information has proven surprisingly difficult to unearth even through the extensive archives held by both national and military authorities.

For times within the book, where appropriate and recorded in official records, I have used the military twenty-four-hour clock. As most times given are British it is also interesting to note that between summer 1940 and 1947, the United Kingdom used British Summer Time (BST, one hour ahead of Greenwich Mean Time) during the winter months, and in summer months adopted BST+1. The government made this decision to support the war effort and later to counter the effect of rationing: extra evening daylight saved lighting fuel and gave time for civilians to return from work before the blackout began. If the time being used is civilian (or from a verbatim account written by military personnel) I have used the more familiar twelve-hour clock method, and it can be considered to adhere to whichever locality to which the text section refers.

*

I am deeply indebted to several people that have helped with material and support for this book but must single out some individuals who have been incredibly generous with their time and information. First, I'd like to thank Tony Chapman, son of Corporal Harry Ralph Chapman of X Troop. Tony generously provided information, personal glimpses and copies of photographs that had belonged to his late father.

I'm also grateful to Tony's nephew Ian Thomason for putting the two of us in touch. Many thanks must go to the writer and literary critic Deirdre Le Faye, the niece of X Troop member Flight Lieutenant Ralph Lucky, who had been something of a man of mystery. His identity was gradually unravelled by Deirdre who provided some absolutely fascinating insight into the man and his family – certainly worthy of their own book. I have also been very fortunate to be in touch with Fabiana Picchi, great-niece of Fortunato Picchi of the Special Operations Executive. She filled in many of the blanks in the story of Fortunato's family before during and after the war and was always ready with quick answers when I hit a roadblock in my research. Many thanks also to Orazio Tinelli, one of the good friends I have made here in Puglia, who helped with understanding the workings of the Carabinieri of which he is an officer. Many thanks to the extremely helpful Sam Stead at the Airborne Assault Museum, Imperial War Museum, Duxford, and its excellent website www.paradata.org.uk. Sam and his co-workers were always on hand to answer questions and help point me in the right direction when I got lost in the story. Thanks also to Graham Fielder for photographing the aqueduct.

I'd also like to thank, as always, my wife Anna who is still vainly trying to teach me Italian and puts up with endless stories about the latest research discovery I have made during the writing of this book. My mum Audrey 'Mumbles' Paterson and my 'kids' Megan and James are also always a source of inspiration to get on with things. As I am finishing this book on the third anniversary of Ian Kilmister's untimely death I would like to dedicate this book to him and also, with the utmost respect, to all the men who took part in the preparation and implementation of Operation Colossus.

Chapter One

'We ought to have . . . 5,000 parachute troops'

By February 1941 the ancient Italian town of Calitri had thus far been largely untouched by the war that had raged through northern Europe and the North African desert. Though young men from the hilltop town had joined the Royal Italian armed forces to fight, the reality of the conflict was distant and remote from everyday life, which continued much as it always had. Italy had been at war with the Allies since June 1940 and had experienced little success in any theatre of action apart from East Africa where British Somaliland had been successfully invaded during August 1940, though a British counter-attack from both neighbouring Sudan and Kenya had begun during January, presaging yet another military defeat for Mussolini's troops. An abortive attack on Egypt had resulted in Italian forces being hurled back to western Libya by a vastly outnumbered but highly motivated and well-led British and Commonwealth force. The fact that Mussolini had clearly overlooked during June 1940 was that Italy had entered the war militarily unprepared and with its population largely unenthusiastic about his alignment with Nazi Germany.

Calitri lies in the province of Avellino, of the southern Campania region, perched on an elevation that overlooks the Ofanto valley through which its namesake river flows. The area is characterised by rolling mountainous terrain and over a hundred small towns and villages scattered across the rural landscape, Calitri merely one of them in which life was largely unaltered by the war. Whitley and Wellington aircraft of RAF Bomber Command had thus far mounted scattered raids against such distant Italian targets as Milan and Turin, but not ventured into the southern heartland. The astoundingly successful British naval air raid on Taranto during November 1940 had also passed largely unremarked in Calitri save for those who had relatives serving in the Regia Marina. However, late on the night of 10 February 1941, the sound of low-flying bomber engines echoed around a valley unaccustomed to such noises, attracting the attention of what few people were still outdoors. War had finally come to Calitri as forty-one RAF aircrew and thirty-five paratroopers were about to mount the most audacious raid thus far conceived by Britain's Commando forces, and the first attack mounted by the fledgling British airborne force. Their target was a small aqueduct at the foot of the 1,326-metre extinct volcano Mount Vulture east of the Apennine mountain range. The aqueduct spanned the Tragino torrent, one of eleven tributaries that fed the Ofanto River, originating from a heavily wooded elevation to the south and temporarily swollen by melted snow. In an otherwise unremarkable spot, an extraordinary military achievement was about to take place. However, to understand the motivation of this ambitious operation we must first look at the background of Britain's Commandos and the airborne branch that initially grew from this stem before becoming its own elite part of the British Army.

By 6 June 1940 Britain had evacuated its troops from the French Channel coast as Germany's military forces began the final stages of their subjugation of France. Two days previously Operation Dynamo and the lifting of 338,226 men from mainland Europe's beaches and harbours had been completed, though a further 192,000 Allied personnel were still to be rescued from western French ports in Operation Aerial. Though the successful evacuation was indeed victorious in the face of heavy enemy opposition, there was no way to disguise the fact that the British Expeditionary Force had been defeated and Britain now faced the spectre of potential German invasion. Though the British European war effort was now completely defensive, Winston Churchill's unrelenting – and sometimes mis-guided – desire for offensive action against Wehrmacht troops in newly occupied French territory remained undiminished. During one of his unstoppable brainstorming sessions, a minute was dictated to his overworked secretary for despatch to Major-General Hastings 'Pug' Ismay:

Enterprises must be prepared, with specially-trained troops of the hunter class, who can develop a reign of terror down these [French] coasts, first of all on the 'butcher and bolt' policy . . . The passive resistance war, in which we have acquitted ourselves so well, must come to an end.[1]

Ismay held the offices of Secretary of the Chiefs of Staff Committee and Deputy Secretary of the War Cabinet, his role instrumental in linking the military and civilian leaderships of wartime Britain which had just suffered the humiliation of defeat by the Germans in both France and Norway. Though the war against Hitler's Third Reich had begun for Britain on 3 September 1939, until May 1940 the action had been somewhat distant and remote. Although the period was unfairly characterised as the 'Phoney War' due to the lack of ground combat, men of the British and Commonwealth forces had been fighting and dying both in the air and on and under the Atlantic Ocean and North Sea. However, the Phoney War became very real when the front lines established by the British Expeditionary Force in France and Belgium felt the full force of the Germans' military power with their spectacular invasion of the Low Countries and France. The attack began on 10 May and ended with the French armistice on the same day that Churchill sent his note to Ismay. British and Allied troops had also been fighting in Norway since 10 April until that country's surrender two months later. Only Britain, with its Commonwealth contingents and the European troops that had escaped from their homelands to its shores, remained as Germany's last opponent in western Europe.

The seeds of Churchill's 'Striking Companies', as he referred to them, had actually already been sown by Lieutenant-Colonel Dudley Clarke, military assistant to General Sir John Dill, Chief of the Imperial General Staff at the War Office. Clarke had been born in Johannesburg in 1899 and, inspired by childhood recollections of similar Boer forces that had fought the British as well as his own experience attempting to organise an effective response to the 1936 Arab uprising in Palestine, at the end of May 1940 he sketched out an idea for small amphibious raiding parties named after the Boer 'Commandos'. During a subsequent inspection of troops evacuated from Dunkirk, Clarke offered the suggestion to Dill on 5 June, its fortuitous timing leading to it being put into practice the following day in response to Churchill's demand. Clarke, under Brigadier Otto Lunde, was tasked with setting up a new department, MO9, and began to recruit soldiers for what would later become the British Commandos.

A fertile recruiting ground proved to be from within ten 'Independent Companies' that had previously been raised from volunteers from the Territorial Army by the resourceful Lieutenant-Colonel Colin McVean Gubbins, a veteran Military Cross winner of the First World War and major proponent of irregular warfare operations. The Independent Companies were originally intended for Gubbins's favoured guerrilla-style operations and first deployed in Norway during the fight against the invading Wehrmacht. Intended beforehand to support the Finns in their struggle against the Soviet invasion of their country, Finland's surrender on 12 March forestalled their deployment and elements led by Gubbins were instead involved in Norwegian action against German troops around Bodø, Mo and Mosjøen, Gubbins being awarded the DSO for that and his temporary command of 24th Infantry Brigade (Guards) during the fighting. However, the collapse of Allied forces in Norway saw the Independent Companies withdrawn and ultimately disbanded, though contingency planning for future raids on the Norwegian coast was still undertaken by the War Office's research department, MI(R).[2] As the call went out for volunteers for the new Commandos, those men from the Independent Companies who stepped forward were formed on 14 June into No. 11 Independent Company, with an establishment of twenty-five officers and 350 other ranks under the command of Major Ronnie Tod of the Argyll and Sutherland Highlanders. By that date Great Britain and its Allies had already found themselves pitted against a second major European power after Italy declared war on 10 June.

Less than two weeks before the final collapse of France – its Armistice was signed on 22 June – Italy had taken the fatal step of joining the conflict when Mussolini declared war on Britain. France, South Africa, New Zealand, Australia and Canada reciprocated during the course of the next day and Mussolini announced the declaration of war to an enthusiastic gathering of his public from the balcony of Rome's Palazzo Venezia, declaring the moment to be the 'hour of irrevocable destiny' against the western democracies. Awakened from his customary afternoon nap in London and informed of the new development, Winston Churchill reputedly said little except 'people who go to Italy to look at ruins won't have to go as far as Naples and Pompeii in the future.'[3]

Frequently seen as pure political opportunism – not least of all because of Mussolini's own statement that he only needed 'a few thousand dead so that I can sit at the peace conference as a man who has fought' – the move was not without what Rome considered some measure of Allied provocation. A British blockade on German coal imports to Italy had been established on 1 March 1940, Churchill's government being aware of Italy's meagre resources and attempting to bring Italian industry to a standstill. Meanwhile the Mediterranean fleets of Britain and France began working in combination, deploying their twelve to two superiority in capital ships over the Regia Marina. This directly threatened Italy's supply lines to its North African possessions and became a frequent theme of increasingly anti-British rhetoric flowing from Rome in the weeks leading to war. As early as 4 February 1939, Mussolini had declared in an address to a closed session of the Grand Council his opinion that the freedom of a country was proportional to the strength of its navy. Italy was a 'prisoner in the Mediterranean' he claimed. 'The bars of this prison are Corsica, Tunisia, Malta, Cyprus; the sentinels of this prison are Gibraltar and Suez.'[4]

Mussolini's increasing alignment with Nazi Germany, the so-called 'Rome–Berlin axis' foreshadowed the eventual opening of hostilities, though Italy still entered the war terribly ill-prepared. Though externally considered a genuine European power, Italy's economy was largely agricultural and throughout the country there remained high rates of illiteracy and poverty. Its military, though numerically strong, was equipped predominantly with obsolete weaponry and crippled by a lack of both fuel and raw materials with which to modernise. Though in many respects possessed of relatively sophisticated military doctrines, the Italian military was rendered almost completely useless by the inability to enact necessary changes to all three services on land, sea and in the air. Nonetheless, since his appointment as Prime Minister, Benito Mussolini had championed the cause of imperial expansion into a modern day African–Balkan empire controlled by his political will from Rome. It was to this end that Mussolini led his country into war on what appeared to be the prevailing side, despite previously attempting to give at least the illusion of being a voice of moderation and restraint on the diplomatic stage.

While Italy's initial military venture into France near the Mediterranean coast was swiftly checked, British troops attacked and captured Fort Capuzzo in the Italian colony of Libya, prompting Mussolini to order a hastily prepared attack on the British protectorate of Egypt. This, too, though initially successful, would lead to a débâcle the like of which was seldom seen during the Second World War as a counterattack begun in September 1940 by vastly outnumbered British and Commonwealth forces threw Italian troops back to the westernmost reaches of Libya.

However, the battles fought and won on the Libyan sands were small comfort to the citizens of Great Britain who came under increasing threat of invasion as the Luftwaffe was poised to begin its attempt to dominate the skies over the embattled island. At sea, large numbers of destroyers were held in home waters as invasion defence and the resultant slackening of convoy protection aided Karl Dönitz's U-boat campaign. On land, the British Army was in some disarray as it attempted to reconstruct units effectively disarmed by the retreat across the English Channel.

With Britain expelled from the European continent and unable to take the field with conventional arms against German forces, the call for volunteers for the 'Striking Companies' fell on productive ground, the companies that began forming soon being renamed 'Commandos'. Volunteers were requested 'for special service', the nature of which was not indicated but portrayed as 'independent mobile operations'. The letter that was posted out to all British units stated, however, that the men would not be asked to parachute unless they specifically volunteered for it – though this stipulation appears to have slipped through the cracks according to many veterans' recollection – and promised that an officer would privately interview every volunteer to assess their suitability and inform them of their likely duties. By this method, it was reasoned that any man had the opportunity to withdraw his application if he wished, after getting some idea of the service that would be expected of him. Furthermore, all volunteers were to be told that they were liable to be returned to their units at some point, at the discretion of their leaders, and could, in turn, request to be returned at the completion of any operation. The personnel were not originally expected to be continuously employed in special operations over long periods of time, and all kept their original unit designations with the addendum 'on attachment'.

Volunteers were expected to be engaged on fighting duties only, and all ranks would continue to wear their own uniform although a special distinguishing badge would probably be later attached. In general, the stated requirements for service in the Commandos were:

    a. Youth and physical fitness;
    b. Intelligence, self-reliance, and an independent frame of mind;
    c. Ability to swim;
    d. Immunity to seasickness.

Items c and d were found particularly essential in later Commando operations which took on a specifically marine aspect but were obviously less than relevant for the formation of an airborne unit. Additionally, each volunteer had to be a fully trained soldier and those able to drive motor vehicles were thought to be particularly valuable. Officers were expected to display 'personality, tactical ability and imagination'; while other ranks required a 'good standard of general intelligence and independence'. Each Commando was to consist of up to ten individual 'troops', each of two sub-sections totalling a planned establishment of fifty men. In total it was expected to have one captain, two subalterns, four sergeants, eight corporals, twelve lance-corporals and twenty-three privates. Each Commando's desired main characteristics were an ability to operate with twenty-four hours' notice, and the ability to achieve a mission goal by individual action in the event of becoming widely dispersed. Commando units were not heavily armed and therefore not expected to resist determined enemy attack or overcome prepared enemy defensive formations, but rather to use speed, personal ingenuity and dispersion to their advantage.

Except for trained staff officers, personnel of all arms were eligible, but this latitude soon proved to be too broad and was corrected after it was found that too high a proportion of skilled technicians were serving as infantrymen in the Commandos. In fact, so many outstanding men volunteered that some resistance to the Commando idea developed among unit commanders of the Army. As a result, it became necessary to obtain Commando personnel directly from training centres.

From the growing pool of volunteers, officers were selected to lead each new Commando unit, those men in turn given responsibility for the selection of Troop leaders. It was these more junior officers who were then tasked with interviewing and then selecting suitable men from the hundreds of volunteer NCOs and enlisted personnel. With no shortage of volunteers amongst servicemen keen to escape the dull routine of anti-invasion training within Great Britain, the selection process was highly successful and also allowed each individual unit to be given a certain 'identity' provided by the junior officers' selection criteria.

Amongst those who responded was Royal Artillery 2nd Lieutenant Tony Hibbert, one of the many lifted from the French beaches and an early volunteer.

> A yellow-green iridescent film covered the waters of the huge Bay of Dunkirk. Twenty ships sunk with their backs broken were still on fire in the foreground, and the flames of Dunkirk's massive oil tanks reflected downwards from the black clouds above into the sea of phosphorus below. The criss-crossing streams of multi-coloured tracer lit up the sky – ours reaching up to find the German planes, theirs descending to find us. There was an ear-drum-shattering constant thunder of aerial bombs and artillery shells and when they landed round us in the shallow water the fragments performed myriads of outspreading 'ducks and drakes' in lines of green and yellow fire as they touched the phosphorus. This was a Wagnerian setting of Götterdämmerung on a truly Olympian scale. I have never seen anything so beautiful and breath-taking in my life. My mother, a Wagner devotee, would have loved it, though possibly in a quieter setting at Glyndebourne with a bottle of champagne waiting on the lawn. But as an artist what a fantastic Turneresque painting she could have bequeathed us.

In the deep water we found an old Thames Tug, *Sun X*, waiting for us. How we cheered. None of our men had slept for four days and the moment they got on board they all went into a deep coma in spite of all the bombing; one of the bombs almost lifted the tug out of the water but not one of my men even turned over in his sleep. Eventually we reached Ramsgate and within minutes of disembarking the old *Sun* had turned around for another of her mercy runs, followed by our grateful cheers. With only one rail siding on the dock and with ships coming in almost every minute, the military police were herding the men like cattle regardless of rank or unit and were turning around these trains about one every five minutes . . .

In due course, we re-formed at Aberystwyth but since we had no weapons, there was little to do except march up and down the sea front. The only real compensation during this period was the arrival of the Chelsea School of Physical Training for Young Women which had been evacuated to Aberystwyth. These beautiful, healthy girls really kept us on our toes. But some of us were getting very fed up with being inactive and we started applying to join any unit that looked as if it might have some weapons and might get us back into the fight again. I volunteered for Number 2 Commando.[5]

On 9 June, the call for volunteers for 'special service' was officially issued, though there was, at first, no mention of parachute duties as a preliminary War Office investigation into that particular matter was incomplete at that point. Among those who answered the call was Robert Brimer Watson, a Geordie builder who had operated his own construction company near Northampton before joining up on 8 January 1940. Despite being thirty-one years old and in a protected occupation, Watson was determined to serve and enlisted in the Royal Engineers before stepping forward as soon as the call for 'special service' was made. Before long, he was at Ringway aerodrome near Manchester where he discovered that, to his surprise, he was going to become a paratrooper.

Though the parachute had been in existence in one form or another since the Renaissance period the military operational possibility of vertical envelopment was not made a reality until 1 November 1927 when the Italian Army made the first multiple parachute drop at Cinisello Airfield near Milan. Though the Italians had used parachutes to deploy individual agents behind Austrian lines during the First World War, this demonstration involved eleven men who had undertaken training at Centocelle airport in Rome since the previous May. With military staff duly impressed, a parachute school was soon opened at Castel Benito, near Tripoli, Libya, and Italy trained two Libyan battalions to be the core of its airborne forces.

However, it was the Soviet Union that initially truly grasped the potential of insertion by parachute of large infantry units. Indeed, invited German military observers witnessed a demonstration of a sizeable Soviet parachute drop in 1931 when the 1st Paratroop Landing Unit jumped successfully from lumbering transport aircraft during exercises. A second massed exercise open to foreign military observers took place at Kiev in 1935, during which 1,500 men and supporting equipment were successfully parachuted into 'action'. Among the assembled officers were British Major-General Archie Wavell, and the Luftwaffe's Oberst Kurt Student. Wavell, though no doubt impressed by scale of the display, was insufficiently moved to recommend that British forces examine the potential for airborne operations. Student, on the other hand, immediately recognised the latent possibilities of pursuing development of a German parachute arm, the Luftwaffe's *Fallschirmjäger* resulting from Student's ambitious drive to match the Red Army's achievement.

Though the Soviet Union became the first to drop paratroopers in combat when it deployed several small units near Petsamo in November 1939 during the Russo-Finnish War, it was the *Fallschirmjäger* who later sent shockwaves rippling across the world during 1940. Their first highly successful airborne assault took place at daybreak on 9 April, when ninety-six men were dropped on the Danish island of Masnedø, storming the barely manned coastal fortress and taking control of the Storstrøm Bridge in order to allow the advance of ground troops of the 198th Infantry Division. *Fallschirmjäger* operations were mounted in Denmark and Norway, but it was their use in the seizure of bridges in the Netherlands and the supposedly impregnable Belgian fort of Eben-Emael on 10 May that demonstrated beyond any doubt the capabilities of airborne troops, albeit thus far deployed in relatively small units.

In Westminster on 4 June 1940 the Member of Parliament for Aberdeen North, George Garro Jones, pressed the Secretary of State for War, Anthony Eden, on the issue of airborne troops in the House of Commons. During the course of a heated debate Eden evaded the question of whether British military planners had embarked on a course of establishing their own airborne forces like those so capably handled by Germany. Nonetheless, an internal memo within the War Office was generated that day, entitled 'Creation of a Parachute Corps':

> This idea has real possibilities at the present time. The objection will come from the R.A.F. e.g. provision of special equipment and troop-carrying aircraft. Will you make a short preliminary investigation into the possibilities of putting it into effect?[6]

The following day, perhaps galvanised by the exchange, which echoed sentiments that Churchill had harboured since the First World war regarding the efficacy of airborne soldiers, the Prime Minister despatched a lengthy note to Ismay on allocating Australian troops due in the United Kingdom to 'Strike Companies' including his first mention of an airborne unit of 'a scale equal to 5,000'. This initial wish crystallised into a more direct request written shortly thereafter:

> We ought to have a corps of at least 5,000 parachute troops, including a proportion of Australians, New Zealanders and Canadians, together with some trustworthy people from Norway and France. I see more difficulty in selecting and employing Danes, Dutch and Belgians. I hear something is being done already to form such a corps but only I believe on a very small scale. Advantage must be taken of the summer to train three forces, who can, none the less, play their part meanwhile as shock troops in home defences. Pray let me have a note from the War Office on the subject.[7]

The War Office subsequently formalised the overall Commando organisation on 20 June 1940 and simultaneously authorised the establishment of a parachute Commando of 500 men, but left room for expansion if required. Churchill's memorandum issued to Ismay two days later, on 22 June, confirmed the formation of Britain's first airborne unit, No 2. (Parachute) Commando, though the number of men that were instructed to be trained differed significantly from the War Office figure and would later become an annoyance to Churchill. This was illustrated on 6 August after the Chiefs of Staff informed Churchill that 500 men were at that time being trained as parachute troops. The Prime Minister's reply was simply a note written in the returned report's margin baldly stating, 'I said five thousand.'

Though the War Office had confirmed the new venture, it still regarded the role of the airborne soldier as essentially that of a Commando force, made up of small raiding parties capable of sabotage or perhaps airfield or port seizure. Churchill's ambition, on the other hand, was of a much larger scale; something to match or even surpass the German airborne establishment. However, offensively minded as always, Churchill had also championed the use of shock troops to be employed in any way that was possible to get to grips with the enemy, especially at Britain's darkest hours. He had become increasingly concerned in June 1940 that the decidedly defensive posture that Britain had been forced to adopt had the potential to undermine morale severely within the armed forces. On 25 June 1940 the Chief of the Imperial General Staff reported to the War Cabinet that:

> A Memorandum had been widely circulated emphasising the need for instilling the offensive spirit into all ranks. The morale of the Army had inevitably suffered as a result of the series of retreats which had been forced upon them through no fault of their own, and every effort was being made to bring morale up to the highest possible level.[8]

While the new Commando formations began training, 115 men of the existing No. 11 Company – formed from men who had volunteered from the now-disbanded Independent Companies – took part in the first hastily organised Commando raid of the war. Operation Collar took place on the night of 24/25 June and was intended to reconnoitre four Pas de Calais coastal locations and capture prisoners. The raid achieved only modest success with few enemy troops encountered: two German sentries were killed and the entire attacking force was successfully evacuated with only Lieutenant-Colonel Dudley Clarke lightly injured in the ear. This mission was followed on 14 July by Operation Ambassador in which Major Tod led 100 men of No. 11 Independent Company into action alongside forty men from the newly formed No. 3 Commando under the command of Lieutenant-Colonel John Durnford-Slater. This time the target was Guernsey and an attack on the captured island's newly established Luftwaffe airfield.

Unfortunately, the raid quickly devolved into a near fiasco, beset with equipment problems and faulty navigation, achieving none of its goals but losing four men captured from the attacking force as well as a pair of officers who had been landed on Guernsey in advance of the raid and ultimately forced to surrender after failing to rendezvous with the RAF rescue launches that had been detached to retrieve them.

The disastrous mission created an unexpected question mark over the future of Britain's Commando service, Churchill's fury at the 'silly fiasco' being freely expressed to his Army commanders. However, the lessons learned from the débâcle ultimately paid dividends. There were no more hurriedly concocted operations and as No. 11 Independent Company was disbanded and its men absorbed into the first twelve forming Commando units, training became more rigorous and structured. Two days after the raid, Admiral of the Fleet Sir Roger Keyes became Director of Combined Operations, with his headquarters responsible both for operational planning and the development of ideas and equipment with which to harass the enemy in any way possible. Keyes had planned and led the famous 1918 raids on the German submarine pens in the Belgian ports of Zeebrugge and Ostend during the previous war and was a vigorous and bold leader, the perfect man for the job of heading the Commando service. By autumn 1940, more than 2,000 men had volunteered for Commando training, spread between twelve separate Commandos and placed under the organisational umbrella of Brigadier J. C. Haydon's Special Service Brigade.

One of the new Special Service troops was Welshman Arthur 'Taff' Lawley, who had become a miner after leaving school but soon tired of life down the pit and opted instead to join the Army, serving with the South Wales Borderers in Egypt and Palestine during 1936. Following time spent on the Army reserve list and a period working for London Transport, he immediately volunteered for active service at the outbreak of war with Germany and joined the Royal Army Service Corps as a driving instructor. As soon as he heard the call for Special Service volunteers, the 35-year-old Lawley stepped forward and was accepted at his existing rank of sergeant for No. 2 Commando, consisting initially of two troops of men taken from Northern Command, and another two from Southern Command.

Lance-Corporal Harold Nelson Tomlin was another early recruit. He had joined the Army in October 1939, not long after the death of his first wife, and after training was posted as a sapper to the 21st Field Company, Royal Engineers, in which unit he soon became a veteran of the battle for France. Following his return to Britain, Tomlin quickly became bored by the routine of anti-invasion duties.

> After returning from Dunkirk, the Royal Engineers were involved in works. The defences around the coast had to be made stronger, so we were then . . . near Skegness on anti-paratroop patrol, two hours before dawn and two hours after dusk. And we used to sit in a coach waiting for [German] paratroopers to land. And then, presumably, they would ring us and let us know and we would be on our way to do whatever we had to do. I don't know if we were really in a regular unit because the Army was in a bit of a state after Dunkirk and I suppose they got all the R.E. to go to the coast and repair coastal defences and you were a sort of job lot.
>
> So we had to sit in this coach, thirty-two of us, And when you think of thirty-two people lighting up Woodbines and God knows what else at some unearthly hour of the morning . . . and then this thing came around from Mister Churchill asking for volunteers . . . for Special Services. Didn't say for what. And of course, when we went for them nobody had any idea it was for parachuting. Could have been Commandos of any description. [I volunteered] because I was fed up with sitting in that coach in the morning with those bloody cigarettes going all the time, and I could see no future in it. It's terrible to get up that early in the morning, two hours before dawn and then sit in the coach with everyone smoking all the

time. So, when that came round I put my name down for it and was fortunate to be one of the first to go.[9]

Though unaware of it at the time, Tomlin was posted to No. 2 Commando that had begun formation on 22 June, the same day that Winston Churchill promoted the idea of the creation of an airborne force. Second Lieutenant Anthony Deane-Drummond of the Royal Corps of Signals was also among those who answered the call for volunteers.

We all came back from Dunkirk on 3 June 1940 and were based in Lincolnshire awaiting the German invasion. The media hype at the time painted the evacuation as a great success. It skated over what had happened and that the superb but tiny British Army had been defeated and flung off the Continent. Naturally I was glad to have survived, but stories in the newspapers and on the radio rankled. It was time to do something more active. At about this period every Army unit was bombarded with letters asking for volunteers for special service or the Commandos. Commanding Officers were specifically instructed to send forward the names of all volunteers. But [Brigadier] Ambrose Pratt did not agree. He let it be known that he would first select those officers he thought suitable and who would then be allowed to volunteer. Fortunately, he chose me and two officers from the gunner regiments. We all went for the interview, but I was the only one to be accepted. Two days later, in July 1940, I joined No. 2 Commando, later called 11 Special Air Service Battalion, and later still to become 1st Parachute Battalion.[10]

Major John Frank Rock, Royal Engineers, had also recently returned from Dunkirk where he had been brigade major of the 11th Infantry Brigade (4th Infantry Division). Rock was summoned from his post in Scotland to the War Office in Whitehall and tasked with immediately taking charge of the Army's part of creating an airborne force. His instructions on exactly how he was to go about such a task were vague in the extreme and he later recorded in his personal diary: 'It was impossible to obtain information as to policy or task.'[11] Indeed, the sole practical guidance given to Rock seems to have been the supply of small items of captured German *Fallschirmjäger* uniform and equipment.

Born in 1905, the son of a naval surgeon killed in action during the First World War, Rock had been commissioned into the Royal Engineers in 1925. Posted for a period to Ceylon for construction work he also served as an instructor at the School of Engineering. By 1938 he had completed courses in mounted duties, anti-aircraft defence, air photography and small arms and was also a trained interpreter in four languages, including German. However, of parachuting and airborne operations, he had no experience whatsoever and not an inkling of where to begin. Fortunately, not only was Rock an energetic leader and possessed of clear thinking and determination, he was assisted by an equally dynamic personality in Captain Martin Lindsay. Born the same year as Rock to Scottish nobility and a military family, Lindsay was a former Army officer who had left the military after mounting a successful polar exploration expedition, to become a potential Conservative Party candidate for Parliament. Re-enlisting at the outbreak of war, he had served in a staff appointment during the Norwegian campaign due to his knowledge of Arctic conditions, for which he was Mentioned in Despatches.

The two army officers were posted to a new parachute training school that had been opened just two days previously by the Royal Air Force at Ringway Airfield, near Manchester.

However, although the Army command appeared relatively keen on the development of this new airborne force, albeit unsure of exactly how to do so, the Royal Air Force was distinctly not so. Prevailing Air Ministry prejudice against such a formation significantly hampered the airborne unit's growth rate, as the Director of Combined Operations had far less direct control over the development of parachute troops due to the fact that Ringway, and its parachute school, was directly subordinate to the Air Ministry and not the Army or Combined Operations. Earlier in June an urgent conference convened at the Air Ministry had agreed to the establishment of a parachute training centre but acknowledged that the RAF simply did not have the machines to mount an airborne transport operation of the scale demanded by Churchill. The RAF's emphasis was on the bombing of Germany and any diversion of potential bomber strength in lieu of dedicated transport aircraft was considered detrimental to the overall war effort. Furthermore, what resources there were for aircraft construction could not be justifiably side-tracked to the production of a suitable number of dedicated transport aircraft. In effect, the RAF was far more interested in the development of glider-borne infantry than parachutists. An unnamed RAF officer ruefully expressed the general lack of enthusiasm for the new parachute venture when he apparently stated that 'It will be necessary to cover in six months what the Germans have covered in six years.' Nonetheless a suitable venue for such training was required and had been quickly found. Manchester Corporation's Ringway civil airport had been taken over by the RAF during 1939 and the Station Commander, Wing Commander Joseph Blackford, was an officer of the RAF's Directorate of Military Co-operation. Ringway was chosen as the centre for the new training establishment, named the Central Landing School, perhaps the very name reflecting the Air Ministry's desire for glider training to become the primary thrust.

However, despite RAF reservations, the kind of British inter-service cooperation that would be required to bring Churchill's demands rapidly to fruition had actually already been long established and allowed the successful maintenance of Britain's far-flung imperial reaches. During 1936, a committee formed to revise the existing Combined Operations Manual had recommended the creation of the Inter-Service Training and Development Centre (ISTDC) to develop new techniques and equipment to enhance cooperation between the three services. Unfortunately, the ISTDC became focussed almost exclusively on amphibious operations to the detriment of both the Army and Royal Air Force, protests from the War Office and Air Ministry achieving little before the outbreak of hostilities with Germany.

The Royal Air Force despatched an equally impressive officer to oversee its part of the training requirements at Ringway. Royal Air Force Volunteer Reserve Pilot Officer Louis Strange, DSO, MC, DFC, was a First World War flying veteran who had exercised his inventiveness to the fullest extent during that conflict by modifying his reconnaissance aircraft to accommodate machine guns and bombs from the war's outset. He was able to mount the RFC's first tactical bombing mission against Courtrai railway station, for which he received the Military Cross. He was also a man of considerable skill and bravery as evidenced by the following incident that took place in 1915. Strange had adapted his Martinsyde S.1 scout plane to carry a Lewis gun mounted above the top wing. While attacking a German spotter aircraft on 10 May 1915 he was compelled to change ammunition drums on the Lewis gun and, to do so, was forced to stand in his cockpit. As soon as he was on his feet, he lost control of the aircraft, which flipped over and went into a flat spin. Strange was thrown from the cockpit and left hanging on to the ammunition drum as his only contact with the plummeting aircraft. As he later recalled: 'I kept on kicking upwards behind me until at last I got one foot and then the other hooked inside the cockpit. Somehow, I got the stick between my legs again, and jammed on full aileron and elevator; I do not know exactly what happened then, but the trick was done. The machine came over the right way up, and I fell off the top plane and into my seat with a bump.' He returned to base without further incident but was reprimanded by his Commanding Officer for 'unnecessary damage' to the aircraft's instrument panel and seat while attempting to get back into the cockpit. By the end of the First World War, Strange had been awarded both the Distinguished Flying Cross and the Distinguished Service Order alongside his Military Cross

At the outbreak of the Second World War, too old for a regular commission, on 18 April 1940 Strange returned to duty as a 48-year-old pilot officer in the Royal Air Force Volunteer Reserve and was posted to 24 Squadron, the only RAF transport and communication unit at that time. There he once again distinguished himself after being posted to Merville as Aerodrome Control Officer, tasked with saving as much equipment as possible before the German advance. A patched-up Hurricane, using cannibalised parts from two others and carrying no armament, was the last airworthy aircraft on the field as German troops approached in plain sight from the aerodrome control tower. Though unfamiliar with the aircraft, Strange took to its cockpit and lifted off for England where every machine would matter for the inevitable coming battle against the Luftwaffe. Forced to climb by heavy ground fire he then encountered Bf 109 fighters that gave chase,

Strange diving to treetop level and using all of his skills to keep ahead of them until he was over the Channel and within range of Royal Navy ships that provided covering fire. With the enemy fighters driven off, Strange took his damaged aircraft to RAF Manston and in doing so he added a bar to his Distinguished Flying Cross in the process.

The Air Ministry officially recognised the Parachute Training Centre as coming into being on 21 June, placed under the administrative control of 22 Group, but held under operational authority of the Director of Plans, the Air Ministry post held by Air Commodore John C. Slessor. He too harboured grave doubts about Churchill's intention to create an airborne arm, articulated in a letter dated 4 July 1940 to Lieutenant-General Alan Bourne, Adjutant-General of the Royal Marines and recently appointed to the post of 'Commander of Raiding Operations on Coasts in Enemy Occupation, and Adviser to the Chiefs of Staff on Combined Operations'.

> I am rather uneasy about the air side of the development of parachute troops and am afraid that if we are not careful it will be a case of more haste less speed. I am also afraid that if we try to go too fast, we may have unnecessary training casualties which will be a set back to the development of parachute units. The fact is that, until two or three weeks ago when the Prime Minister told us to develop five thousand parachute troops, we had, rightly or wrongly, not made any preparations, either in the sphere of aircraft or personnel, to raise any parachute troops at all. That may show lamentable lack of foresight on the part of the Air and General Staffs in the past, but we need not worry about that now. The point is that the development of what amounts to a completely new arm of the service, requiring a technique which we have never considered, material which we have never thought of providing, and special personnel whom we have never thought of training, is a thing that cannot be done in the twinkling of an eye.[12]

Nonetheless, preparations continued despite the doubts of officialdom. The aircraft establishment was to number six Whitley bombers, estimated to be capable of carrying up to twelve paratroopers and 1,000 pounds of additional equipment each. The reason for the

Air Ministry's conclusion that these were the 'only aircraft' suitable for the task remains unclear. Six RAF officers, commanded by Squadron Leader Donald Ross Shore, and sixty-six other ranks were posted to Ringway, but an additional request for an instructional staff of four sergeants and four corporals was refused. Louis Strange was also posted to Ringway on 23 June for 'parachuting duties' alongside six other pilots. Initially Strange had been despatched to tour the half-completed airport with its hangars and buildings still under construction at the behest of the Air Ministry to assess officially its readiness for training use.

Perhaps intuitively sensing that he was likely to be attached to the new training installation, Strange himself insisted to his superiors that he was too junior in rank to take charge of the establishment. However, the intended commanding officer of the school, Squadron Leader Shore, had somewhat ironically broken his leg in a test parachute jump at Henlow and was unable to take charge as required. Rapidly promoted to Squadron Leader (confirmed by 22 Group on 1 July), Strange instead took the post as commander of Ringway's Central Landing School and awaited the arrival of his Army counterpart, Major Rock, and the first detachment of troops arriving on 27 June.

> 'We know nothing about training parachutists,' admitted Louis Strange, whose initiative had by then promoted him to spokesman for the fliers.
>
> 'Neither do I,' said John Rock.
>
> The following day Louis borrowed a Leopard Moth from Wing Commander Nigel Norman, at the time commanding an Army Co-Operation Wing at Ringway and hurried to the Air Ministry via Hendon. He eventually managed to track down responsibility for the parachute training project to the Director of Combined Operations, whose Deputy (Air) was an old friend, Group Captain Bowman.[13]

Strange was familiar with the process of circumventing tiresome official procedure, much to the chagrin of his more hidebound superiors. When asked directly whether he believed that the Prime Minister's number of 5,000 trained parachutists could be reached within three months, he replied confidently that large-scale training could indeed be achieved if those in authority could provide quick policy decisions and equipment authorisation. He further asserted that he could begin training the first batch of 100 men at Ringway within a week if he was able to 'take decisions that might not be covered by RAF regulations'.

In the meantime, instructions were issued from the War Office to each of Britain's Home Commands to form nine letter-designated fifty-man troops between them. Furthermore, Southern Command was given the task of selecting a suitable commanding officer for No. 2 Commando and so, as men began to arrive at Ringway from their parent units, they were placed under the command of newly promoted Lieutenant-Colonel Charles 'Ivor' Jackson on 3 July.

Jackson appeared an unusual choice on the face of it, being a member of the Royal Tank Corps into which he had been commissioned as a lieutenant in 1925. However, he did have experience in aerial matters having been granted a temporary commission as a flying officer and seconded to the RAF for four years beginning in July 1927 after being posted to No. 2 Flying Training School at Digby. Upon completion of his flying training Jackson had then been posted to No. 4 (Army Co-operation) Squadron where he remained until 1931 and a return to the Royal Tank Corps. A second two-year secondment to the RAF began in July 1936 after he had been promoted to captain. During January 1940 he served with a tank demonstration unit of the 6th Royal Tank Regiment in Egypt before being posted back to Britain the following month. He was promoted on 1 February to major before being given command of No. 2 Commando with his final promotion to (temporary) lieutenant-colonel. However, at least one veteran of the early days of No. 2 Commando held an alternative view. According to Tony Hibbert, Jackson: 'should never ever have been appointed to that position. He was a tank officer and he had not succeeded in any of his appointments previously. And I think they just said, "for Christ's sake . . . what are we going to do with this old boy? We'll give him 2 Commando."'

Jackson's effectiveness as a commanding officer has received much critical reappraisal, particularly with the hindsight provided following his replacement in June 1941 by Major Eric Down, the new commanding officer being determined to convert what was considered by many within the traditionalist British Army as a somewhat maverick unit into an elite infantry formation. Training had largely revolved around small-scale Commando-type missions to that point, whereas Down's remit was the establishment of what would become the highly disciplined Airborne Division.[14]

Nonetheless, in mid-1940 under Jackson's leadership the first gathered units – B Troop, under Captain Bailey, and C Troop, under Captain Robert Parks-Smith, Royal Marines – who collectively had already undertaken ten days' training in map reading and initiative tests before travelling to the Cheshire town of Knutsford, south-west of Manchester and only five miles or so from Ringway's Central Landing School as the crow flies. The unit would soon consist of four Troops – A to D – and as there were no established barracks available for the sudden influx of men they were billeted in civilian houses in Knutsford. The Royal George Hotel on King Street served as the officers' mess, while Jackson established his headquarters next to a local fish and chip shop. There they prepared to begin training on 9 July in whatever rudimentary form Major Rock and Squadron Leader Strange had managed to create between them.

Despite being dropped in the deep end, the extent of Rock's clear-sightedness regarding his impending task is illustrated by minutes of a meeting held during June when issues regarding extra pay for airborne soldiers, the development of specialised jump clothing along patterns provided by captured German equipment, provision of gloves, anklets and 'jock straps' for personal jump protection, fully redesigned battledress trousers, provision of specialist parachute packers, and acquisition of ideally equipped aircraft were all raised by Rock even at that early stage. Meanwhile, nine men of the Army Physical Training Corps, led by Regimental Sergeant-Major Mansie, were brought in to Ringway to begin training the assembled volunteers, though none of the instructors possessed parachute experience.

The Air Ministry had accepted responsibility to design and provide parachutes and all launching accessories separately. As the man responsible for the actual parachute training, Strange had already deduced that the standard existing British pilot's parachute was too small for the requirements of a fully kitted soldier. The RAF had first adopted the parachute as basic pilot escape equipment in 1918, not long after the service had been born from the amalgamation of the Royal Flying Corps and Royal Naval Air Service, the eventual design of the canopy being settled at twenty-four feet in diameter. American parachute pioneer Leslie Irvin had initially provided twenty-eight-foot diameter parachutes, though these were thereafter relegated to training duties as they were considered too bulky in the cramped confines of an aircraft cockpit. It was these larger 'Irving chutes' that Strange considered viable for the use of No. 2 Commando and he personally travelled to the RAF's parachute training unit – the Parachute Development Flight – that had been formed in 1920 at Henlow, Bedfordshire to seek some out.[15] An Air Ministry memorandum dated 20 June stated that only eleven serviceable Irving chutes were available within the United Kingdom, as well as three repairable ones. While an order had been placed for 10,000 new parachutes – estimated to be available within two months if all other parachute type manufacture ceased, and five if it did not – Strange commandeered the entire stock at Henlow for use at Ringway. Furthermore, with the station commander's permission, he addressed the assembled staff and called for volunteers for the role of parachute instructors. Ten men from the team of safety-equipment and fabric workers came forward and were immediately transferred to Ringway to begin their new career as jumping instructors.

> 'Their names, which should never be lost to Air Force or Airborne history,' wrote Louis Strange who would thereafter hold these airmen in the highest esteem, 'are as follows: Terry Oakes, Paddy Gavin, Bill Pacey, Kim Campbell, Lofty Humphries, Frankie Chambers, Taff Roberts, Bill Walton, Paddy Wicklow, Harry Harwood.'[16]

Before long, Warrant Officer Bill Brereton was brought in from Henlow to take charge of the RAF jumping instructors. Strange also sought experienced parachute packers and enlisted professional parachutists who had inhabited the travelling air circus circuit that had gained popularity between the wars, notably Bruce Williams who had made aerial drops for the famous Cobham's Flying Circus and was already serving as a sergeant air gunner, and had survived the ditching of his Bolton Paul Defiant in the English Channel.[17] He was the first of three circus jumpers to join Strange, as recalled by another, Acting Pilot Officer Henry 'Harry' Ward:

> When war broke out in 1939, I put in for a commission and got it. In 1940, I went down to the Air Ministry and there was my old friend Leslie Hollinghurst. He had been made a Group Captain, and he told me they were opening a parachute school near Ringway, Manchester. Within a month I was there. I met up with my old Air Circus friends: Louis Strange was our CO, and our chief pilot on the Air Show, E. B. Fielding, was in charge of flying. Bruce Williams and Bill Hire, who used to parachute with me, completed the team. So, there were five of us, all from civil aviation. Nobody else knew anything about parachuting, and we didn't know much about the military. We were to train Army volunteers who were sent in batches, and we had to do it from three old Whitley bombers, which weren't ideal for the purpose![18]

While ground training of the Commandos began almost immediately, by 8 July the CLS core staff numbered eleven including Strange and Rock, and comprised an adjutant, intelligence officer, chief flying instructor and three pilots, chief and assistant chief landing instructors and a chief physical training instructor. This allowed Strange to delegate various responsibilities between them while he concentrated on drawing up an initial parachute training syllabus.

While awaiting the arrival of the modified Whitley bombers, jump training began on the ground using a range of improvised apparatus intended to simulate the effect of landing by parachute. Two of Ringway's hangars were commandeered for the purpose inside which rough aircraft replicas were constructed in order to familiarise the students with the techniques required both to emplane and to exit safely. Furthermore, to simulate the effects of a hard landing, early recruits simply jumped from the tailgate of a moving truck or from a raised platform, their descent from the latter brought to a sudden halt by means of an attached rope which quickly earned the platform the nickname of 'The Gallows'.

The Whitley aircraft themselves finally began to arrive, although only one had received any form of modification to allow the egress of paratroopers. Despite an Air Ministry conference of 10 June that had established that the Whitley would require modification by the fitting of a side door in the 'manner of the Junkers Ju 52' for parachutist use, one of the Whitleys had instead had its rear gun turret removed by the Parachute Development Flight; the Air Ministry cited the side-door concept as liable to weaken the aircraft's structural integrity. The new design required the jumper to crawl through the fuselage and stand in the empty gun cockpit, holding on to steel bars and facing forward with his back to the open air. Once the parachute ripcord was pulled, the billowing canopy would drag its wearer backwards clear of the aircraft. It was a hair-raising experience, and though Strange at first considered it the easiest way to introduce novices to parachuting, the terrifying effect that this method had on novice parachutists proved detrimental as well as being impractical for the rapid exit of multiple men.

Instead the retractable ventral 'dustbin' gun turret was removed leaving a circular hole in the fuselage through which men could drop feet first. Aircraftman Terry Oakes was the first to experience 'going through the hole' when Strange organised a practice drop at RAF Bassingbourn near Cambridge. Oakes landed on the station's fire tender, while the rest of the first load of parachutists managed to make landfall on, or at least near, the aerodrome. The system was a go.

Though not perfect, this method became *de rigeur* until the introduction of Dakota transport aircraft for parachute units. With five men seated on either side of the aperture the aircraft were capable of relatively quick exits. Each man's ripcord was attached to a strongpoint within the aircraft and the paratroops would fall with body erect and arms rigidly held at the sides in rapid succession through the thirty-inch-wide hole. However, the hole itself was nearly three feet deep and the drop was not simply a matter of slipping cleanly into mid-air from the aircraft.

> One of the difficulties of 'hole jumping' was to make a completely clean exit without touching the sides. If you pushed too hard, your face encountered the rear edge as you went out. If you slid out too gently, the parachute on your back bounced you off your side of the hole so that your face again met the far

side! Nor did the slipstream help, for as it acted first on the legs of the parachutist as he emerged from the aircraft; it tended to topple him over unless he went out perfectly straight. As may be imagined, there were quite a few bruised and bleeding faces walking about Knutsford and Ringway in those days, disfigured by what came to be called a 'Whitley kiss'.[19]

Corporal Harry Ralph Chapman – known throughout his life, and hereafter in these pages, as Ralph Chapman – later recounted to his son that one particularly tall member of the first batch of trainee parachutists seemed destined to hit his face every time he jumped.

The final piece of the jigsaw for Strange to find was a suitable dropping zone for parachute training. Ringway itself was a functioning air base and therefore unsuitable for extensive parachuting. Scanning an Ordnance Survey map of the immediate area revealed Tatton Park: 2,000 acres of landscaped deer park containing the mansion Tatton Hall, owned by Maurice Egerton, the 4th Baron Egerton. As fortune would have it, Maurice Egerton had been an aviator before his naval service in the First World War and was an acquaintance of Strange's. Lord Egerton readily agreed to Strange's direct proposal to use his land as a practice drop zone, and an official request passed to the Air Ministry on 7 July was approved the following day on the condition that the owner agreed and that there would be no financial cost to the Air Ministry. All other flying was prohibited within two miles of the park and planned anti-invasion measures such as the establishment of anti-glider obstructions cancelled.

The first dummy drops at Tatton Park using sandbags were made on 11 July, before a group of the RAF parachute instructors, and Strange himself, made their initial live drops two days later, the entire process being considered top secret and a carefully guarded exercise. In fact, the details of the drop were so secret that most of Manchester was there to watch after the local anti-aircraft defences had been informed, who had in turn informed the Observer Corps, who informed the Police and the Home Guard, who appear to have informed everybody for miles around. In total eight descents were made, two from the rear turret position using the 'pull off' method, and eight through the fuselage aperture. Fourteen more descents were made during the following day, including by six Army personnel including Rock. And with these inaugural jumps, the Central Landing School was considered fully operational.

Flight Lieutenant Denis Hornsey, DFC, of No. 78 Squadron was one of the pilots taking part in the parachute training drops.

> We did our 'live' dropping practice at Tatton Park. On the first day there was a 40-mph wind blowing and a consultation was held with the Army as to whether the exercise should go ahead. The leader of the detachment, a tough Scotsman with the rank of Major, expressed the view that a little wind would add reality to the proceedings. It did. The Major was dragged across a field by his parachute and through a pond, ending up in a hedge. His second-in-command lodged up in a tree, and one of his men struck a post with sufficient force to break two ribs and an ankle. Nothing daunted the Army who pronounced it 'a very good day' and, to our respect, turned up next morning in readiness for some more of the same punishment.[20]

Away from the growing pains of No. 2 Commando, events had already been put into motion which would have a direct bearing on Operation Colossus. At the outbreak of war, German and Austrian nationals resident in Britain were officially classed as enemy aliens. To assess each case, the British Home Office's 'Aliens Department' established internment tribunals throughout the country to examine some 70,000 registered aliens over the age of sixteen in order to divide them into one of three categories: Category A, to be interned; Category B, exempt from internment but subject to restrictions; and Category C, exempt from both internment and restrictions. By February 1940 the task was nearly complete with only 6,700 people classified Category B and 569 interned as Category A. Internment camps for the latter were set up across the UK, the largest on the Isle of Man, though others were dotted in and around Glasgow, Liverpool, Manchester, Bury, Huyton, Sutton Coldfield, London, Kempton Park, Lingfield, Seaton and Paignton.

However, by May 1940 with invasion fever at an all-time high in Great Britain, a further 7,000 alien residents in the southern parts of England were interned, regardless of their previously designated category. When Mussolini finally plunged his country into the war there were in the region of 19,000 Italians living in Great Britain. Orders were immediately issued to arrest approximately 4,100 Italian men aged between seventeen and sixty who had lived in Great Britain for less than twenty years and whose reliability was considered suspect, Churchill infamously ordering the authorities to 'Collar the lot!' Arrested under the Defence of the Realm Act Regulation 18b, they were held in detention without trial, the majority of them on the Isle of Man. Perhaps 700 of those interned were indeed committed fascists, but the rest included prominent Italian socialist leaders, many apolitical restaurant workers, and a number of Jews.

At 175 Sussex Gardens, a Georgian townhouse converted to boarding house on a leafy road in London's Paddington, police arrived to arrest Fortunato Picchi. An unassuming looking man, five-foot-tall and balding at the age of forty-three, Picchi had rented a room at the address from Florence Lantieri since his arrival in London from Italy in November 1921. Mrs Lantieri, English wife of an Italian resident, remembered him as a genial little man, whose two great passions were watching his beloved Arsenal football team play on a Saturday afternoon and walking his Alsatian dog Billy in Hyde Park. Picchi had been born in the small Tuscan village of Carmignano in August 1896, one of eleven children (two of whom died in infancy) to Giovacchino Ferdinando and Jacopina Pazzi Picchi, his father a textile worker who had passed away by the time of the Second World War. A veteran of the First World War, Fortunato had served as a *soldato* in the Italian 64th Infantry Regiment during its advance into Macedonia where he had been wounded and decorated for gallantry in action.

Following his demobilisation from the Army in 1919, Fortunato worked as a hotel porter, waiter, and junior chef before pursuit of more gainful employment led him to England in November 1921. His first job after arrival and settling in Sussex Gardens was at the Hyde Park Hotel in Knightsbridge, followed by a stint at the Ritz on Piccadilly, and the job of head waiter at London's Ambassador's Club off Regent Street. Following some trans-Atlantic voyages as a restaurant waiter on the White Star liner RMS *Majestic*, Picchi settled for a period as head waiter in banqueting at the Savoy Hotel on the

Strand. There he worked beneath Ettore Zavattoni, a man apparently rampantly pro-fascist and also later arrested by Special Branch along with Loreto Santarelli, the Savoy's restaurant manager, who had been under surveillance since 1935 as MI5 mistakenly believed he headed a fascist cell in London.[21] By then Picchi had already moved on. During September 1939 the Savoy had downsized its staff and Picchi had been among those to go, finding new employment as head waiter in Flemings Hotel, Mayfair, until his arrest. He spent the next six months in Douglas, Isle of Man, in what was dubbed the 'Palace Camp', consisting of thirty requisitioned seafront hotels and boarding houses surrounded by barbed wire and patrolled by armed British Army sentries.

When Mussolini's military venture in Egypt began to misfire badly, the British Chiefs of Staff became increasingly convinced that Italy was the 'soft underbelly' of the Axis, the Italian population being considered by British intelligence to be largely opposed to war on the side of Nazi Germany. They considered the Italians' psychology 'not suited for war' and felt that pressure applied in the right areas could possibly persuade the entire nation to abandon their support for the fascist regime and could potentially lead to Italy's withdrawal from the war entirely. Coupled with offensive operations on land in North and East Africa, and a highly successful aerial torpedo attack on the Italian fleet in Taranto during the night of 11/12 November, increasing attention was to be given by the newly established Special Operations Executive to clandestine operations within Italy. Indeed, in a memorandum entitled 'Subversive Activities in Relation to Strategy' dated 25 November 1940, the British Chiefs of Staffs Committee issued a directive to SOE that the 'elimination of Italy' from the Axis was to be of primary strategic importance.

Designed to conduct sabotage, espionage and reconnaissance in occupied Europe, the Special Operations Executive first came into being during July 1940 under the responsibility of Hugh Dalton, the Minister of Economic Warfare. This new organisation was created by the merger of three existing secret departments whose work frequently overlapped. Following the German annexation of Austria in 1938, the British Foreign Office had established a propaganda organisation known as Department E.H. (named after its London headquarters at

84 Moorgate, Electra House), funded by the SIS (Secret Intelligence Service) and run by Canadian newspaper magnate Sir Campbell Stuart. Later that same month, the SIS formed Section D, under Major Laurence Grand, RE, to 'plan, prepare and when necessary carry out sabotage and other clandestine operations, as opposed to the gathering of intelligence'.[22] Finally, in December of the same year, the War Office established a working group known as GS(R) under Lieutenant-Colonel Jo Holland, tasked with more military means of waging irregular warfare than the 'agent centric' work which concerned Section D. Renamed MI(R) in early 1939, on 16 October 1940 the office was formally abolished as the merger between all three services was complete and the Special Operation Executive emerged fully functional. Initially, SOE was divided into three broad sections: SO1, which dealt with propaganda; SO2 (Operations); and SO3 (Research).[23] While Grand and Holland both returned to regular Army posts, Holland's direct subordinate, Acting Brigadier Colin Gubbins – formerly of the Independent Companies – took charge as Director of Operations and Training, Special Operations Executive. He was largely responsible for SOE's subsequent success, remaining in command until the war's end.

Hugh Dalton, head of the service as Minister of Economic Warfare, had an intimate knowledge of Italy and Italians. He had served on the Italian front during the First World War as a lieutenant in the Royal Artillery manning siege guns during 1917 and 1918.[24] Between the wars he was a frequent visitor to Italy for diplomatic reasons, and met Mussolini in person during December 1932, a man whose initial dynamic impression generated great respect from Dalton. However, with Great Britain now at war with fascist Italy, Dalton threw his considerable energies into shaping strategies by which it could be defeated.

Guaranteed to ruffle the volatile Dalton's feathers was a letter from Henry Hopkinson (private secretary to the Permanent Under-Secretary of State for Foreign Affairs, Sir Alexander Cadogan) to Gladwyn Jebb, a close friend of Dalton's who in August 1940 had been appointed Chief Executive Officer of the Special Operations Executive. Hopkinson indelicately enquired as to exactly what activities SOE was coordinating in Italy now that the moment for the intensification of such activities seemed 'particularly favourable'. Passed down the chain of command, the brief answer which found its way to Dalton's desk was: nothing. There had been no recruiting of anti-fascist Italian nationals to SOE, no concerted effort at investigating espionage possibilities within the country and no sub-section appointed to do so within the near future. Furious, Dalton ordered an immediate concentration of ideas on how best to strike at Italy. It was somewhat fortuitous timing as only days later Churchill levelled the same inquiry at Dalton's office. The Minister was forced to conceded that little had thus far been achieved, though he was able to offer the idea of despatching future agents to the industrial north for potential sabotage missions.

> P.M. says, 'They will all be killed.' I say, 'No doubt, but if they can add only a little to the confusion and loss of morale, they will help us to a quicker victory.' ... We must by all means hit hard at Italy, I stir up much stink in S.O.2 [Operations Department] on this and order a conference for this afternoon. I am tired of excuses and obstruction. I will, if necessary, sack all the subordinates who are failing to do their job. This is a critical moment of the war. Italy is in the market.[25]

Hurriedly, SOE began to address the matter of acquiring Italian agents. Sir Roger Keyes provided extra impetus during December when he requested 'some good tough and reliable Italians' to accompany his Commandos on potential raids against Italian installations, initially looking perhaps to locate and free political prisoners incarcerated by Mussolini on offshore prison islands. However, Dalton was frustrated by an inability to obtain firm intelligence even regarding on which islands such fiercely anti-fascist men could be held. Instead, he despatched Lieutenant-Commander George Martelli, RNVR, to the Isle of Man for 'toughs and thugs' willing to join SOE. Martelli was an Italian-speaking journalist temporarily commissioned into the Royal Navy Volunteer Reserve and more recently engaged by the Foreign Office to provide intelligence sources for their newly formed Spanish, Portuguese and Italian sections. Though he discovered many anti-fascists amongst the internees, he was less able to locate sufficiently pro-Allied men willing to sign on to his cause:

Italy is still a black spot. Though we are combing all possible sources of supply, we have not [so] far been able (with one exception) to find Italians willing to risk going back home as our agents.[26]

That one exception was Fortunato Picchi.

Chapter Two

Training

The existence of the Central Landing School appears to have caused some measure of confusion among other service branches as to its actual purpose, evidenced not least of all by British military mail. One early recruit, Private Crane, received a letter for the 'Central Sunday School'. Even after the facility had expanded slightly and been renamed 'Central Landing Establishment' in September, mail still arrived for the 'Central Laundry Establishment'. While this may have provoked self-deprecating humour within the offices at Ringway, the task of transforming willing recruits into paratroopers had begun in earnest. Harry Tomlin was among the first wave of volunteers.

> My officers were Deane-Drummond, Christopher Lea and 'Tag' Pritchard. We used to call him 'Tag', but not in his hearing. They were a lively crew. I didn't realise what I'd gotten into until we started jumping. Why didn't they tell us at the beginning? Well, that's the Army, I guess.
>
> We jumped from a platform in the hangars. We had no crash helmets, nothing like that. It was the XI Battalion, Special Air Service, and that's all I can tell you really. They were ragtag and bobtail, from every walk of life. But they were good mates. We took things as they came.
>
> I felt like an old man at first! One night we went into Manchester and someone said, 'This is the bus we want' and of course it just glided past us. Well, to pick up and run with all your limbs aching and your body about to fall apart it's difficult ... and yet, after a fortnight you could have done anything. [Later] we used to climb Ben Nevis every morning for training, and the first one down got the next day off.[1]

From the outset of parachute training at Ringway, it became obvious that specialist protective headgear would be required. The standard British steel helmet was completely impractical and potentially hazardous due to its large rim. The men of No. 2 Commando were provided with leather RAF 'B Type' flying helmets in lieu of any specialised equipment, as even the rudimentary protective helmets of thick rubber, commonly referred to as 'Flash Gordons' due to their resemblance to costumes in the Buster Crabbe films, were some time in the future. After the 'Flash Gordon' would come the first standardised Parachutists' Training Helmet. Under an outer layer of a khaki material was a padded ring of thick rubber over a hardened inner; there were also cloth flaps that could be fastened under the chin. This type of helmet was commonly referred to as a 'Sorbo' after the name of the spongy rubber used.

On 27 July, Admiral Keyes made a brief inspection tour of Ringway to acquaint himself with the situation first hand and review the training regime that Rock and Strange had established as well as the suitability of their equipment. Though satisfied with the men and their officers, he was less enthusiastic about the RAF's stubborn refusal to change from Whitley bombers to a more suitable parachute aircraft:

> It is of the utmost importance that a more suitable plane than the Whitley bomber should be provided at once. After going into the matter with the RAF Officer on my Staff and the Officers Commanding the Training Staff and the troops at Ringway, and myself dropping through the hole in the bottom of a stationary Whitley plane, with a squad of parachutists, I am strongly of the opinion that the Whitley machines are thoroughly unsatisfactory.[2]

Nonetheless, training continued apace as confidence grew in the use of the parachutes. Once men had mastered the art of falling off a high platform onto mats, learning to bend their knees to absorb impact shock, they began jumping from the Whitleys, and occasionally also a Bristol Bombay transport aircraft on loan.

By 25 July a total of 145 jumps had been successfully made without major injury. On that Thursday morning a number of jumps had been completed over Tatton Park with the trainees being taken up in sticks of eight and dropped singly or in 'slow pairs'. One Whitley took to the air carrying an eight-man stick from C Troop, including Welshman Driver Ralph Evans, a volunteer from the Royal Army Service Corps. After Lance-Corporal Doug Jones, RE, had completed his drop, Evans launched himself through the hole in the Whitley's floor and plummeted to his death less than fifty yards from where Strange and Rock were observing from the ground because his parachute failed to deploy properly. The prearranged signal of a red flare arced skyward and all further drops were immediately cancelled, the Whitleys returning to land at what was now a subdued airfield.

The staff were unwilling to let the men of No. 2 Commando kick their heels at Ringway, so they were transferred to Scotland for intensive Commando training while an inquiry was held into the death of Driver Evans, examining any potential shortcomings in the training regime. Both Major Rock and Squadron Leader Strange criticised the use of Whitleys for the delivery of parachutists, Strange urging the type's immediate replacement by the Douglas DC-3, a purpose-designed civilian transport aircraft with a perfect side door exit. Despite Group Captain Geoffrey 'Beery' Bowman, Combined Operations Deputy, later arranging a visit by his commander Roger Keyes to discuss the CLS's most urgent requirements and providing a parachute demonstration with a borrowed DC-3, it would still be two years before the military version – the C-47, or Dakota – would become available to airborne forces. At that point in time the RAF acknowledged the presence of only five DC-3s in the United Kingdom, all belonging to the airline KLM and adapted for tropical use (and therefore more valuable on trans-African routes). A personal approach by Keyes to Churchill failed to break this procurement deadlock. Other aircraft were examined for suitability – particularly the Stirling bomber – but none passed the requirements and on 12 August the RAF's planning department took the opportunity to express a desire instead to move the impetus of training from parachute troops to glider-borne infantry.

> We are using Whitleys for training in the Central Landing School; but, of course, we have not yet got to the stage of bringing in the Whitley Group on the operational side because

the Commandos are not yet trained. Somewhat of an impasse has arisen over the Whitley, largely owing to a fatal accident at Ringway in which a soldier of No. 2 Commando was killed.

It must be admitted that the Whitley is far from ideal technically. The men have to leave the fuselage by a hole in the floor, which is an exceedingly unpleasant performance and has some dangers . . . We are proceeding with dropping training at Ringway with RAF personnel. But at present the Army have declined to continue drops with soldiers . . .

We are beginning to incline to the view that dropping troops from the air by parachute is a clumsy and obsolescent method and that there are far more important possibilities in gliders. The Germans made excellent use of their parachute troops in the Low Countries by exploiting surprise, and by virtue of the fact that they had practically no opposition. But it seems to us at least possible that this may be the last time that parachute troops are used on a serious scale in major operations.[3]

A deficiency had been found in the parachute design itself as it was determined that Driver Evans's canopy and suspension lines had become entangled due to the turbulent slipstream passing below the Whitley fuselage, preventing the parachute from opening. Both Rock and Strange summoned the expertise of their instructors as well as Raymond Quilter of the parachute manufacturing company GQ and representatives of the Irving parachute company. Quilter designed a brand new backpack for the Irving-type parachute in which the rigging lines of the parachute were withdrawn from the bag and fully extended before the canopy was pulled out by the air flow, the rip-cord being replaced by an integral static line connected to the interior of the aircraft, thus eliminating the need for manual deployment by the parachutist. Rapid testing was undertaken of what became known as the GQ X Type 'Statischute', which became the basic design used by British paratroopers for more than twenty years thereafter.

While this had been going on, No. 2 Commando were undergoing the most gruelling training regime that any of their number had experienced at the hands of Scottish instructors including some of the

Lovat Scouts, a British Army unit formed during the Boer War from men of the Scottish Highlands that subsequently developed into the first British sharpshooter unit during the First World War.

Simon Fraser, known as the 17th Lord Lovat and the 25th Chief of the Clan Fraser, was instrumental in establishing the training of the early Commandos:

> And we were lucky I think in Commandos because there were some very good early officers who were all imbued with this determination to take the war back to the enemy. They didn't like the idea of having to retrain on a barrack square and probably not be fit as combatants for a very long time to come . . . Nobody wanted to go on training, marching about on barrack squares, and having very limited facilities to carry out things which obviously could be done if one had boats and could fire off our weapons.
>
> So the Highlands suddenly became a very important area for training volunteers and the Commandos moved into the Western Highlands within a week of the fall of Dunkirk, and the evacuation of Norway, and I was one of the earlier people who was chosen as an instructor along with two or three other Scots Guards officers, including two brothers, David and Bill Stirling, who were my first cousins as it happened. And one of those cousins raised the SAS Regiment after having been an instructor at Lochailort. And we started a training centre at Lochailort which was called the Irregular Warfare School and requisitioned all the deer forests from Achnacarry right out to Knoydart in the far west, so we had 250,000 acres to train over, and we were given as much ammunition and high explosives as was needed for blowing things up and shooting at each other, and we really conducted a war of our own. And the ones that couldn't make it were given the sack and sent back to their regiments, but we did eventually come out as a pretty fine organisation consisting of twelve Commandos.[4]

The men from Ringway were attached to the Special Training Centre (STC) Tor Castle based within a restricted military area, near the castle at Achnacarry – the seat of Sir Donald Walter Cameron of Lochiel,

Chief of the Scottish Clan Cameron, who had already allowed No. 1 Independent Company to train on his grounds – which from 1942 would officially become the School for Irregular Warfare. A Combined Training Centre had already been established at Inverary and Special Training Centre at Lochailort in which other Commando units were learning the amphibious warfare techniques that would later become a hallmark of Commando operations.

Alongside Lord Lovat instructors included 'Mad Mike' Calvert, Spencer Chapman, Peter Kemp, and the Stirling brothers Bill and David; the last two later going on to be instrumental in the development of the Special Air Service in North Africa. Peter Kemp was already a veteran of the Spanish Civil War in which he had fought for Nationalist forces before returning to England severely wounded and decorated with the Spanish Cruz de Guerra and Bar. He would later be part of the Small Scale Raiding Force and SOE, ending the war with the Distinguished Service Order and Military Cross.

Two other formidable instructors were William Ewart Fairbairn and Eric Anthony Sykes, the former an ex-Royal Marine and both of them veterans of the Shanghai Police where they had been involved in hundreds of street fights with violent local gangs. The pair were experts at unarmed combat and were responsible for this aspect of training with the embryonic Commando units, teaching the men to kill by any means possible in a war without rules. The pair would also develop the double-edged Fairbairn–Sykes fighting knife that would later become associated most strongly with the British Commandos.

The training area was in extremely rough Highland terrain, the mountainous countryside reaching altitudes up to 4,000 feet and boasting the heaviest average rainfall in the British Isles. In such terrain it was possible to conduct training that required the greatest physical exertion. At this centre full recognition was given to the imperative need for physical efficiency in war. On many occasions, students were exposed to conditions in which the noise, extreme fatigue, and the mental strain of battle were simulated in a very realistic manner and such training tested the relation between fatigue and mental efficiency, for students were required to consider and render tactical decisions when the going was seemingly unbearable.

Practical and theoretical instruction in map reading was stressed, and both by day and by night map problems that required mountain craft and considerable physical exertion were worked out in the field. The average distance covered in these orienteering tasks was approximately forty miles during which the trainees had to contend with poor visibility, sleep in the rain, build fires with wet fuel, cross swift mountain streams, and move rapidly over exceedingly difficult terrain. In the early days of the training centre, some men unfamiliar with the terrain and training were lost in the Highlands for as many as three days before being recovered.

The use of ground and cover was taught practically in progressive stages. At first the students were required to move towards given objectives over terrain affording good cover. If they exposed themselves unnecessarily, this fact was brought to their attention by bawling NCO instructors in language which rapidly conveyed the latters' displeasure. In later training, the facilities for cover were rendered much more limited. In the middle stages of this work, blank cartridges were fired from an Enfield rifle when a student exposed himself unnecessarily while in the final stage, ball cartridges from rifles and Bren guns were fired so that the bullets fell three to five feet from such a student. This method produced excellent results, compelling the men to take cover naturally and quickly.

The trainees' ability to participate in offensive operations, after enduring hardships and forced marches through strange country at night, was tested in exercises of one to three days' duration, including practice of a rapid withdrawal. The men were taught to live on concentrated rations during these training missions, to take care of themselves in the field under all conditions of weather and climate, and to maintain themselves in a 'fighting condition'.

Instruction was given in firing single shots from the submachine gun while it was set for fully automatic operation; this was to conserve ammunition and yet have the gun immediately ready for fully automatic fire if necessary. Considerable time was also spent in teaching students to fire the rifle and Bren gun from the hip.

> We were based in a forbidden area, Tor Castle. No. 2 Commando was up there doing the boats and goodness knows

what else. There were a lot of mad sods. You know, you could go walking through the woods and all of a sudden, a bloody bullet would go zipping past your ear. And then there was a nice stream there with salmon in it and we used to drop a slab of guncotton in and then pick up half a dozen salmon, dead on the water. They were alright like that, they're just stunned. So, we had quite a good time there really. Fort William was the nearest railway station and when we came away the whole of Fort William turned out to wave us goodbye.[5]

Corporal Ralph Chapman, formerly of 267 Field Company, Royal Engineers, had volunteered for No. 2 Commando after weeks of preparing bridges in Northern Ireland and installations in England, including the Hull docks, for demolition in the event of German landings. Chapman had joined the Territorial Army on 1 May 1939 as he viewed war as inevitable given the rise of Germany's military. Though fascinated by aircraft and flying, he felt it unlikely that he would be able to qualify as a pilot in the RAF given his working-class Midlands background, and he had no affinity for the sea or the Navy at all, in his own words saying, 'the more the firma, the less the terra'. He was mobilised into the Royal Engineers on 2 September 1939. Chapman later recalled shooting deer during exercises in the Highlands and carrying the carcasses back to base so that the trainee Commandos could sell them to Woolworths in Fort William. Chapman also vividly remembered his training by Fairbairn and Sykes and recounted to his son years after the war a tale of losing a weapon (possibly a Lewis gun) overboard from a boat, each man of his section having to take it in turns to dive into the freezing cold loch to recover it. Whilst on holiday in Scotland in the early 1970s with his family he pointed out Lochailort House, saying 'I'm surprised it's still standing considering what we did to it!'

Among the men from Ringway who laboured in the Highlands, Anthony Deane-Drummond particularly prided himself on his athletic ability, challenging his men to race him to the bottom of Ben Nevis after one of their regular climbs to its peak and offering half a crown to anybody that could best him. Generally his money was safe, but on at least one occasion he lost his gamble, Harry Pexton making an all-out effort and beating Deane-Drummond on their last excursion to the Scottish mountain. However, the debt remained unpaid for seventy years, when, after Harry casually mentioned the event to Deane-Drummond's wife at an X Troop reunion in 2001, a card arrived in the post with a half-crown coin secured by a ribbon and the inscription: 'Harry. Better late than never! This silver half-crown is to commemorate the 70th Anniversary of Operation Colossus, Tragino, Italy. 10th February 1941.'

No. 2 Commando was returned to Knutsford and resumed their statischute training at Ringway on 14 August using Whitleys that had once again been cleared for use by the RAF. However, less than two weeks after the re-commencement of drop training a second fatal casualty was suffered when Nottingham-born Trooper Stanley Watts, one of the earliest volunteers, originally from the Royal Horse Guards, was killed in another training accident on 27 August. Jumping was once again suspended, albeit briefly, while that same day Raymond Quilter arrived to examine Watts's statischute, finding a fault in the way that the statischute was secured to the newly introduced back-pack. The solution was developed that day and within forty-eight hours the GQ Company had incorporated the new feature in its manufacturing process. Either unaware of the speed with which the fault had been rectified, or requiring independent corroboration, the War Office signalled Rock to cease all further parachute training until further notice, while Strange received Air Ministry orders to continue. At something of an impasse, the two officers decided on a course of action to enable jumping to resume: Strange placed Rock temporarily under arrest, and training continued.

On 6 September the Central Landing School, now under the command of Group Captain Leslie Gordon 'Stiffy' Harvey, was expanded to become the Central Landing Establishment, boasting a parachute dropping capacity of forty men each week and now comprising three separate sections: Parachute Training Section, under the command of Louis Strange, Glider Training Section, commanded by Squadron Leader Tim Hervey (who had been an airman and Strange's fitter in France during 1915), and Technical Development Section, commanded by Wing Commander Geoffrey Mungo Buxton, a pre-war gliding pioneer. The energetic Wing Commander Sir Nigel

Norman, Officer Commanding No 110 Wing, Ringway, was appointed deputy to Harvey and threw himself into the task of helping prepare Britain's airborne troops.

While Strange and his immediate subordinate and chief instructor, Squadron Leader Jack Benham, created the first training manual for the airborne phase of a paratroopers' deployment, Rock perfected tactical procedures for the troops' ground combat once they had landed, and continued to refine the equipment with which they would operate. Further Army officers also arrived at Ringway: Major John Lander, formerly of the Royal Corps of Signals, taking charge of the selection and modification of weapons and ammunition suitable for dropping alongside the troops, while Captain Bill Brandish of the Royal Irish Fusiliers began instructing infantry tactics.[6]

Training now expanded to include jumping at night using techniques developed by Flight Lieutenant Earl B. Fielden, a former circus flier with parachuting experience. The sensation of parachuting at night proved an entirely new adventure for the men of No. 2 Commando. During one such night drop a trainee was alarmed to see himself drifting towards what appeared to be a crater beneath him, probably caused by one of the increasingly numerous German air raids in the area. Adjusting his trajectory, he was momentarily terrified to see the crater move along with him until he realised that it was the shadow of his own parachute cast by the strong moonlight.

This intense instruction continued apace to the end of 1940, though not without further fatal incident. On 19 November, 25-year-old Corporal Hugh John Carter, a volunteer from 4th Battalion, The Monmouthshire Regiment, became the third training death at Ringway when he fell to earth with an unopened statischute. An immediate investigation discovered that the snap hook at the end of his static line had caught on the edge of the jumping hole in the Whitley floor and been forced open, leaving the statischute unattached as he jumped. Wing Commander Buxton's Technical Development Unit designed and tested a modification to prevent a recurrence and a safety pin was fitted to all static line hooks to prevent the jaws accidentally opening.

Two days after Carter's tragic death, No. 2 Commando was officially redesignated as 11 Special Air Service (SAS) Battalion and a new No. 2 Commando formed from fresh volunteers. Prior to its redesignation the original four troops had been expanded to 450 all ranks mustered in ten separate troops. The rejection rate of volunteers remained understandably high due to refusals to jump, injury or disciplinary matters. If a man refused to jump during training, there was no consequence to him or his service record, other than immediate return to his parent unit. However, once he had qualified with five jumps, and earned the coveted paratrooper wings, such a refusal would be a court-martial offence.[7]

The battalion, remaining under the command of Lieutenant-Colonel Jackson, comprised a Headquarters, Parachute Wing and Glider Wing. However, some confusion remains over the official title of the unit. The commonly used – and generally accepted – '11' is actually a misnomer as the original designation was intended as 'II' in roman numerals, indicating its relationship to the former No. 2 Commando. For clarity's sake, I will continue to use the nomenclature '11 SAS Battalion'. The term Special Air Service is also misunderstood, merely being an airborne derivative of the Commando's 'Special Service' (SS) units. This SAS battalion that was formed on 21 November bears no relation to the famous Special Air Service created by David Stirling in North Africa during 1941, though there is a rather obvious intertwining of the roots that formed both units, the trained mountaineer Stirling having been an instructor in the Highlands during No. 2 Commando's training sessions.

On 3 December thirty-two men of 11 SAS mounted their first demonstration jump as part of fully fledged military manoeuvres before an assembly of officers and dignitaries near the Wiltshire town of Shrewton on Salisbury Plain. The British V Corps was mounting exercises with 1st Armoured Division and 4th Division for three days beginning on the night of 1 December in the area Dorking–Winchester–Salisbury–Cadnam (Hampshire). A 'defending' force of General Auchinleck's Southern Command acting as Germans held the canal between Marlborough and Hungerford which 1st Armoured Division was ordered to seize. Air co-operation was provided to both sides by Lysanders and V Corps commander, acting Lieutenant-General Bernard Montgomery, specifically requested that parachutists drop behind the 'defenders' at West Down near Shrewton.

The parachutists divided into two separate groups of sixteen, each subdivided in half once again. Second in command of 11 SAS Battalion Major Trevor Allan Gordon Pritchard led the first, A Troop, landing east of Pewsey with the objective of securing five crossings over the canal by speed and surprise. Pritchard, son of Major Philip Allan Raymond Pritchard of the Bengal Police and formerly of the Royal Welch Fusiliers had been made temporary major since volunteering for No. 2 Commando. Pritchard – known as 'Tag' to his men when out of earshot and by his fellow officers when within – was a highly popular and effective leader – tall, athletic and dynamic. Anthony Deane-Drummond later described him:

> 'Tag' Pritchard was a regular soldier; he had got out of running a transit camp (hotel keeping he always used to call it) in order to go on active service by volunteering to parachute. In fact, he was rather heavy for a parachutist, having been a good heavyweight boxer in his younger days. In spite of a rather gruff and inarticulate manner, there could not have been a more likeable or a more loyal commanding officer.[8]

The second group of sixteen, designated B Troop, was led by Captain Peter Cleasby-Thompson and contained the parachutist's heavy weapons. Their brief was to move with 'all speed and cover' to seize Shrewton's bridge using 'guerrilla tactics'. Louis Strange flew the leading Whitley for the exercise and the drop itself went without incident.

> A small party from No. 2 (Parachute) Commando came from Ringway to Salisbury and 'sticks' of officers and men of 'A' 'B' 'C' and 'D' troops dropped soon after dawn one morning. As we approached the DZ we could see a vast array of cars and spectators through 'the hole'. The drop was uneventful, the landing 'comic opera'.
>
> As a seething mass of red-tabbed officers pounced on each of the parachutists on landing, shooting questions which varied from the sublime to the ridiculous, reorganisation on the DZ was not particularly easy. However, we eventually left the DZ, followed by squads of spectators.

> The umpires met us, and battle commenced. One party was told they were under heavy fire from a bren-carrier; when the NCO asked, quite reasonably, where the fire was, the umpire parted a mass of spectators, ten files deep, to reveal the said carrier. And so it went on . . .[9]

As the airborne soldiers retrieved weapons from the canisters that had been dropped beside them (designed by Buxton's Technical Branch) they moved as planned towards the target village of Shrewton. Cleasby-Thompson and the heavily burdened men of B Troop chanced upon a large limousine and immediately commandeered it at gunpoint from its startled sergeant driver. The hapless man was ordered to carry as many men as possible into the village, slipping past sentries guarding the bridge over the River Till in the process. A truck was also seized, and the remaining men carried hidden beneath the tarpaulin covering its back to join in successfully taking and holding Shrewton. The audacity of the airborne attack impressed the high-ranking observers, including Prince Olaf of Norway, whose car Cleasby-Thompson had stolen. The limousine was duly returned to the Prince outside the Plume of Feathers inn from where Prince Olaf bought B Troop's Corporal Derry Fletcher and Lance-Corporal Harry Pexton, standing guard over the vehicle, a pint of beer each.

One of the men who distinguished himself that day was Sergeant Percy Priestly Clements. Clements had enlisted in the Leicestershire Regiment in August 1928, serving with 2nd Battalion in Germany before being drafted into the 1st Battalion and transferred to India from September 1930. Always a naturally fit man, Clements had represented the battalion in both football and rugby; he was promoted to sergeant during 1939. He had immediately volunteered for special service when the call had been made:

> Among the seven of us who volunteered were Sergeant Cook, Corporals Lymer and Shutt . . . Shortly after our first interview, three of us were notified that we had been selected for this new branch of the service, and Corporals Shutt [later promoted to Sergeant and part of X Troop] and Scott and I duly presented ourselves at a Northern aerodrome. Better pens than mine have described the training undergone by paratroops, yet I would

like to add that after six months ground and air training, I felt fitter than I'd ever been before . . .

[Towards the end of 1940] the first demonstration was given to the General Staff. This took place on a perfect day, and I'm sure we left behind a very good impression, both on the ground and in the minds of the spectators. On this particular day I set up records for low drops and getting from plane to ground. But I was too scared to think of that at the time. In fact, my fright was so great that I just sat there limply in the harness and waited for the bang. Imagine my surprise when I landed perfectly with the chute covering me like a shroud.[10]

Despite Clements's self-deprecating prose, the men of 11 SAS Battalion had been imbued with the swagger and pride that is necessary for an elite military formation. Their training had been more arduous than any yet undertaken by the British Army and they rightfully felt ready for more than endless drills and demonstration drops. The battalion's duties towards the end of 1940 and beginning of 1941 primarily consisted of performing such demonstrations on behalf of the Central Landing Establishment as it struggled for resources and to complete the training of more recent recruits. With not a sniff of action against the enemy yet, morale began to suffer with several requests for transfer being put forward by men frustrated by inactivity at Ringway while fighting was raging in North Africa. Finally, during December, the first indications of a possible operation in planning began to reach the SAS officers and signs pointed to at least part of 11 SAS Battalion finally being used in anger early in 1941.

Chapter Three

The Target

By the end of 1940 and beginning of the new year, the only ground combat being waged by Allied forces was against the Italians in North Africa. Though the war against Germany had continued unabated in the air and at sea, a sense of idleness overcame many officers and men who had braced themselves for an impending German invasion that never materialised. At the very top, Churchill too fretted about the apparent inactivity of Britain's fledgling special service units.

However, in North Africa, the Italian Tenth Army forces had been forced to retreat pell-mell before the British advance of Operation Compass – as always it was a difficult proposition for any commander to withdraw a non-motorised force before a mechanised enemy. Nevertheless, although completely outclassed by their Allied attackers, the Tenth Army maintained a numerically significant Italian military presence, albeit crumbling rapidly. In East Africa, Italian forces in Eritrea, Ethiopia and Italian Somaliland had adopted an inevitably defensive posture after early success and in the face of impending British counter-attack from surrounding territories. With Italian forces also heavily involved in fighting the Greek Army in Albania, Mussolini's troops had become embroiled in a war that most did not want, and all were unprepared and under-equipped for. Now more than ever Italy appeared an obvious weak point at which to strike against the Axis powers.

Six months earlier, during June 1940, W. G. Ardley of the British engineering firm George Kent and Sons had approached the Air Ministry with information about the Pugliese aqueduct that supplied water for vast swathes of southern Italy. The Italian region of Puglia forms the back of the boot of the Italian peninsula bordered by the

Adriatic Sea, extending from the Gargano spur to the town of Santa Maria di Leuca at the very tip of the Italian heel and curving around the Ionian Sea coast to Calabria. While Italy's industry was mostly located in the northern parts of the peninsula, Ardley reasoned that the vital supply heads, transit and military ports of Bari, Brindisi and Taranto, which were heavily involved in maintaining Italian forces in Albania, Libya and Cyrenaica were completely reliant on the aqueduct for the supply of water for industrial purposes as well as the maintenance of the local population and military presence. Puglia was an infamously arid region of which the Roman poet Horace once wrote that it had a 'thirst that rises to the stars'. The lack of water in Puglia rendered the population susceptible to outbreaks of typhus and cholera as people drank from shallow cisterns and wells often containing polluted water. A report written for the Chamber of Deputies regarding the proposed Pugliese Aqueduct Bill by representative De Cesare described the nature of the region starved of such a precious commodity as fresh water:

> Crossing the plain of the Tavoliere or the wastelands of the high plateau in the summer months, through arid grasslands and parched stubble reflecting a blinding light, beaten by a sun that raises the temperature above forty degrees and suffocated by the föhn wind, kilometre after kilometre without finding a stream from which to drink, only at the occasional *masserie* [farm house], at the bottom of some barrel or bucket of warm and unhealthful water drawn from wells or polluted ponds, will the traveller find something to drink ... One drinks polluted water almost everywhere, with detritus floating in it, which is visible. The water itself has a yellowish colour, but a warm temperature, and a flavour that only the need, even more so than any habit, makes tolerable.[1]

Frederick II, King of Italy, first initiated investigation into the problem of supplying water to the parched south during the thirteenth century but not until 1868 did a junior government engineer, Camillo Rosalba from Salerno, first advocated the construction of channels running along the side of the southern Apennine mountain range to carry water from the Sele River to Caposele in the province of Avellino.

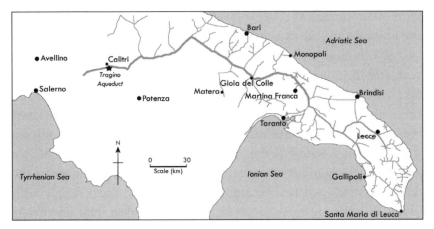

The Pugliese Aqueduct System, 1941.

Rosalba thereupon expanded his idea and created the original design for the Pugliese Aqueduct to provide water from the Sele headwaters to the entire southern region of Italy. Initial surveying of the proposed aqueduct route began in 1901 and construction commenced within five years.

The design was masterful, with water drawn from the head of the Sele River, some 400 metres above sea level in the mountains near Avellino in the Campania region, and channelled east rather than following the natural flow of the river west to the Gulf of Salerno some sixty-four kilometres distant. The Apennine mountain range was to be pierced by a 15-kilometre-long tunnel to bring the water to the eastern side before running towards the six provinces that comprise Puglia where an interwoven web of water conduits stretched to each corner of the region.

To this day the Pugliese aqueduct continues to provide the region's water, totalling 2,189 kilometres of primary and secondary lines. As well as less elaborate tunnels through mountains along the route, the waterway required numerous aqueducts, those traversing major valleys being primarily of a masonry arch design while the smaller ones were built from reinforced concrete.

The entire aqueduct system attracted considerable international attention and numerous articles were found in related periodicals, such as the London-based journal *The Engineer*. Work on the ambitious 'Roman scale' project, was temporarily halted by the First

World War, though Bari began receiving water from the Sele by 1915; the fountain in Piazza Umberto gushing water for the first time on 24 April. Taranto was successfully linked to the system the following year and Brindisi by 1918. In 1927, construction of the 'Grande Sifone Leccese' was completed which allowed the arrival of water in Lecce and beyond. Finally, in 1939, the Pugliese aqueduct reached the small town of Santa Maria di Leuca, where Mussolini ordered a monumental waterfall that reached the Ionian Sea, flanked by a grand Roman column transported from the capital. Citizens of the region greeted each newly completed part of the water supply with near rapturous joy and did not hesitate to abandon their previously maintained water cisterns, which soon fell into disrepair. Despite warnings from government agencies to keep functioning wells and cisterns operational in case of disruption of the single Pugliese aqueduct supply, the ancient sources were abandoned and, in some cases, destroyed. Any interruption in the main supply could therefore theoretically bring Puglia rapidly to its knees.

Alongside the complicated pipework and pumping systems, metering was an important part of the entire project to keep control of the water flow throughout the structure. The London engineering firm George Kent and Sons specialised in such equipment and supplied flume and metering equipment to the Italian construction firms. It was through this technical connection to the Pugliese aqueduct building project that Ardley was able to identify the potential vulnerability of this water supply to the crucial southern ports and the two million local inhabitants. He singled out the relatively small main-line aqueduct that crossed the Tragino torrent near Calitri. If this were destroyed by bombing, he reasoned, the interrupted water supply would dislocate Italy's war effort and perhaps also serve to provoke alarm and despondency in a civilian population already wearied by bad news from the front that was being passed around by word of mouth as official sources steadfastly refused to publish the facts of Italy's failing war effort.

It was not until December 1940 that the Air Ministry staff revisited Ardley's idea, though they rapidly deemed the small aqueduct an unsuitable target for bombers due to its extreme range and relatively small profile. Instead, the proposal was transferred to Admiral Keyes at

Combined Operations. A meeting between Keyes and the Combined Operations staff, Colonel Sir Jonathan Roberts Davidson – a First World War veteran and Chief Engineer of the London Metropolitan Water Board, with previous aqueduct design experience – and Ardley resulted in the conclusions that demolition of a single main aqueduct could significantly disrupt the Italian military, lower civilian morale and hamper fire-fighting in the Puglia region should the main harbours subsequently become the target of bombing attacks. Ideally, any destruction undertaken by Combined Operations troops would be compounded by an RAF bombing raid on Italian reconstruction efforts, although this was not essential for the plan's overall viability. The Special Operations Executive was also consulted as to whether it believed the objective could be completed by clandestine agent work, though it declined, reasoning that it had neither the trained personnel nor material to mount such an operation. Instead, it would provide whatever support it could for any mission mounted by Keyes's men. The decision was soon taken to deploy a small group of the highly trained men from 11 SAS Battalion for the task, and planning got under way almost immediately. The plan was examined on 4 January 1941 by the Chiefs of Staff who approved and designated it Project T. A summarised memorandum was sent to Churchill four days later in which they outlined the project, stating that they considered there to be 'reasonable chances of success'. The following day, their answer was received in an inked notation made by the Prime Minister in the margin: 'I approve.'[2] With the official green light received, planning began in earnest for what was now given the fresh codename Operation Colossus.

The plan coordinated by Keyes and his staff took relatively quick shape, the formalised Operation Instruction No. 1 finally being issued to senior officers only on 25 January 1941 once training of a selected element of 11 SAS Battalion had already begun in earnest.

The Plan in Outline.

The operation is to take place during February moon, i.e. between the 9th and 16th of February. A ground force of 36 officers and other ranks will be employed, to be known as 'X' Troop, and consisting of a demolition party R.E. and a covering party from No. 11 Special Air Service Battalion. These will be carried in Whitley aircraft and will be dropped from a low height in the neighbourhood of the bridge.

After the operation the troops will make their way to the coast where C-in-C. Mediterranean is being asked to provide a submarine on the night of D.5 and again on D.9 night *if necessary.*

Preliminary air action in the neighbourhood will be necessary . . . as will subsequent bombing to delay repairs to the bridge.[3]

The idea was for the Whitleys to stage through Malta before mounting the attack and for the men to be subsequently recovered by submarine from the Italian Tyrrhenian Sea coast, though, according to General Ismay, it was 'left to the Commander-in-Chief Mediterranean's discretion to make the best possible arrangements to get the party off'. The troops and aircraft of Operation Colossus were initially thought to be needed in Malta by 4 February, not providing much time for preparation.

Somewhat baffling given the important nature of this first projected parachute raid to be mounted by British forces, was the lack of firm intelligence regarding the target aqueduct. While exact dimensional schematics of it had featured in Italian engineering magazines during construction, the material of which it was comprised remained unknown and was incorrectly assumed to be masonry despite various constructions along the length of the Pugliese aqueduct being analytically described with data and technical drawings. Likewise, only a single photo existed with which to plan the attack, taken in 1928 and showing the temporary buildings erected by the construction crew along the bank of the Tragino. So little was known of the target that British planners were not even aware of the existence of a second, smaller aqueduct of the same form and construction barely 200 metres to the east over a tiny tributary of the main Tragino torrent.

Early in January 1941 Lieutenant-Colonel Jackson called his men to parade on the open ground at Shaw Heath in Knutsford before informing them about the impending operation. He told the assembled troops that a top-secret mission was being planned to involve a deep-penetration strike in enemy territory. Though evacuation of the attacking party was being arranged, he informed them that there was no guarantee that escape could be made, and the likelihood of capture was high. In this event, though they would go into action in British battledress, there was also the possibility that they would be treated as saboteurs rather than soldiers and handled accordingly. Royal Engineer, Lance-Corporal Harry Tomlin was among the men paraded that day:

> We were all keen to get on operations. When Major Pritchard said, well, we've got an operation, all those that want to be on it take one step forward and of course everybody took one step forward. So, he said, I'm sorry, I can't accept all of you, I only need so many of you, so we'll have to choose who we want . . . and I happened to be one of those chosen. I was a lance-corporal.[4]

With every man volunteering for the operation, the task fell to the assigned officers to assemble the group that they would lead into action. Jackson had placed his second-in-command, Major Trevor 'Tag' Pritchard, designated 'Attack Commander – Ground' for the operation, in charge and instructed him to select five officers, who in turn would choose 'five good men' each, who would comprise their individual sections. Three men would also be selected to form an operational reserve in case of accidents or any other reason for a reduction in numbers. Though Pritchard and Jackson were aware of the mission target, this information was kept strictly confidential, though the demolition nature of the raid would require half of the party to be comprised of engineers.

Major Rock took part in the planning aspect of the raid itself, using his experience as an officer of the Royal Engineers. The ideal was to destroy the aqueduct bridge so that repairs would take at least one month. Composed of four spans estimated at seventy feet each, the structure was carried on three piers, mistakenly thought to be made of masonry due to a short description written in the London *Engineering Journal* of 1928. The decision was made that the best method of destroying the aqueduct would be charges attached to all three piers. Should insufficient stores or men arrive to complete this task, then a secondary option of destroying two piers was viable. Rock considered that 'No attempt would be made to blow only one pier, for the effort would not be worth-while.'[5]

After some deliberation Pritchard selected Captain Gerrard Francis Kirkpatrick Daly of the Royal Engineers as the chief demolition officer. Aged twenty-four, Daly came from a family with a military tradition and after graduating with honours from Cambridge University had also been a pre-war graduate of the Woolwich Military Academy. Small in stature and studiously quiet, he had seen action in France during the retreat to Dunkirk where he had demonstrated an unshakeable calm and fortitude that stood him in good stead for his Commando training. To act as his assistant demolition officer, 2nd Lieutenant George Paterson, a 21-year-old Scots-Canadian of the Royal Engineers, was also selected. As tall as Daly was short, Paterson stood well over six feet and had interrupted his studies at Edinburgh University to volunteer for military service at the outbreak of war. Initially assigned to the development of chemical warfare, he immediately volunteered for the Commandos lest he become stranded in a laboratory for the duration of hostilities.

To lead three covering sections of infantry Pritchard chose Captain Christopher Lea, of the Lancashire Fusiliers, Lieutenant Anthony Deane-Drummond, of the Royal Corps of Signals, and 2nd Lieutenant Geoffrey Jowett, newly commissioned into the Highland Light Infantry. Twenty-two-year-old 'Christoph' (as he was known to his family) Lea had served as a brigade intelligence officer and been sent to France with the Lancashire Fusiliers at the outbreak of war, writing home during the months of inactivity of the Western Front that he was 'getting too much food and drink, though not enough exercise' and asking for books on Roman law to be sent by his family. Following the German attack on 10 May, Lea was wounded in the wrist during the retreat to Dunkirk. Standing six foot three and 'both lanky and languid', Lea was another who hailed from a military family, his brother George having been commissioned into the Lancashire Fusiliers in 1933 and served in Britain, China, and India before the Second World War. Christopher had attended the interview process for screening volunteers for the Commandos as soon as the request went out, and was accepted after being interviewed by

Captain Cleasby-Thompson, also of the Lancashire Fusiliers.

The 23-year-old son of a retired colonel and tea planter, Anthony Deane-Drummond grew up in a village in the Cotswolds and was educated at Marlborough before going to the Royal Military Academy, Woolwich. He then joined the Royal Corps of Signals because of his love of horse-riding and knowledge that two 'chargers' were the automatic right of every officer in the unit. Commissioned in 1937, he was commanding an artillery signal section at the outbreak of war and went to France as part of the British Expeditionary Force.

Geoff Jowett was another Scots-Canadian, small and stocky with a large bristling moustache who looked older than his twenty-nine years. More Sottish than the Scots, he wore his emotions on his sleeve and was always seen with his nearly bald head crowned by the bonnet of his Highland regiment. Jowett was, like Paterson, informal with his men, generally addressing them by their Christian names and even allowing them to do likewise. A strong swimmer, Jowett proved to be adept in combat and prided himself on being more aggressive and bloodthirsty than his peers, earning the nickname 'Killer Jowett'.

The final officer enrolled in Pritchard's group was 2nd Lieutenant Davies, training alongside his peers for the forthcoming operation, but to be held in reserve along with two enlisted men, Corporal Rowe and Lance-Corporal Humphries.[6]

In total, after a number of names were considered for the main party, thirty-eight officers and men were selected and formed into a brand-new unit named 'X Troop' (those marked with an asterisk held as reserve):

> Major Pritchard, Captain Lea, Captain Daly, Lieutenant Deane-Drummond, 2nd Lieutenant Patterson, 2nd Lieutenant Jowett, 2nd Lieutenant Davies*, Sergeant P. P. Clements, Sergeant Edward William 'Little Jock' Durie, Sergeant Arthur 'Taff' Lawley, Sergeant Joe Shutt, Sergeant John 'Big Jock' Walker, Corporal Ralph Chapman, Bombardier William Alfred Dennis, Corporal Derry Fletcher, Corporal J. E. Grice, Corporal Philip Julian, Corporal Peter O'Brien, Corporal Rowe*, Lance-Corporal Harry Boulter, Lance-Corporal Douglas 'Flash'

Henderson, Lance-Corporal Humphries*, Lance-Corporal Doug E. Jones, Lance-Corporal Jim E. Maher, Lance-Corporal Harry Pexton, Lance-Corporal Harry Tomlin, Lance-Corporal Robert Brimer 'Mad Bob' Watson, Sapper 'Jock' W. Crawford, Sapper R. Davidson, Private Ernest Humphrey, Private Nicola Nastri, Sapper Alf Parker, Sapper James Parker, Sapper Owen D. J. Phillips, Driver Glyn Pryor (RE), Sapper Alan B. Ross, Private Albert Samuels and Sapper David L. Struthers.

Among X Troop was one man born of Italian parents, capable of understanding the language and speaking it fluently: nineteen-year-old Private Nicola Nastri, a Londoner with a broad Cockney accent when he spoke English. Of small stature – local children used to good-naturedly call Nicola and his six brothers the 'seven dwarves' – his features were unmistakeably Italian and to disguise his heritage in the event of capture, he was assigned the name 'John Tristan', the assumed surname a near anagram of his real name. Nastri had come to volunteer for special services by a most peculiar route. Called up to serve in the British Army on 2 September 1939 and enlisted into the Oxfordshire & Buckinghamshire Light Infantry, he was distraught to be informed that his Italian father faced internment following the declaration of war by Italy on 10 June 1940. Requesting an interview with his commanding officer, Nastri was told that his superior would 'look into the matter'. The following day Nicola reported once again to his commanding officer and was told that if he would be prepared to volunteer for a 'special service unit' then the CO would 'see what he could do' regarding his father Without a second thought, Nicola did exactly that and his father, at that time tearfully preparing for internment and separation from his close-knit family, was instead informed that though he was to surrender his family's wireless set, register as an alien, report to the local police once a week and not venture more than five miles from his home, he would no longer be interned.

After the selection of X Troop was complete, Pritchard and his men were immediately segregated from the rest of 11 SAS and moved from their various billets in Knutsford into a large wooden building within the boundary of Ringway aerodrome. Until the operation was over, they were to be kept in isolation, allowed off the aerodrome to visit a local pub in the evenings, but under strict supervision by plain-clothes security men who remained vigilant for any potential security breach. The final choice of men by Pritchard's officers didn't stop those left behind from doing their best to be included in whatever action was about to begin. Tony Hibbert was among those not chosen:

> We didn't hear of the special training that they had been up to, but the word got around that there was a special operation on and that Major 'Tag' Pritchard would be commanding it. We couldn't get to Tag because he and the troop had been isolated, but all of us, by fair means or foul, managed to get little chits to him pointing out that the operation would be a total and utter waste of time unless we, personally, were included in the party. As you can imagine, our approaches weren't very productive.
>
> Everyone was terribly disappointed that they hadn't been included ... We were all very fit and immensely keen and proud to belong to this special unit; we were quite sure that there were no other troops in the whole British Army in the same league ...[7]

There then began six weeks of intensive training for the already physically fit men of X Troop, including the construction of a forty-foot-long wooden mock-up of the aqueduct structure – which the troops mistakenly believed was simply a bridge – erected behind Lord Egerton's house at Tatton Park and kept under constant armed guard. The troop was divided into two separate components: No. 1 Party containing the infantrymen that would provide cover for No. 2 Party, comprised of the Royal Engineers. The days were long and difficult, generally beginning with thirty minutes of PT before breakfast, a daily three-mile run and fifteen-mile quick march in full equipment. An example schedule for the days between Saturday 25 January and Tuesday 28 January was as follows:

No. 1 Party				No. 2 Party
Date	Time	Detail	Place	
Sat. 25 Jan.	0845	To Tatton Park by bus (work on Mock Up)	Outside Hut	As for No. 1 Party
	1045	March back to dinner		Remain Tatton Park under orders of Captain Daly for rest of day.
	1400	Personnel for night dropping to pack 'chutes		
	1500	Lecture	Decontamination Room	
	1530	Container Drill	Decontamination Room	
	2000	Personnel for night drops to stand by in Parachute Packing Room.		
Sun. 26 Jan.	1000	Run and PT	Outside Hut	As ordered by Captain Daly
	1130	Aircraft Drill	Outside Armoury	
	1430	Container Drill	Outside Armoury	
	1900	Container Drill	Outside Armoury	
Mon. 27 Jan.	0730	Run and PT	Outside Hut	As for No. 1 Party
	0930	Individual Stalking	Tatton Park by bus	As ordered by Captain Daly for rest of day
	1215	Section Stalking		
	1430	Aircraft Drill	Outside Armoury	
	1600	Lecture (Equipment)		
	1845	Individual and Section Stalking	Tatton Park	
Tue. 28 Jan.	0730	Run and PT	Outside Hut	As for No. 1 Party
	0930	Rehearsal	Tatton Park by bus	

Among the lectures delivered to X Troop was one by a visiting officer from MI9, given to officers, warrant officers and sergeants, dealing not only with escape and evasion, but also a system of code communication which could be used in normal correspondence in the event of capture and imprisonment. The War Office's MI9 department had been established in 1939, its objectives officially listed as:

1. The facilitation of escapes by British prisoners of war, thereby returning service personnel to action and causing the enemy to deploy additional manpower on guard duties.
2. The return to the United Kingdom of those who succeeded in evading capture in enemy-occupied territory.
3. Collection and distribution of information.
4. Denial of information to the enemy.
5. Maintaining morale of British prisoners of war in enemy prison camps.

Those receiving the lectures were expected to pass on all required information to their subordinates, with the exception of details regarding coded communication. Given the delicate and secret nature of those instructions, they were limited to a select number of officers and non-commissioned officers and subsequently used to great effect by those men in the months after Operation Colossus.

During early January, two additional men were brought into X Troop from outside, both middle-aged, both sporting medal ribbons from the First World War and both surrounded by a certain air of mystery as far as their new comrades were concerned. As part of preparation for the mission Keyes had added a request to SOE for two Italian agents, fit and willing to be landed by parachute as part of a raiding mission on the Italian mainland. Lieutenant-Commander Martelli had located five possible candidates from his combing of the internees on the Isle of Man; all five were removed and transferred to Scotland where they began Commando training near Lochailort. Known to SOE as 'the Quins', two were soon found unsuitable as an SOE observer, Canadian John Macalister, found them hard working but far too docile and passive to be useful agents for subversion activities. The pair were returned to the normal civilian lives that they had had before internment. A third, Rinaldo Purisiol, had taken part in the Spanish Civil War with the Republican International Brigade and was considered potentially useful, as was the fourth Emilio Salsilli, another veteran of Spain, noted as a convinced Communist, tough, brave and completely ruthless. The last was Picchi and though he possessed none of the more recent fighting experience that his two compatriots shared, his honest and heartfelt desire to assist the British forces in ridding Italy of 'the odious dictatorship' of Benito Mussolini's fascists made him stand head and shoulders above the others. Special Operations Executive NCO Lance-Corporal Searle, assigned to observe the Italian potential recruits, later wrote a report on Picchi in which he stated:

> An idealist, apart from politics, who is in many ways more English than the English. An excellent worker and organiser who cannot allow failure. Wants, above all things, for everyone to be treated fairly, and according to their just desserts. Is prepared to share in all England's trials and has no desire to be treated in any way differently from the English soldier. Has a real security sense.[8]

His assessment of the middle-aged Italian was corroborated once all three possible Italians had moved to a billet near Ringway by another SOE operative, Pilot Officer L. P. R. Roche, an administrative member of the RAF granted his rank for the duration of hostilities.[9]

> I stayed with Picchi, Purisiol and Salsilli at the same hotel from 23.1.41 to 26.1.41 inclusive. All spoke freely to me of their various experiences from which the following was gathered ... [Picchi] claims to have no politics himself, but against Dictators and attached to his country ... speaks excellent English (with accent). Quite intelligent, inclined to talk too much about his keenness to do a job in the war for Britain. Appears genuinely grateful for opportunity given him here, and for his treatment, during and after internment. He seems quite fit and moderate in his habits. Appears to be keen and have 'guts'.[10]

It was at that point that Keyes declared that only one man was needed for the forthcoming operation, and Picchi was selected to be that man. Before he was inducted into X Troop he received an alias designed to safeguard him in the event of capture in Italy, being disguised as a member of the Free French forces, Private Pierre Dupont, serial number 3846154.

A second latecomer also arrived during early January and this one was greeted with even greater suspicion regarding his identity. Forty-four-year-old Pilot Officer Ralph Henry Lucky, MC (serial number 79272) of the Royal Air Force Volunteer Reserve, arrived at Ringway as the fortieth member of X Troop. Fluent in many languages, including Italian, Lucky possessed a calm demeanour and sported the medal ribbon of the Military Cross, though no record exists of a 'Ralph Lucky' winning such a decoration during the previous war. This was because his given name was Raoul Lucovich, and he was a foreign volunteer who had enlisted during the First World War in the 22nd Battalion, London Regiment (serial number 682573), subsequently to be commissioned in a different unit and shortly thereafter decorated for valour.

The Lucovich family had originated in Montenegro, though during the nineteenth century had become spread far and wide; Raoul's father, Gino Antonio Lucovich had been born in Cheshire on 1 December 1861. Gino Antonio subsequently married a French woman and qualified as an engineer, working in the construction of railways in the Balkans where Raoul and his sister Alice-Henriette were born, the former on 4 March 1897.

A medical student at Paris University at the outbreak of the First World War, Raoul already harboured a thirst for adventure and, being too young to join the Royal Flying Corps, had instead enlisted in the French Flying Services with which he served from 14 August 1914 to February 1916. He attended the school of aerial gunnery in France and, later, the No. 1 School of Aerial Gunnery in Hythe, Kent, that had been established in 1916 by Major Louis Strange. For reasons that remain unknown, Raoul then transferred to, and saw action, with the British Army during 1916, first as a corporal with the 22nd (County of London) Battalion, London Regiment (The Queen's) before being commissioned as a 2nd Lieutenant on 19 February 1917 and transferred to the 10th Battalion, Worcestershire Regiment. On 4 July 1917, during the Battle for Messines, Lucovich was badly wounded in action after crawling from shell hole to shell hole to seize a vital position known as Cutting Farm. The *London Gazette* of 17 September 1917 includes the full citation of his Military Cross awarded for his actions that day:

For conspicuous gallantry and devotion to duty on several occasions. In broad daylight and under full view of the enemy he crawled forward 700 yards up to the enemy's line and brought back information which enabled his Commanding Officer to occupy commanding positions previous to the attack. The same evening, he led forward his platoon under heavy fire, established an advanced post of great tactical value and remained in command of it, although wounded, for two nights. A few nights later he was severely wounded but with great pluck and devotion refused to have his wounds dressed until all his wounded men had been attended to. His gallantry was beyond all praise.

In May 1918, Raoul returned to the air when he transferred to the brand-new Royal Air Force, created by the amalgamation of the Royal Flying Corps and Royal Naval Air Service. After attending the No. 1 School of Aerial Navigation and Bomb Dropping situated immediately adjacent to Stonehenge, he joined 115 Squadron at Castle Bromwich Aerodrome on 29 August 1918 as the squadron transferred to Roville-aux-Chênes in the Vosges, north-east France. There 115 Squadron formed part of the Independent Air Force; the RAF's strategic bombing force of nine squadrons created to strike German railways, aerodromes, and industrial centres without the need for co-ordination with the Army or Navy. 115 squadron operated twelve three-man-crew Handley Page O/400 aircraft which were used for night bombing and on 22 September, following a raid on the Morhange aerodrome and Leininen rail station, Raoul was hospitalised for a week before returning to active service in the rank of lieutenant until the war's end.

In March 1919, Raoul Lucovich returned to Britain, posted to No. 2 RAF Depot, Uxbridge, before being demobilised on 25 August. He relocated to Egypt where he worked alongside his father Gino who was a director of the Egyptian Irrigation Company and manager of the sugar factory at Nag Hamadi in 1919, living in a rather grand, walled residential compound on the western bank of the Nile, at the centre of social life in the Egyptian region between Abydos and Dendera.[11] With a passing resemblance to Ronald Coleman and possessed of an extraordinary confidence, the self-professed ladies' man appeared to flourish in Egypt. He married a Frenchwoman named Lucienne, apparently the girlfriend of another man that Ralph particularly disliked, perhaps providing impetus to his own seduction of her. Nonetheless, he clearly yearned for further military adventure and Lucienne disappears from Raoul's story before 1939, though whether through death or divorce is unclear.

On the outbreak of the Second World War, Raoul Lucovich – now going under the pseudonym Ralph Henry Lucky, a surname derived from the nickname frequently given him during the previous war – enlisted once again, initially into the Military Pioneer Corps where he was appointed acting company sergeant-major. However, fluent in French, Arabic and Italian, he was considered more useful elsewhere and was discharged from the Army on 13 May 1940, granted an RAF commission for the duration of hostilities on the following day as a pilot officer on probation, and attached to RAF Intelligence – no doubt due not only to his impeccable service record, but his language capabilities. Frequently referred to in written works about Operation Colossus as flight lieutenant, Lucky remained a pilot officer during the raid and was only confirmed in his appointment and promoted to the war substantive rank of flying officer (equivalent to an Army lieutenant and still one rank below flight lieutenant) on 14 May 1941 after the raid on the Tragino aqueduct was over. He would not reach flight lieutenant until the war's end, as we shall see later.

It is unclear how much of the training regime both men were involved in, or on exactly which date they officially joined X Troop, though Deane-Drummond remembered the arrival of Lucky and Picchi in fond terms.

> Early in January we were joined by two Italian interpreters, Flight Lieutenant [*sic*] Lucky and Sergeant Pichi [*sic*]. Both were about forty-five which is a healthy age to start parachuting. Sergeant Pichi was perhaps the most surprising member of our party – and certainly not the least courageous . . . He was fanatical, both in his hatred of the Fascists and his love of Italy. Uniform did not change him much. He was still the suave and polite little man, with a bald top to his head and a slight middle-age spread, who might be expected to be in charge of

the banquets at the Savoy, and no one would have recognised him as the hero he proved to be.[12]

The method by which demolition of the aqueduct would be achieved had been honed by repeated practice against the model at Tatton Park. By use of ladders, a top row of charges was hung around each pylon by steel wire passing through grooves in steel angle plates at each corner and pulled tight by means of a ratchet. The angle plates themselves had toothed claws to cling to the surface and provide some grip while the wire was being tightened. A second, bottom row of charges was then suspended from the same steel wire. Each row of charges was bound to the pier by a length of alpine cord, windlassed tight once in position and divided into four tins of guncotton held on a 1⅝-inch pine board with steel sheet brackets at each end and a small webbing loop riveted to the bracket at top and bottom. To these loops was tied a length of cord attached to a small hook and eye, adjustable in length by means of a sheepshank knot. The hooks of the upper charge boards were placed on the steel wire and board height adjusted accordingly while the lower board hung from the bottom webbing loop of the board above.

All charges were to be fired simultaneously to avert the risk of one charge explosion dislodging adjacent charge boards and one guncotton slab of the centre tin on each charge board was provided with a primer and three feet of cordtex; a type of detonating cord generally used in mining and resembling an electrical extension cord, with an explosive core of pentaerythritol tetranitrate (PETN) inside plastic coating, its velocity of detonation rated at 6,000–7,000 metres per second, making it perfect to group a sequence of explosives together. A main ring of cordtex was then taken around both rows of charge boards on each pier and from there to a junction box at the foot of each pier. The cordtex lead from each charge board was then taped to the ring-main with insulation tape. These three separate junction boxes were in turn connected in series with cordtex and a cordtex lead taken from each junction box to a firing point fifty yards from the aqueduct where a detonator and six feet of safety fuse were used for ignition.

While the men trained and rehearsed their individual parts of the operation, Wing Commander Norman was informed that he would accompany the air party from Britain. From the time of arrival at Malta until the departure of the force to carry out the attack 'or such alternative movement as may be ordered', he was to assume full command and complete responsibility for decisions affecting the combined operation. Norman was to be known as Operation Controller for Colossus and immediately set about attempting to procure the necessary aircraft with which to mount this ambitious operation. However, he immediately met with resistance as the Air Ministry attempted to provide a mixed bag of Bombay and Whitley aircraft due to a 'lack of operational aircraft'. Though the Bristol Bombay had occasionally been used in parachute training, valued because of its side door exit rather than the Whitley's hole, the Whitley possessed a greater range and maximum speed. Furthermore, the logistical complication of preparing men and equipment to be dropped from two separate aircraft types was an unwelcome millstone around Ringway's neck and Norman protested vigorously to the Air Ministry that the mission was already difficult enough without adding an extra hindrance. Though RAF Bomber Command was loath to release front-line bombers for alternative use, eight new Whitley V aircraft and crews from 51 and 78 Squadrons were belatedly handed over to Norman's control, flown from RAF Dishford, North Yorkshire, to Ringway on 15 January. The Whitleys of 51 Squadron had already seen action over Italy, taking part in the first bombing raid on the Italian mainland when the marshalling yards in Turin were attacked on 11 June 1940.

The man designated Attack Commander – Air for the RAF bombers attached to the operation was Flight Lieutenant James Brian 'Willie' Tait, given full command and responsibility for the combined force while airborne. Tait had been commissioned as a pilot officer into the RAF on 1 August 1936 and joined 51 Squadron where he was promoted to flying officer on 1 February 1938. Tait was active on bombing operations from the war's beginning, including several long-distance raids on Berlin (where his bomb-aimer Sergeant Ronald Walker pinpointed and bombed Hitler's Chancellery in the face of intense anti-aircraft fire) and the first British air raid on Turin for which he was awarded the Distinguished Flying Cross. Promoted to flight lieutenant on 1 February 1940, Tait's experience made him the perfect choice for the role of Air Commander. The roster of aircraft and crews attached to Operation Colossus were:

'D' (#T4236), 78 Squadron: *Captain*, Sergeant Holden; *Second Pilot*, Sergeant Williams; *Navigator*, Sergeant Stevens; *Wireless Operator*, Sergeant Barton; *Rear Gunner*, Sergeant Balcombe.

'E' (#N1525), 78 Squadron: *Captain*, Pilot Officer Robinson; *Second Pilot*, Sergeant Hatcher; *Navigator*, Sergeant Nolan; *Wireless Operator*, Sergeant Diamond; *Rear Gunner*, Sergeant Gurmin.

'J' (#T4215), 78 Squadron: *Captain*, Sub-Lieutenant Hoad, RN; *Second Pilot*, Sergeant Smith; *Navigator*, Pilot Officer Houghton; *Wireless Operator*, Sergeant Markland; *Rear Gunner*, Flying Officer Webb.[13]

'K' (#P5015) 51 Squadron: *Captain*, Flight Lieutenant Tait; *Second Pilot*, Pilot Officer Purley; *Supernumerary Second Pilot*, Sergeant Sharp; *Navigator*, Pilot Officer Alabaster; *Wireless Operator*, Sergeant Patterson; *Rear Gunner*, Pilot Officer Careless.

'N' (#T4165), 51 Squadron: *Captain*, Sergeant Lashbrook; *Second Pilot*, Pilot Officer Hawley; *Navigator*, Pilot Officer Way; *Wireless Operator*, Sergeant Green; *Rear Gunner*, Flight Lieutenant Williams (Central Landing Establishment).

'R' (#T4166), 78 Squadron, *Captain*, Sergeant Ennis; *Second Pilot*, Pilot Officer Stubbs; *Navigator*, Sergeant Edgar; *Wireless Operator*, Sergeant Graham; *Rear Gunner*, Sergeant Billing.

'S' (#T4167), 78 Squadron: *Captain*, Pilot Officer Wotherspoon; *Second Pilot*, Sergeant Southam; *Navigator*, Sergeant Meddings; *Wireless Operator*, Sergeant Albon; *Rear Gunner*, Sergeant Hodges.

'W' (#T4235) 78 Squadron: *Captain*, Flight Lieutenant Williams (RNZAF); *Second Pilot*, Sergeant Hornsey; *Navigator*, Sergeant Walker; *Wireless Operator*, Sergeant Kershaw; *Rear Gunner*, Pilot Officer McLeod.

Sergeant Denis Hornsey later recalled:

> On our second day at Ringway we were all assembled in the CO's office and were told that the object of our mission was now to be disclosed . . . 'I need hardly say that this is a mission in which the greatest secrecy is necessary. All operations are top secret but this one is more than top secret. In fact, it is my

unpleasant task to mention to you that anybody found guilty of disclosing details of this operation, whether by carelessness or intent, will be instantly shot. Some clues have already leaked out through injudicious talking. It will go ill with those responsible when we find out who they are.'

Step by step he unfolded the plan. We were to fly to Mildenhall to get our aircraft bombed up and loaded with the necessary supplies and stores. We would then fly to Malta and, when the weather was favourable, operate from there. Meanwhile, our aircraft had to be converted for the carriage and dropping of parachute troops, and we had to train on other aircraft, with the troops we were to drop, while the modification work proceeded. Any spare time had to be spent studying and familiarising ourselves with the model [of the aqueduct] until we knew it by heart and could recognise the dropping zone from any angle.[14]

The RAF plan for the attack counted six aircraft carrying the men and equipment of X Troop, while two others ('R' and 'S') were armed with a pair of 500-pound and six 250-pound bombs each for a diversionary raid on Foggia. Two of the troop-carrying aircraft ('J' and 'K') would also carry a single 250-pound bomb apiece to add to the attack on Foggia and hopefully confuse Italian observers as to the likely reason for the British presence in the skies over southern Italy. For six of the bomber crews the requirements of Operation Colossus presented a totally different procedure to that which they had grown accustomed to. Dropping parachutists from a low level and using a low-speed approach was a different discipline to the high-level night bombing in which they had thus far been employed.

While the Whitley Vs themselves were modified with long-distance fuel tanks, and the provision of the universal bomb racks required for the equipment containers, both parachutists and aircrews trained hard in cold winter conditions using other aircraft. The Whitleys' jumping holes were closed by a pair of semi-circular hatches that sat flush with the inner deck, covered by large sorbo-rubber mats when in flight. Hinged at the fuselage wall, these were lifted and secured in place when only five minutes from the drop zone as the men prepared to jump. With practice, a stick of eight men could clear the Whitley within fifteen seconds, jumping alternately from front and rear.

Sergeant Wally Lashbrook was the pilot of Whitley 'N' of 51 Squadron:

> It was in January 1941 when eight of the more experienced Whitley crews – two from 51 Squadron and six from 78 Squadron – were sent to Ringway to practice Paratroop dropping, prior to carrying out 'Operation Colossus'. I was privileged to be selected to Captain one of the Crews.
>
> Squadron Leader [temporary promotion to Squadron Leader was made on 1 March 1941, confirmed shortly thereafter] Willie Tait, an admirable leader, was the senior officer and was responsible for the crews. Dropping practice was carried out initially on Whitley IIs, drops being made from as low as 300 feet. Once proficient, we finished the course flying the particular Whitley Vs which we were expected to use on the job. The morale among the paratroops was very high in spite of suffering the odd broken bone and occasionally finishing up in a tree. I knew of no one refusing to jump. We were however unfortunate in having one fatality; he fell into an iced-over lake and was drowned.[15]

In fact, several drops were made at a height below 300 feet because of wind buffeting the transporting aircraft, the subsequent landings being particularly hard for men whose statischutes had little time in the air to deploy fully to arrest their descent. The latest training death at Ringway occurred on 22 January when 21-year-old Bombardier William Alfred Dennis, of the Royal Artillery before joining No. 2 Commando, landed in an ice-covered pond at Tatton Park during one of the practice drops and drowned in only three feet of water as he became stuck in thick glutinous mud, fatally weighed down by equipment.

Nonetheless, X Troop refined its abilities with repeated mock parachute attacks on the replica 'bridge' in Tatton Park. Before long, they were able to drop successfully and then move by hand nearly half a ton of guncotton explosives against the target's supporting stanchions within half an hour.[16] Each parachutist was armed with only a pistol as he exited the aircraft, all heavier equipment being dropped separately in containers. This procedure was copied from the German model, and would later prove disastrous for many *Fallschirmjäger* involved in the battle for Crete, but was subsequently abandoned by Allied parachute forces which would go on to drop men armed with their principal weapons.

However, in 1939, the RAF possessed two simple pieces of equipment for dropping stores to Army units, though neither was suitable for the parachutists' needs. The first was a small metal container about 30 inches long and 12 inches in diameter with a lid at one end only. Suspended after dropping by a 10 ft diameter parachute it could carry up to 150 lb of equipment. The second was a wooden beam to which small boxes or crates were attached, dropped and suspended by a single parachute and once again able to hold approximately 150 lb of equipment. Both were carried in aircraft bomb bays and could not be dropped at speeds above 120 mph. However, neither could hold a rifle and both were found to be time consuming to unpack on the ground. The Central Landing Establishment was therefore tasked with designing a new series of containers in time for Colossus. Their initial design used a large cylindrical canvas bag with internal wooden supports provided to retain the cylindrical shape. It was this canvas container that was most likely used in Operation Colossus. Designed to be carried on any aircraft fitted with a universal bomb rack and dropped mechanically, the container was also equipped with a small light for recovery at night. Eventually, a single cylinder of wooden panels on a metal framework with large hinged access doors secured by three latches was developed, named the 'CLE container' after the Central Landing Establishment, but later revised to stand for 'Container Light Equipment'. This CLE Mk 1 could be internally divided into sections by removable wooden partitions.[17] That was, however, some time in the future and the canvas equipment containers supplied to X Troop were also given coloured parachutes to aid identification, and recommended to be released in the middle of the stick of men to reduce the risk of loss.

Twenty-five containers were to be provided for heavier weapons to be used by No. 1 Party as well as the equipment judged to be required for the demolition of the Tragino aqueduct by No. 2 Party. After exhaustive trials and calculations, the kit list was finalised officially as follows:

Tools

Mash hammers	6
Cold chisels	10
Entrenching tools	5
Saws, hand, 26-inch	5
Tensioners	5

Detonating Agents

Cordtex drums	5
Primers	111
Detonators	36
Safety fuse	162 ft

Guncotton

2,240 lb, wet slabs = 160 boxes (14 lb each)

Rope

Spunyarn	10 lb
Whipping twine	5 balls
Alpine cord	1,000 ft
Steel wire rope	300 ft

General

Insulating tape	18 rolls
Angle plates	20
Sandbags	150

Demolition Equipment

Item	Three piers	Spare for Operation	Spare	Total
Charge boards, complete with end plates, cordage, sheepshank, top hook and short hook	30	12	2	44
Angle plates	12	8	1	21
Balloon cable strops, soldered to ratchet tensioners	3	2	1	6
Pairs of ladders, strengthened and fixed together to extend	6	4	–	10
Alpine rope strops	6	4	–	10
Windlass sticks	6	4	–	10

The standard container as supplied was modified slightly to carry two loaded charge boards, while each pair of ladders was lashed together with a harness and fitted with its own parachute as a self-contained equipment bundle, small elements of the demolition stores in turn being lashed to each individual ladder rung.

Though the location of their target remained a closely guarded secret, the parachutists were also shown a scale model of the aqueduct – still believed by the men to be a bridge – and the surrounding terrain in order to familiarise themselves with the 'bridge', drop zone and surroundings. The detailed and accurate model had been produced by Flying Officer David Iain McMonnies of the Ringway staff and was held under lock and key in Harvey's office. Rumours spread throughout X Troop that they were to be dropped in France, or Albania, or North Africa as a spearhead for Wavell's advance or, most likely, against Italian forces in Abyssinia. This latter destination was part of the official cover story, the rumour helped in large part by the occasional 'careless' leaving of maps pinpointing a railway bridge within Italian-held Abyssinia. Malta would be the natural staging point for just such an attack, enabling the official cover story to remain intact until the very last moment, none of X Troop correctly guessing that the target was deep within Italy itself.

The culmination of the hard training came on the final night of 30 January with a full 'dress rehearsal' attack on the aqueduct mock up in Tatton Park. Between the hours of 1630 and 2000, X Troop emplaned with packed equipment containers aboard six of the Whitley Vs and made their drop on a cloudy night during which a strong breeze was blowing. Unfortunately, though designed to test their capabilities fully and provide a last-minute boost in confidence, the exercise was a shambles. The poor weather conditions resulted in most of the men being dropped too far from the target; several were blown into the tall trees fringing Tatton Park and had to be rescued by men of the Knutsford fire service, while those who landed near their planned drop zones were frequently dragged across the ground by their statischute canopies in the stiff breeze. Major Pritchard caught his leg in the guidelines lines of his statischute as it deployed but managed to free it in time to avert any potential harm. Some of the containers were also blown across the ground behind their statischutes, chased by desperate rag-tag groups of men who had managed to free themselves of their own troublesome canopies.

> From this minor fiasco we deduced that the operation was
> not feasible in a strong wind, and that though landing in a

tree rarely did anyone any material harm, it was often quite impossible to get down without outside help.[18]

One of X Troop was fortunate to miss this débâcle. On 24 January, Deane-Drummond had departed Ringway in charge of an advance party to prepare the logistics required for X Troop at their staging base of Malta and to act as liaison between Pritchard's command and the local Army, Air Force and Navy chiefs. He was accompanied by a small group of six RAF personnel – Sergeant Patterson (Fitter I), Corporal Albert Henry Hope (Fitter II), Corporal Alfred Jackson (Wireless and Electrical Mechanic), a Leading Aircraftman Electrician, Leading Aircraftman Instrument maker and Leading Aircraftman Machamee (Armourer) – all familiar with the Whitley Vs soon to be bound for Malta. They also took with them two of X Troop's Bren gun containers and 636 pounds of engine, aircraft and maintenance spares for the Whitleys. Deane-Drummond and the RAF men left for Plymouth from where they were to be transported by RAAF Sunderland flying boat to the island bastion deep within the Mediterranean. Bad weather, however, prevented their departure until the last day of January whereupon the Sunderland flew to Gibraltar for an overnight stop before continuing onward to Malta the following day. Before departing Britain, Deane-Drummond became the first officer of X Troop apart from Pritchard to receive full information regarding their target, escape route and method of extraction from Italy.

Indeed, this latter issue had dogged the idea of using paratroops for raiding missions as far back as July 1940. At that time, both Keyes and his chief advisor, Royal Marine Lieutenant-General Alan Bourne, had harboured grave reservations about the utility of such troops – Bourne's air advisor had already told him at that time that extraction by aircraft of a large body of men was not in any sense a practical option. Therefore, missions would have to be mounted within reasonable distance of a shoreline from which naval extraction could be used. Both naval officers tended to believe that such raids were probably better handled by seaborne forces, though they continued to back the development of airborne troops without prejudice.

It appears that Keyes was so certain that X Troop faced insurmountable problems in being successfully lifted from the Italian

mainland that in London he went as far as to write a brief minute
to be presented to each of the Chiefs of Staff. In it he proposed
delivering a diplomatic warning to Italy, at the appropriate moment,
in which the raiders would be identified as serving British soldiers
– not saboteurs or spies – and therefore subject to the provisions of
the Geneva Convention. In the event of this not being adhered to,
retaliatory action could be taken by British authorities against Italian
prisoners. This grave proposal was discussed by the Chiefs of Staff on
6 February but quickly rejected as impracticable after General Sir John
Dill listed his own opposition to the idea.

> There are two reasons why I consider it unwise to adopt
> D.C.O.'s suggestion.
> 1. If the threat is to reach the Italian authorities in time to
> prevent any men captured being shot out of hand or otherwise
> maltreated (if indeed this is likely to happen), it would have to
> reach them just before or after the operation is undertaken. This
> would be bound to prejudice secrecy. There will, moreover, be
> two opportunities for men to be picked up by submarine, the
> second occurring some four days after the first, and we want
> to give anyone who misses the first every chance of getting the
> second; we should accordingly be ill-advised to let the Italians
> know officially how the operation had been carried out until
> several days afterwards.
> 2. It is dangerous to adopt a policy which might lead to
> reprisals and counter-reprisals. The Germans hold some
> 40,000 British prisoners and they are bound to be the winners
> in any contest of this nature.[19]

Deane-Drummond later recalled that as he went over the details of
the Colossus plan with the originators of the operation, he reasoned
that the chance of successfully demolishing the Tragino aqueduct was
very high. However, successful extraction depended entirely on their
being able to march the sixty or so miles through enemy territory in
the middle of winter in order to make rendezvous with the submarine
HMS *Triumph* on the coast of the Tyrrhenian Sea. The Admiralty had
determined that it was aboard this large T-Class submarine that the
raiders would be evacuated; Lieutenant-Commander Wilfrid John

Wentworth 'Sammy' Woods planned to bring *Triumph* from Malta to the Gulf of Salerno and wait near the mouth of the Sele River on the night of 15/16 February to make rendezvous, returning two nights later (rather than the originally planned four) if no contact had been made at the first attempt. The mountainous landscape between Tragino and the Gulf of Salerno coastline was relatively inhospitable, especially during the winter months. However, the men of X Troop – with perhaps the exceptions of Picchi and Lucky – had already trained to peak physical fitness at Ringway and in the Scottish Highlands, so the distance itself was not considered to pose insurmountable problems. Nevertheless, though population centres may have been sparse in the area, the likelihood of escaping discovery by Italian civilians seemed remote to Deane-Drummond. The stark fact facing X Troop was that they would have a maximum of just seven days to cover the entire distance between the aqueduct and rendezvous point while remaining undetected to stand any chance of being successfully evacuated.

Chapter Four

Malta

The Whitleys were first to fly from Ringway to the Bomber Command airfield in Suffolk that would be their point of departure from Britain.

> We completed our training on 1st February 1941 and departed immediately for Mildenhall. On arrival over the airfield, we were greeted by light flak from some enthusiastic air gunners who mistakenly thought we were German Dorniers. The error was quickly rectified, and we all landed safely.
>
> We were soon assembled in the Briefing Room and informed we were on a special mission and would not be allowed out of camp etc. etc. We were then told that we were to fly direct to Malta and, from there, drop the thirty-six paratroops on an aqueduct in Southern Italy. The aim was to destroy the aqueduct and thus deprive the area of a high percentage of its fresh water. This would also be the first time any Allied forces had been dropped on enemy territory in uniform.
>
> We were shown a landscape model of the dropping area, together with the approaches to the valley, which were studied at length by pilots and navigators. We were told that on our route out we were to keep to the west of Marseilles, Corsica and Sardinia, continuing south to the coast of Tunisia, a further 50 miles on that course before turning east to a [dead reckoning] position due south of Malta, then turn north to the Island. This would prevent the enemy from knowing of our arrival.[1]

The Whitleys were subject to a complete overhaul and fitted with extra fuel tanks inside the fuselage. Due to this additional encumbrance, the ground crew recalculated each aircraft's trim and the ideal weight of bombs required in the front bomb bay to counter-act the additional load and enable the bomber's nose to be kept level in flight.

Behind them, still in Ringway, X Troop underwent final container drills, lectures and spent time on the shooting range before they too travelled by bus to Mildenhall where they were again sequestered away on the aerodrome. Once they were established in their temporary accommodation their tunics were collected from them and taken to have escape gear sewn into the lining. Each man now had a significnt sum of Italian lire secreted in various parts of his tunic alongside an array of material designed by Colin Hutton of MI9. These included a small flexible hacksaw blade hidden above the left breast pocket and two one-foot square silk maps of northern and southern Italy sewn inside the sleeve lining. Furthermore, a collar stud manufactured by the technical engineering firm headed by the elderly Blunt Brothers on Old Kent Road in London – who generally manufactured bomb sights – was attached to each tunic, sporting a removable white plastic cover that could be chipped away to reveal a small 'pillbox' escape compass measuring under 7 mm in diameter. Additionally, each officer had ten gold sovereign coins sewn into his tunic linings.

Finally, by 7 February, all preparations for Colossus had been com-pleted and the men were paraded once more, this time in a Mildenhall hangar before the Chief of Combined Operations. They noted that Keyes spent considerable time in conversation not only with 'Tag' Pritchard but also the somewhat mysterious Pilot Officer Lucky who remained somewhat enigmatic to the remainder of X Troop, though apparently acquainted with Keyes. Rumours that he had been attached to the unit by SOE increased, though Picchi was in actual fact the sole representative of that shadowy organisation. Eventually, Keyes addressed the assembled men:

> You are setting off on a very important job, and I should like
> you to know that I have been assured that no better, fitter and
> braver men could have been selected than you to play this very
> vital role. You have been specially trained for a job like this and
> provided with every piece of equipment you should require.

I know that you will tackle this job with determination and enthusiasm, and with a bit of luck I am sure you will pull it off. We shall be waiting to hear how you have got on, waiting to learn what British paratroopers can do.

I decided that I just couldn't let you go without coming here to say goodbye to you. We are very proud of you.[2]

Unexpectedly, Keyes then stood ramrod straight and saluted the men of X Troop before shaking each man's hand and then turning away, apparently overheard by the soldier nearest to him to have muttered 'What a pity.'

Whatever feelings Keyes's somewhat unusual behaviour may have stirred within the men of X Troop were quickly put aside as they prepared to leave Britain. To that point, it remained only the officers who were aware that Malta was their initial destination, this forward operational base under almost constant aerial bombardment by the Italian and German air forces. The route itself was difficult and would take the Whitleys over considerable lengths of enemy territory and the featureless Mediterranean Sea, though Tait's hand-picked crews were considered more than equal to the challenge. Amidst melting snow scattered on the ground at Mildenhall, the parachutists began emplaning, each Whitley taking a maximum of five members of X Troop aboard, as well as some extra RAF personnel: Flight Lieutenant Bruce Williams of CLS was taken to supervise maintenance of the supplied statichutes as well as using his qualified air gunner credentials and flying as part of a Whitley's operational crew, and Wing Commander Norman, who during the flight acted as an extra observer aboard Whitley 'E' flown by Pilot Officer Robinson. This aircraft also carried Corporal Gray, an RAF engine fitter familiar with the particular Rolls Royce engines that equipped the Whitley V, which had not been seen in Malta before.

The aircrew themselves remained most concerned not about their flight route, though it passed over German-held territory, nor the prospect of such a long-distance flight, but the added complication of the heavy load each Whitley carried. The fuselage was crammed with stores ranging from spare tail wheels and propeller blades to oil seals and washers, and they, along with the extra fuel tanks, weighed each aircraft down considerably. Hornsey recalled that his Whitley was

> crammed tight with spares of every description, to say nothing
> of hot water bottles and thermos flasks for each one of the five
> parachute troops we were carrying . . . The crew's cabin was
> chock-a-block with kit and suitcases – so much so that it all
> had to be piled in after we got in. When the front hatch was
> closed a suitcase had to be put on it and a six-foot-long spare
> propeller blade across it, so that our chances of getting out, if
> our overloaded aircraft got into difficulties, were negligible.[3]

The aircraft were so heavy at take-off that Norman had to stay in the front turret of Robinson's Whitley until his aircraft had gained enough height to allow adjustment of the bomber's trim.

The flight began at 2200 hours and was long and cold, though X Troop had enough extra equipment to pass the journey in as much comfort as possible. Each man was provided with the quilted kapok lining from a 'Sidcot suit', a flying overall developed in 1917 to protect pilots in open cockpits exposed to harsh elements and low temperatures. The men wore full battledress, a gaberdine jacket, balaclava, flying helmet, silk inner gloves under woollen outers, and one of three pairs of socks that had been issued. Furthermore, they were provided with a thick sleeping bag (no boots to be worn when in the bag), an RAF Everhot bag – chemical heating pads to be placed inside boots – lilo, thermos flask, food and chewing gum, hot water bottles (for urination), Mae West lifejacket, statischute and two paper bags in the event of air sickness. Each man also wore two haversacks, standard rimmed steel helmet and respirator which were taken off as soon as they had entered the aircraft. The statischute could also be removed on orders of the aircraft commander for use as a pillow during the transit flight.

Specific instructions were given to the passengers on their distribution throughout the aircraft for the flight. At take-off, one soldier was to be positioned lying on the floor beneath the 155-gallon fuel tank in the fuselage roof that lay over the spar centre section. Two others were to be sitting facing forward, resting on the two auxiliary fuel tanks installed in the front fuselage and the remaining men were seated facing aft with their backs to the fuel tanks and knees beneath their chins. Once the aircraft had reached their operational heights, and at the discretion of the captain, the paratroopers were instructed to stand down, lying on the floor of the Whitley in their sleeping bags along the length of the fuselage.

The Whitleys were superbly navigated, using visible reservoirs near Marseilles as a transit point before heading over the Mediterranean Sea to reach Tabarka on the Tunisian coast. From there they used the waypoint of the Cape Bon lighthouse to calculate their final course to Luqa, Malta. They attracted only a solitary Bf 109 fighter over France, which was successfully kept at bay by gunfire from Flying Officer Webb's rear turret on Whitley 'J' and evaded, as well as some unfocussed flak that posed no significant threat. Wally Lashbrook recalled the outbound flight that covered 1,400 miles, much of it over occupied France:

> On the 7th February, we took off in our Whitleys. They had been fitted with an Auto Pilot and overload petrol tanks. We were carrying our six [*sic*] paratroops down the fuselage [Captain Daly, Corporal Julian, Lance-Corporal Boulter, Private Humphrey and Sapper Struthers]; each Para had an air mattress and a sleeping bag. With no windows to observe the outside world, sleep was the obvious way to pass the long night. Flying by Auto Pilot proved more of a hazard than doing the job yourself. After droning on and on for close on eight hours, we were approaching the Tunisian coast.
>
> It was in the light of early dawn. There was a huge black hulk ahead of us – 'cloud build up' – I said to myself. All was quiet inside the aircraft, perhaps slight snores from the second pilot. We were getting very close to 'the Hulk' when he woke up and screamed at me 'Look out – bloody mountains!'. I clapped on full left rudder and hard aileron. I was still pulling back on the stick when the Whitley, now almost on its wingtip, sank into the 'Hulk'. My subsequent remarks to that pilot cannot be printed.
>
> Back on course, we continued as per flight plan, landing on Malta after 10 hours 45 minutes airborne. Much to the surprise of the resident RAF, all eight Whitleys landed safely.

We were given a quick debriefing and sent to take up residence with the submarine boys in the Lazzeretto Barracks at Sliema. After listening to those boys telling of their experiences at being depth charged while probing the approaches to Tripoli, we were thankful we were only an aircrew from Bomber Command.[4]

Deane-Drummond had already exchanged the misery of a harsh British winter for Malta's blazing sun, landing at the seaplane base of Kalafrana and being immediately taken to the island's Governor, General William Dobbie, in whose house he spent his first night ashore. He carried with him six letters outlining the operation to be hand-delivered to naval and air commanders of Malta (and through them their superiors commanding Mediterranean and Middle East respectively) and the captain of the 1st Submarine Flotilla. He also possessed two 'packages' of maps and intelligence material. 'Package A' held forty-four enlargements of a geological map of the target area and eight complete maps, while 'Package B' carried larger-scale maps of the Italian region, both packages delivered in person to Air Officer Commanding Malta for safe custody until the arrival of the remainder of X Troop. Any future communication by the RAF in connection with the operation was ordered sent in cypher and, if possible, not by wireless as secrecy remained of paramount importance to the potential success of Colossus. The young lieutenant had been instructed to arrange viewing of any available aerial reconnaissance photographs – there were none as yet – and liaise with Vice-Admiral Malta regarding the rendezvous point for the withdrawal of the paratroopers. He also wasted no time in trying to secure the necessary billets for himself, the six RAF men who had accompanied him, and the incoming X Troop, Whitley crews and extra personnel. However, under frequent German and Italian aerial bombardment, conditions on Malta were difficult at best. The aircraft carrier HMS *Illustrious* had been severely damaged in action and continued to attract fierce German and Italian bombing raids while lying in Valetta's Grand Harbour, its crew unexpectedly requiring housing ashore and making Deane-Drummond's hunt for a suitable location more difficult than expected. Eventually he found ideal room in the disused quarantine hospital of Lazaretto on Mauel

Island, currently lodging Royal Navy submarine personnel, including the men from HMS *Triumph*.

> When the men arrived, they were highly amused by suddenly talking about mess decks and hammocks instead of mess rooms and beds. They were not so amused when they found that they had actually to sleep in them. In addition to the accommodation, which was the main worry, all the explosives and other stores that we wanted had to be drawn up and arrangements made to transport them to the airfield. I was in Malta about forty-eight hours before the main party arrived, but those forty-eight hours seemed to pass in a flash.[5]

The incoming Whitleys began landing at 0900 hours on Saturday 8 February when they were received by the RAF Station Commander, Wing Commander Robert Carter Jonas, and commanding officer of 148 Squadron's Wellington bombers, Squadron Leader Patrick Foss. Operational instructions had allowed for the loss of up to four aircraft either through enemy action or other causes and still enable the attack to be mounted. In that event and with only four Whitleys being available, each would carry eight men into action. However, every aircraft arrived intact, and all were soon pushed into sandstone blast pens to minimise possible damage by air raids. That afternoon the men of X Troop were allocated their accommodation and allowed a certain amount of free time in Valetta to make local purchases.

While in Malta, X Troop were given rations and pay from the island's stores, also drawing the necessary demolition materials from the main island armoury. While the Whitley crews procured incendiary and high explosive bombs as well as 18-volt starter batteries from Luqa airfield, X Troop took possession of 2,240 lb of guncotton wet slabs in tins, fifty dry primers, four cordtex drums as well as wire, chisels, hammers, entrenching tools and empty sandbags, all of which needed to be carefully packed in the canvas and wooden containers brought from Britain.

The mission was originally scheduled for the following night, although after a conference held between Tait, Pritchard and Norman, the decision was taken to postpone due to potentially adverse weather conditions, the Tatton Park fiasco no doubt lurking in the officers' minds. During the following Sunday morning, all aircrew were excused duties as the Whitleys were serviced and had repairs made to minor damage inflicted by flying rock splinters blown across the airfield by Axis bombs. Fortunately, the thick sandstone walls minimised the effect of the enemy air attacks which had only recently reached a fresh crescendo with the transfer of Luftwaffe units to the Mediterranean theatre. During the afternoon all equipment was checked and repacked into the containers for loading inside the Whitley bomb bays; the container parachutes were also examined and freshly repacked to ensure optimal performance. Only those containers carrying rations and the Slingsby extendible ladders were left unstowed until the following day. General Dobbie also inspected the paraded men of X Troop and wished them his personal congratulations and luck for their forthcoming mission. That morning, RAF 69 Squadron mounted a photo-reconnaissance mission over the Tragino aqueduct, also covering a swathe of countryside between there and the Sele River mouth; this was new information as previously the only photographic evidence of the target was the single photo taken during its construction and published during the 1920s by Italian engineering journals.

The man tasked with this crucial photo-reconnaissance flight was Adrian Warburton, fast becoming legendary within the Royal Air Force. Warburton had been commissioned into the RAF on 3 September 1939 as an acting pilot officer, his rank confirmed on 31 October. Upon completion of training he was posted to 608 Squadron, flying the four-seater Blackburn B26 Botha reconnaissance and torpedo bomber on North Sea patrols. This particular aircraft design, which had only just entered service, immediately proved a complete failure: underpowered, unstable and with poor visibility for its crew. Warburton's outspoken criticism of the aircraft, however, appears to have been unwelcome, and he was swiftly despatched to the 'backwater' of Malta, transferred as an observer, rather than a pilot. There he joined 431 Flight, a small RAF detachment that had formed in September 1940 at Luqa airfield and flew reconnaissance sorties over the Mediterranean with a trio of twin-engine Martin Maryland light bombers. Within four days of arrival, he had his pilot status restored.

'Warby' was considered something of an oddball in 431 Flight, avoiding the officer's mess but maintaining a good and informal rapport with the enlisted men serving alongside him. However, his masterful flying and bravery in the air were indisputable. Unorthodox – to say the least – in his administrative procedures on the ground, he proved fearless in action and on 30 October 1940, Warburton and his two crewmen shot down an Italian CANT Z.506B seaplane. Three days later, they nearly fell victim to an attack by four Italian aircraft and Warburton was hit by a spent bullet which caused no serious injury but rendered him unconscious. Sergeant Frank Bastard took control and managed to keep the aircraft flying (for which he received the Distinguished Flying Medal) until Warburton had sufficiently recovered. On 10 November, a concentration of Italian battleships and cruisers was detected in Taranto, leading Admiral Andrew Cunningham to plan an audacious night attack by Fleet Air Arm Swordfish torpedo bombers. Warburton flew a reconnaissance mission on 11 November immediately prior to the attack. As Warburton circled the harbour several times, the cameras aboard the Maryland failed, so he flew so low that his observer was able to read off the names of the battleships. Guided by this intelligence, the Fleet Air Arm launched the successful Taranto raid that same night; Warburton was subsequently promoted to flying officer on 3 December and awarded the Distinguished Flying Cross in January 1941. Jack Vowles, a wartime NCO who serviced Warburton's aircraft in Malta, later recalled his friendship with the young officer. 'Warby was never a swaggerer. There was some jealousy about his awards, but he never cared about medals. He was driven by an absolute determination to get the job done. If he did a job badly – and that was extremely rare – he would refuel and go back straight away to do it again.'[6]

This time there was no mishap and Warby's photographs were swiftly developed and passed to the officers of Operation Colossus by 1930 hours. To their surprise there were two aqueducts visible in the photographs, only a few hundred metres apart. The primary target remained as expected, but over a small rise to the west lay a second smaller aqueduct of similar construction that crossed a small stream tributary of the Tragino – the Fosse della Cinestra – which flowed past several small farm houses. Though relatively unimportant to the mission itself, the lack of such information displays a rather shocking gap in British intelligence-gathering for the impending operation, especially considering the stakes being played for by such a risky deep penetration into enemy territory. Nonetheless, the mission plan remained unaltered; the main target would be the eastern aqueduct around which all planning had already revolved.

Maps and copies of the photographs were issued to the officers, and at least some enlisted men also received copies later after they had finally been fully briefed on the operation and its objective. Using Warburton's photographs of the landscape stretching from the Tragino to the Tyrrhenian coast, Major Pritchard conferred at length with Lieutenant-Commander Woods, the captain of HMS *Triumph*, which had been assigned the task of extracting the paratroopers from the Italian shoreline. Their rendezvous schedule was reconfirmed, and light signals agreed, the information being passed on to the other officers of X Troop. Pritchard planned that, following the demolition of the aqueduct, X Troop would divide into four separate groups for the trek to the coast. While the rendezvous point had been firmly agreed with the Royal Navy, the route by which each group reached that location was left to the discretion of the officers in command.

Like that issued to the men before their transit flight to Malta, the equipment carried into action and worn aboard the aircraft by X Troop had been worked out minutely and meticulously listed in written instructions issued to Pritchard.

> *All ranks were to wear the following:*
> Battledress (with special trousers and less their parachute
>   badge)
> Boots (with thick rubber soles)
> Socks
> Braces or belt
> Underclothing
> Shirt
> Two haversacks with slings special
> Waist belt with Colt in holster and 18 rounds of ammunition
>   in pouch
> Helmets: both balaclava and flying

Gloves, woollen

Gaberdine jacket

Anklets and kneepads

Identity discs

Pullover

All ranks were to carry in their pockets:

Field dressing

AB64 (British Army paybook)

Clasp knife

Two grenades

One box of matches in tin container and waterproof

Plaster and iodine pencil

Chewing gum

A little toilet paper

Four Other Ranks only: a pair of pliers

No letters or diaries were to be carried.

Each man was to carry in two haversacks:

Groundsheet

One spare pair of socks

Mess tin and four days' special rations

Small enamel mug

Torch

Nothing else was to be put in these haversacks.

In addition to twelve water bottles (empty), twelve filled stoves and twelve filled petrol containers were to be carried in haversacks, divided among the thirty-six personnel of the party. Every officer and man would therefore have *one* of these, under arrangements made by Officer Commanding X Troop. All officers and NCOs were to wear compasses and watches and carry field message forms, and pencil and rubber. Officers to wear field glasses and carry maps. Each of the escaping parties was to carry in addition to their weapons:

1 sextant and tables

60 feet of rope

2 elastic bandages, 2 pairs of spare bootlaces

1 razor, blades, brush, soap and comb.

Each man was given a supply of cigarettes, and one man in five carried a small solid-fuel stove that was smokeless. Those of the Royal Engineers also each carried a tin containing cotton wool and a dozen detonators. The Sidcot suit, Mae West, steel helmet and respirators that each man had carried to Malta from Britain were to be left behind, and this time boots were kept on and there was to be no removal of their statischutes during their outbound flight, though the men were allowed to unfasten the harness straps between their legs in order to get comfortable.

The men of X Troop were not heavily armed for the operation as there seemed little likelihood of fighting a pitched battle with enemy troops. Instead, each officer carried a Colt .38 service revolver and each man a Colt .32 semi-automatic. For heavier weapons to be used by No. 2 Party, seven Thompson submachine guns were provided, one container holding four and four bandoliers of sixteen magazines each, a second holding a further three of the heavy American sub-machine guns and the associated magazines. A single Bren gun was also included in its own container, along with a 'hat box' of twelve magazines. The containers were carefully filled, an RAF report later commenting that they were 'better packed than in previous trials, and nearly all bomb doors were completely shut'.

The special rations provided for the mission included hard-tack biscuits, oatmeal, chocolate, raisins, and pemmican, a concentrated mixture of fat and protein that had been used as a source of nutrition by native Americans. Adopted by both European explorers and subsequently the military, it constituted the men's iron rations, requiring little or no preparation in the field. Pemmican could be eaten raw, crumbled and stewed, or fried according to each man's taste and abilities, though the general consensus among the men of X Troop was that it was barely edible:

> Pemmican, which is the old polar explorers' standby, is made
> of meat extract, with added fat, and tastes like concentrated
> greasy Bovril. Personally, I found it quite nauseating although
> it may well be ideal for Arctic expeditions.[7]

The men had been encouraged during training to forage for dandelion shoots, grass nettles, and other herbs to be combined with their pemmican and oatmeal into a stew, the herbs contributing vitamin C to the mix. While standard Army rations were used during most of their training, pemmican was substituted during tactical operations because of its small bulk and light weight. It was impressed on the students that the ration was entirely sufficient to maintain them in satisfactory physical condition during short operations, and to enable them to perform their assigned tasks without undue hunger and fatigue. Whether it was palatable or not remained open to debate.

With weather reports indicating perfect conditions for the night of 10 February the RAF crews were given refresher briefings on the target area by Wing Commander Norman. All spares that had been carried from Britain were removed from the Whitleys and final servicing and the loading of the last containers was completed by 1430 hours. Once these final steps had been completed aboard the aircraft, Pritchard briefed his men in full on the nature of their mission, passing on all available intelligence and going over all relevant signals information. The speculation that had been rife throughout X Troop was finally laid to rest as they were informed that their target was the Tragino aqueduct in Italy, the men cheering boisterously at news of the audacious goal inside an enemy country. The operational requirements were laid out to each man, though only the assembled officers were later briefed in private on the planned extraction by HMS *Triumph*.

At about 1700 hours, the men of X Troop were given hot tea and an unappetising final meal of hardboiled eggs and meat, sitting confined within a hangar at Luqa airfield in full jumping gear minus only their statischutes. After they were transported by trucks to the waiting aircraft, Pritchard addressed his men one more time while on the tarmac. 'You are pioneers', he said, 'or guinea pigs – and you can choose which word you prefer.' In high spirits and singing 'Oh! What a surprise for the Duce!' the men emplaned, squeezing themselves down the narrow Whitley fuselages to take their allocated positions for take-off, similar to those used on the outward flight from Britain.

The men were distributed between six of the eight aircraft allocated to Colossus; three for the demolition party and three for the covering party while the remaining two Whitleys were assigned to the diversionary attack on Foggia. Take off from Luqa airfield was timed to allow assembly of the three sub-flights during the last hours of daylight and before the expected night raid by Axis bombers. The Whitleys taxied out of their sandstone blast pens and waited at the end of the flarepath in the half-light of dusk, then were finally given permission to take off. All aircraft climbed out to sea over the southern Maltese coast, none permitted northwards until darkness had fallen.

The initial aircraft to lift off were those of the covering party, the first of which took to the air at 1740 hours: Flight Lieutenant Tait's Whitley 'K' (carrying Pritchard, Lea, Lucky, Walker, Pexton and James Parker) followed by Flight Lieutenant Williams's 'W' (carrying Jowett, Clements, Fletcher, Grice, Nastri alias Tristan, and Samuel) and Sergeant Wally Lashbrook's 'N' (carrying Deane-Drummond, Lawley, Shutt, Boulter, Henderson and Picchi alias Dupont). Ten minutes later the demolition party were scheduled to lift off in Sub-Lieutenant Hoad's 'J' (carrying Daly, Chapman, Tomlin, Davidson, Alf Parker and Pryor), Pilot Officer Robinson's 'E' (carrying Paterson, O'Brien, Maher, Jones, Watson, Struthers) and Sergeant Holden's 'D' (with Durie, Julian, Humphrey, Crawford, Phillips and Ross). Finally, the two diversionary aircraft – Pilot Officer Jack Wotherspoon's 'S' and Sergeant Ennis's 'R' – both carrying full bomb loads, lifted off at 1800 hours. However, a last-minute complication forced the delay of Hoad's Whitley, originally aircraft number four in the departure schedule. Harold Tomlin recalled what happened:

> There were six in my Whitley for the operation, Captain Daly and five others, but just before we left Malta one of the fellas in the plane, right at the tail end of it said he was ill. So, Captain Daly said, well if he's ill shove him off before we take off, so he was pushed out and we were one short when we took off. But we managed. I don't know [what was wrong with him] he got back to England all right anyway, but nobody knew what happened to him. I think he was just . . . you know . . . it had to happen to somebody. Somebody had to say they're not going.[8]

The unfortunate man was Corporal Ralph Chapman (serial number 2094113), a Royal Engineer who had joined K Troop, No. 2 Commando, from 267th Field Company in August 1940. Selected for X Troop by Daly, Chapman had excelled in training and his son Tony Chapman remembered his father saying that he had reached his physical peak during his time with X Troop, going from a weight of about 10 stone (140 pounds) at enlistment to 13 stone (192 pounds) carried on his 5 feet 8 inch frame by the time of Operation Colossus. Some accounts state that Chapman later claimed to be overcome by the aircraft's exhaust fumes, others that he complained of severe stomach pains once aboard the Whitley. If the latter, it was probably what was known locally as 'Malta Dog', a stomach complaint endemic to the island with resultant effects similar to dysentery. Caused by ingestion of unpasteurised milk or undercooked meat from infected animals, it could become almost completely debilitating within a matter of days. With no time to lose, Chapman was hurriedly disembarked and returned to his barracks, it being considered too late in the day to equip any of the reserve troops to take his place. Daly's aircraft finally lifted off at 1817 hours with only five paratroopers aboard. The delay proved to have severe consequences.

Why Chapman missed the mission has never been fully explained, and Harry passed away in Bromsgrove, Worcestershire in 1998. However, his subsequent service record indicates no black mark from missing the operation. Chapman was returned to Britain and granted six days' leave on 22 February, remaining in 11 SAS Battalion until 29 June 1941 when he was posted to the 107th Army Field Company, Royal Engineers. The fact that he remained with the unit for months after Colossus indicates no disciplinary procedures were either sought or required, in turn suggesting that his medical complaint was genuine. Chapman later told his son that the main reason he opted to return to the Royal Engineers is that he did not like the way that his unit was gravitating towards the role of airborne infantry in the months following Colossus. It is worth noting that it was not unusual for men to return to their parent service after a period in the Commandos, as stipulated in the original formation parameters of Britain's Special Services. On 27 February 1943 Chapman embarked for North Africa and took part in the closing stages of the battle against German and Italian forces, including the fierce fighting around Medjes el Bab in Tunisia. Subsequently he landed in Italy, surviving the sinking of a landing ship tank, and became embroiled in the relentless grind of the Allied campaign as it crept up the Italian peninsula, in almost constant action, including heavily involvement in the fighting at Anzio in 1944.

Chapman's son remembers hearing only sporadic stories from his father of his part in the Second World War.

> I am unable to cast any light on the specific circumstances of my father's departure from the 'plane. In common with many of his generation he was always very reluctant to talk about his experiences during the war, and this included his time with X Troop ... It was probably only in his 70s that I got much insight about the war in general from him. At that time, he was becoming troubled by recurrent nightmares of clearing land mines at Medjes el Bab. He had been doing this at night with the Germans firing intersecting machine guns over the minefield. The nightmarish part for him was that earlier on there had been an infantry charge through the minefield and there were body parts strewn about which he would reach out and touch. He saw the war as a great waste of human life and was very forgiving towards the Germans and Italians, something which marked him out somewhat from many of that generation ... As an individual he always appeared fearless although he would always say that anyone who wasn't frightened in a dangerous situation was a hazard and that it was simply a matter of controlling fear. He always displayed great determination in the face of any adversity; I can never recall him giving up on any physical or mental task. He did have an explosive temper in which he would display a very controlled but fearsome aggression. In retrospect I put this down, at least in part, to post-traumatic stress disorder.[9]

Ralph Chapman's European war ended in Tel Aviv where his company was resting and refitting. Victory over Japan was declared as they were in Port Said being made ready for transfer to the Far East. The months before his demobilisation at the rank of warrant officer II on 26 March 1946 were spent defusing improvised explosive devices in Palestine left by the Zionist paramilitary organisation, the Irgun.

Chapter Five

The Raid

The eight Whitleys took off from Malta, each sub-flight making rendezvous south of the island albeit with aircraft 'J' lagging significantly behind and unable to join the loose formation maintained by the remaining seven, contact held by use of brief radio transmissions. The Whitleys' course crossed the Sicilian coast near Agrigento, heading almost due north to pass near Palermo. Scattered cloud was encountered over the Mediterranean and fog over Sicily itself, though the first sign of flak was not seen until near Palermo as the bombers passed the northern coast. Landfall on the main Italian coast was not particularly accurate, although all seven of the main Whitley group were able to detect the dull red glow of Vesuvius and then follow the Sele River which strongly reflected the light of the moon.

Coupled with the environmental conditions was the fact that although partial blackout regulations had been issued throughout Italy on 13 June 1940 by the Ministry of War, they were of a complexity that baffled most ordinary Italian citizens unused to stringent instructions regarding their day to day conduct. Instead of initiating a single system for the entire country, three levels of blackout and anti-aircraft provisions were introduced: P ('prominent'), M ('medium') and S ('scarce'), leading to wholesale confusion and the frequent widespread ignoring of the regulations in their entirety. As a result, numbers of brightly burning lights in towns and city suburbs conveniently aided the bombers' navigation. A light was also seen in one signal box north of the dropping zone on the rail track that traced the contour of the Ofanto River, and those of a single car that approached the bridge opposite Calitri. Aboard the aircraft, the men of X Troop passed the time in whatever way they could. Some slept, others played cards, read books, talked or just ran yet again over their instructions for the mission to follow:

> I remember the night; it was a very clear moonlit one. We were a crew of five and carried six paratroops, their leader being Lieutenant Deane-Drummond ... Our dropping height was 300 ft. As far as I remember, we flew to the coast at 9,000 ft. then descended gradually to about 500 ft. and down to 300 ft. just before the turn into the dropping area. By then we were roughly line astern.[1]

The disposition of the incoming aircraft adhered to a carefully prepared control system. All dropping was synchronised to ensure that either all or none of the aircraft dropped in the event of extreme weather conditions, while also minimising the potential for collision between aircraft occupying the relatively small area over the dropping zone. Fortunately, although banks of thick fog lay at the base of some valleys and mountain passes between the Gulf of Salerno and the Tragino, the visibility was perfect and, with large patches of snow reflecting the moon's light, every detail of the final approach was clearly visible allowing easy identification of the objective and its surrounding landscape.

The 'Attack Commander, Air' – Tait in Whitley 'K' – arrived at the rendezvous point over the prominent landmark of Mount Vulture at 2125 hours, soon joined by the remaining two Whitleys of the first sub-flight that had lifted off on schedule. The aircraft circled, stepped off at agreed heights to minimise any risk of accidental collision. Tait broke formation and made a preliminary reconnaissance of the dropping zone after which he selected an appropriate 'zero hour' for the dropping operation to begin. Finding the target area clear, Tait broadcast 2135 hours as the chosen time, each aircraft being allocated five minutes to complete its runs over the landing zone. However, uncertain that all aircraft had reached Mount Vulture, as his original chosen time rapidly approached Tait allowed the first two aircraft of the covering party to make their dropping runs over the target, while rebroadcasting a revised zero hour of 2200 hours to the second sub-flight carrying the engineers. Either due to a lack of communication, or in line with Tait's original plan, Lashbrook's 'N' adhered to the

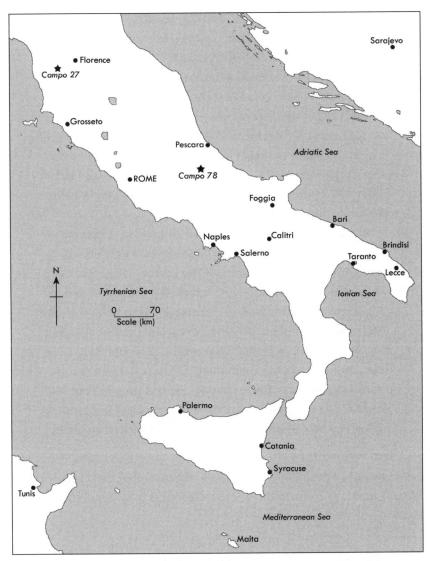

Italy, showing the target location and prisoner of war camps where some of X Troop were later held.

original zero hour and successfully dropped Deane-Drummond and his party; the agreed signal 'operations completed' was then transmitted, bringing in Flight Lieutenant Williams's 'W' which also dropped its troops at 2140 hours:

All eyes to the left. I suddenly saw the valley entrance, just like the briefing model. We turned in reduced speed by dropping

30-degree flap, then switched the warning light to 'Red' indicating to the paras that we were five minutes from the target. Just before we reached the bridge, we turned it to 'Green'. Without hesitation, they were away. First Nos. 1, 2 and 3 paras, then the containers, followed by Nos. 4, 5 and 6. As we turned to climb out of the valley it was great to see the parachutes of the soldiers and containers floating down around the target. It is interesting to note that Lieutenant Deane Drummond . . . who dropped as No. 5, says in his memoirs that he landed about 100 yards from the aqueduct. It was 40 minutes before any of the other teams joined him.

The side of the valley loomed up to meet us. I opened up to full throttle and for one horrible moment I didn't think we were going to make it. I swear if the undercarriage had been down, the wheels would have struck the rim. After gaining height and raising the flaps, our next task was to find a suitable diversionary target on which to drop our two bombs. As I flew over Calitri, it looked so peaceful. It would have been sheer murder to bomb such a target. After circling the town, I followed a railway line to a junction and dropped our 250 pounders on the station. We then set course for Malta, landing back at our base at Luqa, after being airborne for seven hours.[2]

A last-minute intercom failure between Deane-Drummond in the fuselage and Lashbrook in the cockpit almost foiled their timely drop. Fifteen minutes from target the paratroopers had been successfully alerted, but then only silence followed.

After what seemed like a very long fifteen minutes, we were astounded to see the rear gunner [Flight Lieutenant Bruce Williams of the Central Landing Establishment] come through from his perch in the tail and shout out, 'You are due to drop in under a minute. Get cracking.' The intercom had failed at the last minute, and for about ten seconds there was a pandemonium while we wrestled with the doors.[3]

Deane-Drummond's drop was nearly perfect. The aircraft aiming point had been designated as Hill 427, north-west of the aqueduct, the Whitley approaching on a line that bisected this feature and the target itself. The first two troopers, sitting with legs dangling through the open fuselage hatch buffeted by the icy blast of fast-moving air, watched the lights of Calitri flash by underneath before only seconds later the green light above them switched on and they threw themselves downwards, snatched away by the slipstream. The first three men dropped smoothly, after which Sergeant Lawley, acting as despatcher, pressed the button to release the four containers, followed by two more men and then Lawley himself simply unplugging his headphone set and stepping through the hole. Dropping from such a low altitude, each man had little more than fifteen seconds to survey his surroundings before he hit the ground. Deane-Drummond, who had been the fifth man to leave the aircraft, was gratified to see all containers and every one of his men swinging gently from their parachutes down to earth as the noise of the Whitley engines receded southwards. Aboard, Bruce Williams had returned to his rear gun turret and called out the parachutes that he saw over the intercom as Lashbrook threw his engines into maximum power to clear the edges of the valley safely. To Deane-Drummond the terrain looked familiar from Warburton's photographs and the landscape models with which they had worked in Britain, though he noted that the surrounding countryside appeared wilder and more contoured than he had expected. His section's primary task was to secure the small cluster of farmhouses nearby and any occupants found, and he saw them plainly silhouetted in the moonlight before his feet landed on the ploughed hillside only 100 yards above the aqueduct in what he remembered as the best landing he had ever made.

Untangling himself from the cumbersome parachute that lay sprawled across the ground, the young officer was swiftly joined by Lawley and three of his men who had made equally perfect drops, all exchanging the agreed recognition passwords 'Heil Hitler' and its reply 'Viva Duce'. Together they secured the four containers: two holding explosives, one a Bren gun and the last with four Thompson submachine guns. However, as Deane-Drummond's group gathered together it became apparent that one man was missing. Lance-Corporal Harry Boulter had made a smooth exit from the Whitley but had been unable to steer his statichute far from its original course

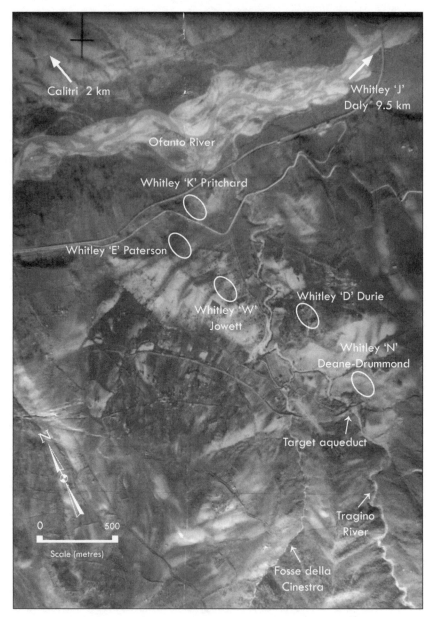

Calitri 2 km

Whitley 'J'
Daly 9.5 km

Ofanto River

Whitley 'K' Pritchard

Whitley 'E' Paterson

Whitley 'D' Durie

Whitley 'W'
Jowett

Whitley 'N'
Deane-Drummond

Target aqueduct

N

0   500

Scale (metres)

Tragino
River

Fosse della
Cinestra

The target area and the drop zones on the night of the attack.

and landed heavily on rocks along the bank of the Tragino, badly
fracturing his ankle.

Fortunato Picchi, alias Dupont, was among Deane-Drummond's
party and he and one other were immediately sent uphill to secure a

pair of small buildings, little more than shacks but potentially holding some of the people who tilled the surrounding fields. While Deane-Drummond waited at the aqueduct, 'Taff' Lawley took the last able-bodied man of the group to the west to search the small group of main farm buildings, instructed to bring any occupants to the aqueduct itself. Somewhat disturbingly for this first group, there appeared no sign of the remainder of X Troop following them in to the dropping zone and nagging doubts fuelled by the tension of the moment must have planted kernels of worry within the paratroopers' minds that they were perhaps the only men to have made it to the target. Isolated as they had been in the Whitley's fuselage, they had no way of knowing that zero hour had been pushed back for four of the other aircraft, while above them Williams's 'W' had already overflown the drop zone once and was coming around for a second pass at the target, leading to another unexpected slight delay.

Within 'W', Sergeant Percy Clements was sitting with his feet in the hole, ready to be the first man of his stick out of their aircraft. Williams had already told the paratroopers that he would pass over the target once or twice before giving the signal to jump; Clements had been able to see the aqueduct on at least one of the passes made. The intercom was functioning perfectly between the pilot and the man acting as despatcher and Clements tensed himself at the one-minute warning until the green light flickered on above his head. Immediately he launched himself forward, only to be frantically grabbed by the remaining men of his section as the light almost instantly flashed back to red. The Whitley had strayed too far over the river and was rapidly approaching an escarpment, Williams heaving the Whitley into a tight turning climb, circling for a second attempt. Unable to pull Clements back into the aircraft as the slipstream clutched at his lower body, the men grimly held on to him for nearly five interminable minutes before the green light shone once more and they let go, all six men successfully leaving the aircraft, although one of the weapons containers refused to be dislodged from its bomb bay.

Clements himself landed only eighty yards from the target aqueduct:

> The ground was ploughed and with lots of water in furrows, and I made my softest drop ever. But whilst in the air I'd been

able to pick out only two other 'chutes, and when the section closed, we found that our arms containers had failed to drop. After contacting No. 1 section at the aqueduct, we discovered that theirs, too, had failed to drop. So we felt much happier when No. 3 section came up and reported present and correct, and we all shared their quota of arms. No. 4 and 5 planes came over with the R.E. and explosives, and the job was started.[4]

Tait's own aircraft dropped Pritchard and his five accompanying men without problem, although prematurely as it transpired, Pritchard landing nearly a mile from the aqueduct on pebbles near the southern bank of the Ofanto River. Lance-Corporal Harry Pexton came down in the upper branches of a fourteen-foot tree but was fortunately able to free himself without assistance; perhaps the débâcle of the final training drop at Ringway had prepared him for such an eventuality after his rescue by the Knutsford fire brigade. However, a single container had failed to release, stuck within the starboard central bomb bay and depriving X Troop of its three Thompson submachine guns. Collecting the remainder of the containers, which held explosives, food and a ladder, Pritchard and his men immediately began moving towards the Tragino aqueduct, wary of possible encounters with Italian troops or civilians while running crouched across the foreign countryside.

Meanwhile, according to previously published accounts, back at the farmhouses near the aqueduct Lawley had been poised to enter the first farm building when its door was flung open and a man emerged silhouetted in the bright light spilling from the house interior. With him was a small dog, barking excitedly and freezing the blood in the British paratroopers' veins lest it detect their presence. However, both man and dog briefly disappeared into a nearby outbuilding, re-emerging to return to the house and close the door firmly behind them, betraying no sense of the two men's presence. With an audible sigh of relief, Lawley proceeded to lead his companion to the door before pushing it sharply open, Thompson menacingly pointed to the occupants beyond. It was a simple stone-floored room, lit by a dim paraffin light with a small fire burning for warmth. Facing the two Britons were a middle-aged man and another slightly younger, as well as a woman and several children. Lawley assured them in English that they meant no harm to any of the people gathered and the Italians' brief shock soon gave way to gabbled replies and questions, all of them lost on the two paratroopers who possessed no grasp of Italian. In reply, Lawley stretched out his hand to the elder man reassuring him by handshake that they faced no danger, motioning them outside but allowing them to don warmer clothes before exiting while his companion searched the few other rooms for any stragglers.

The second house entered by Lawley yielded another family group, this time including an Italian soldier in uniform who lunged for a nearby shotgun as Lawley once again stretched out his hand to signal no ill intentions towards the occupants of the house. Kicking the shotgun out of the Italian soldier's grasp, Lawley's levelled Thompson eloquently described the balance of power in the room, and the dejected Italian allowed himself to be led from the house to join the other civilians gathered outside. They were moved through the snowy farmyard towards the aqueduct, where Deane-Drummond continued to await the arrival of the remainder of X Troop.

Interestingly, years after the war, Nicola Nastri's younger brother Victor visited the Tragino aqueduct and met an old *contadino* who recalled being aware of the aircraft and going outside into the night air to watch the paratroopers descend *before* the arrival of Lawley. If so, then they were obviously aware of the paratroopers' presence before Lawley's entry into the houses. This seems quite likely as the presence of bombers at low altitude overhead would have been hard to miss in the still night air, and extremely unusual for that part of Italy in early 1941. With the occupants already outside, all that Lawley and his comrade had to do was round them up and take them to the aqueduct. The elderly peasant told Victor:

> It was such a bright moonlit night, when suddenly these white frothy graceful apparitions came floating down through the stars. I called my mother, and some of the other children. They came running out as did the other farmers in the area. We all gazed up at the sky, not understanding at all. Then someone said that they were angels floating down from heaven. Some fell to their knees and genuflected. It was a sight that I have never forgotten.[5]

In various fragments of information written in Italy about the raid, several of the people rounded up by Lawley later claimed to have initially believed that the paratroopers were Germans, engaged on some form of exercise. It is highly possible that the last thing expected by people who lived alongside the Tragino would be the presence of enemy troops in their corner of Italy. This, however, remains unsubstantiated as all the participants are no longer with us to answer such questions.

With the three covering parties already having dropped, the second wave of engineers began to jump. With Captain Daly's under-manned 'J' lagging, Paterson's five sappers were the next men to land, Paterson himself acting as despatcher aboard Whitley 'E' but frustrated after the first three men had launched themselves through the hole by an inability to release the containers. Repeatedly he hammered on the button on the hand-held control, before abandoning the attempt lest they overshoot the drop zone and sending his two remaining men through into the cold night air followed by himself as the last man out, fretting about the potential loss of weapons and explosives being carried back to Malta within the Whitley bomb bays. However, Pilot Officer Robinson circled the drop zone once more, his rear gunner taking the role of despatcher to drop the containers successfully, five holding explosives and the sixth a ladder.

Paterson wasn't the only man of his section to be alarmed during his brief fifteen-second descent. Below him Lance-Corporal Doug Jones narrowly missed a line of tall trees, managing to pull hard on the canopy's guidelines and head away from them, lifting his knees to clear the topmost branches, but landing in an almost horizontal position in the middle of the freezing waters of the Tragino river. Thoughts of the fate that had befallen Bombardier Dennis, drowned at Tatton Park in less than three feet of water, no doubt raced through his mind and if his canopy had landed on top of him, he might well have been in serious jeopardy. However, although the shock of sudden submersion caused momentary panic, he spluttered to the surface in what proved to be shallow but fast-moving water, his canopy carried away from him by the current. Gathering his senses, he banged hard on the quick-release buckle and let the statischute pull free, half wading and half crawling towards the bank where he vomited his unexpected mouthfuls of water before hauling himself to his feet and beginning to head to the aqueduct at a slow jog, knowing that he needed to get the blood circulating through his freezing body.

Aboard Sergeant Holden's Whitley 'D' there was no mistaking the drop zone, clearly visible and already dotted with scattered white parachutes on the ground. Sergeant 'Little Jock' Durie (so-named because he had been born in Brechin, Scotland, and was shorter than Sergeant John 'Big Jock' Walker) acted as despatcher as his men landed west of the narrow unpaved road that straggled towards the aqueduct not far from the western bank of the Tragino. All six containers carrying explosives and another ladder were successfully dropped alongside the men, who gathered them together before racing for the aqueduct, planning to return for the heavy explosives once the rendezvous with the rest of X Troop had been made. The arrival of the aircraft brought a wave of relief to Deane-Drummond and his men already at the target, now guarding the group of nearly two dozen Italian civilians and the single dispirited enemy soldier:

> Forty minutes later, at 10.15 pm, we heard more planes overhead. I expect one of the pilots had spotted our white parachutes on the ground and he fired off two green Very lights to attract the others. One by one they turned for a run in over Calitri and we saw the parachutes floating down in the silent night. We were all mighty relieved to see it happen in front of us, as were our Italian peasants who were grouped near the aqueduct. They also had front row seats and continually crossed themselves in amazement as they saw something they had never seen before. The Italian children jumped with excitement and clapped their hands. '*Angeli, angeli*' they shouted while their parents looked on in awe. No angels these, however, even though they were later to give part of their chocolate ration to the children.[6]

Above them and to the north-east, Tait remained circling over Mount Vulture awaiting possible visual reports of 'operations completed' by any aircraft that might have experienced wireless transmitter failure, though there were none, and by 2245 hours all Whitleys except for the tardy 'J' had left the area. This final aircraft dropped its paratroopers at 2330 hours, significantly late and, unfortunately, wide of the target area by a large margin. Hoad's 'J' had made a bad landfall on the Italian west coast and proceeded to follow the wrong river until coming within sight of the waters of the Adriatic Sea glistening in the moonlight. Navigator Pilot Officer James Thomas Houghton, RAFVR, frantically recalculated the aircraft's position and the Whitley arrived near Mount Vulture at approximately 2315 hours. Unfortunately, to make matters worse, none of the aircraft's containers (carrying explosives and a ladder) released when Daly and his four men were dropped, although even if they had they would have been no use. The five men drifted silently by parachute into a broad valley that sloped upwards to Mount Vulture; seven miles north-east of the aqueduct near the town of Monticchio Bagni. Harry Tomlin was one of the luckless paratroopers.

> We were carrying sidearms, revolver, and whatever else the troop was taking with them. But of course, we never got anything from our plane. I don't know where he dropped our things. The flight was all right, but of course the first thing one does after a flight like that, is, you have to go to the toilet . . . And of course, we were in a line across the field, there were five of us, just having a wee. Nobody else about. I wondered where the hell the others had got to, we didn't see any more. And then we started to climb up the mountainside and we heard an explosion, and Captain Daly said, 'Well that's it . . . it's gone off. There's no point in going towards it any more. Turn back the other way and go for the coast.' We were in the wrong valley.

While Daly's men were still flying towards their incorrect dropping zone, the remainder of X Troop had begun assembling at the aqueduct. Boulter had been found painfully dragging himself towards the aqueduct and was helped into a sheltered spot by other men who then raced ahead as their orders dictated. On Pritchard's arrival Deane-Drummond briefed him swiftly on events thus far, including the Italians held under guard and the lack of Captain Daly, head of the demolition party. Much to everybody's relief, one of the nagging questions regarding the target had also been answered: it was unguarded and there appeared to be no enemy troops in the vicinity save for one man visiting his family and now under guard. Most of the heavy explosive bundles had been left with their containers, the small location lights attached to the wooden frames still burning, which would allow their relocation and collection. Realising that dragging the heavy slabs of guncotton to the aqueduct would unnecessarily tire his men, Pritchard ordered the more able-bodied Italians to be pressed into service as porters alongside the sweating sappers, while the women, children and older men were secured in one of the farm houses from which they had come. The covering parties were fanned out as they had rehearsed repeatedly at Tatton Park on the mock bridge, taking up firing positions in the event of the arrival of any curious enemy troops. 'Killer' Jowett and his men formed a loose line strung across the Tragino immediately north of where the Fosse della Cinestra joined the main torrent. To his west, Deane-Drummond and his party guarded the farmhouses to which they had returned some of the civilians and watched the approach road that trailed off towards Calitri. Near the smaller of the two aqueducts, Lea watched the western approaches with two of his men from the top of a small ridge that crowned the one of the farm's ploughed fields, hiding in scrubby bushes that provided at least minimal cover. The remainder of Lea's men remained near the target aqueduct itself, warily monitoring the abandoned shacks to the east for any sign of movement.

The hour now belonged to the sappers, With Picchi and Lucky translating the orders to the captured Italians, the British were surprised at how willingly they took part in the retrieval of the guncotton from the scattered containers. Apparently, they told the two interpreters, nothing of any interest ever happened in this part of Italy and the excitement of the evening would give them something to talk about for years to come. Whether the single Italian soldier was as content as his civilian counterparts is not known. The task of lugging the fifty-pound slabs of guncotton into place was arduous and Pritchard remained at the aqueduct as sweating groups of sappers and Italians began carrying the demolition equipment to the target. Apart from muttered curses and the occasional good-natured jokes exchanged at low volume between the working sappers, the night was still and quiet, broken only by the farm's dogs barking interminably, something that was not strange in the Italian night, dogs being frequently used to keep foxes and wolves away from livestock. While the repetitive barking may have grated on the paratroopers' nerves, to local inhabitants it would have barely raised an eyebrow.

Before long, it became obvious that Captain Daly was seriously overdue, and Pritchard pulled Paterson aside and passed the task on to him as Daly's deputy. Paterson had already made a preliminary inspection of the aqueduct itself, finding it similar to the model with which they had become familiar, though not as squat as predicted, the central pier standing mid-stream almost thirty feet high. Yet, a more urgent doubt had begun to germinate at the back of his mind since studying Warburton's reconnaissance photographs in Malta. All indications given by W. G. Ardley of the London engineering firm that had first brought the aqueduct to the Air Ministry's attention were that the structure was made of masonry, the carried guncotton being ample to blow out the entire central span by destroying at least two supporting piers. However, the sheer scale and width of the aqueduct had already led Paterson to believe that this was unlikely construction material, rather that the structure required more strength to carry the quantity of water that flowed over the centre span.

Standing beside one of the piers, Paterson, assisted by Sergeant Drury, took a hammer and chisel and began chipping its surface, soon realising his worst fear. While masonry would present little problem to the explosive power of the guncotton, the Tragino aqueduct was built from reinforced concrete, a far more resistant material than they had been led to believe. To make matters worse, Daly and his missing party were meant to bring five containers of guncotton, leaving an amount of explosive that Paterson was not even sure could achieve the desired destruction that they had travelled so far to inflict on Italy's straining war machine.

The guncotton could indeed be blown, but to what effect? Indeed Major Rock's initial summation of the method by which the aqueduct was to be destroyed had stipulated that: 'Should they prove to be reinforced concrete, no attempt would be made to blow them, but the reinforced concrete girders of the aqueduct were to be blown at midspan on two adjacent spans on either side of an end pier, these piers having roller bearings.'[7]

Operation Colossus could yet be an entirely futile endeavour.

The blocking positions adopted by the attack force while the charges were laid, with the locations of the aqueducts and the small bridge.

As events unfolded on the ground in Italy, the Whitleys were already headed home, the last of them landing back at Luqa airfield on Malta by 0200 hours the following morning as Hoad brought his aircraft safely back from its extended flight. Low cloud had obscured the island on approach and all aircraft required W/T guidance. Diversionary bombs carried by Sergeant Ennis's 'R' had been successfully dropped on target at Foggia, hitting the railway station and yard and setting fire to a petrol-carrying train, the trucks exploding and creating a major conflagration that spread to some adjacent stationary trains. Machine-gun fire from Ennis's rear gunner sprayed men seen to be trying to move the damaged train away from the blaze, making them scurry visibly for cover. The other aircraft carrying smaller bomb loads alongside their cargo of containers had also dropped them on scattered targets, the entire family of five of the agricultural expert Domenico Rorro unfortunately being killed when several bombs were dropped on Monteverde. However, one of the Whitleys was missing. Aircraft 'S', flown by Lancashireman Pilot Officer Jack Wotherspoon, designated one of the diversionary raiders bound for Foggia, reported a port engine failure not long after passing the Italian coast, then jettisoning bombs and turning back for Malta until the starboard engine began to overheat dramatically. With little alternative, the entire crew bailed out near Battipaglia after Sergeant Basil Albon sent a hurried message in the RAF's basic 'Syko' code to Malta, reporting their predicament and requesting extraction if possible from the point that they were likely to land, near the mouth of the Sele River at almost the exact location planned for the rendezvous between the withdrawing paratroopers and HMS *Triumph*.[8]

Meanwhile back at Tragino the sappers continued their task of piling guncotton at the aqueduct as the covering party scanned the surrounding countryside for any signs that their arrival had been detected. Suddenly, a lone figure on a bicycle appeared before Deane-Drummond.

> Our orders were to give warning of anybody coming up the valley and, if necessary, to prevent interference with the parties carrying the explosives ... As it happened the only man in uniform who appeared was the local station master from Calitri station. He was duly impressed into the labour gang and made quite a good porter, as was only proper. His biggest worry was that he would be late taking over from his relief and might get the sack. If he was sacked, he would be put in the army and sent to the front, which he pointed out was far too terrible a punishment for kind people like us to inflict on him. We told him that his skilled labour was required, but that if he liked we would give him a certificate to say that he had been detained against his will. This cheered him up tremendously and from then on nobody could stop him talking. He said he might even get a medal for his heroic labours. We heard later

that most of these civilians were awarded medals for their brave conduct in the face of the enemy.[9]

As the explosives were gathered, Paterson weighed possible courses of action after his discovery that the aqueduct was far more robust than they had been led to believe. Daly's original demolition plan called for a minimum of two of the three piers and one of the abutments to be destroyed, which would conceivably have collapsed the entire length of the aqueduct and caused severe delays in reconstruction, possibly putting it out of commission for an entire month. However, this was virtually impossible given the amount of explosive on hand. Instead, Paterson planned to use nearly all available guncotton on a single pier. With good fortune and the help of gravity he hoped that this could also bring down enough of the span, or even one or both neighbouring piers, and achieve much the same result. Daly's containers still aboard Hoad's Whitley were the only ones containing explosives that had not dropped but even some of those that had been successfully parachuted were now proving difficult to recover as the small battery-powered lights began to go out, rendering them difficult to locate. In total Paterson reckoned that he had approximately 800 pounds of guncotton to work with rather than the originally loaded 2,240 pounds. Nonetheless, it would have to suffice.

Improvising, Paterson decided to use 640 pounds against the westernmost pier and 160 pounds on the adjacent abutment. The sappers Doug Jones and Robert 'Mad Bob' Watson stood on a pair of ladders to string the steel cable half way up the structure of the pier and wrap it around the column using the notched angle plates, the sheepshanks and hooks facilitating the hanging of charge boards, top and bottom, each with four boxes of explosives attached. By this method the pier was completely encircled by explosives. The other sappers lifted the heavy planks into place or piled the allocated guncotton into position against the abutment.

As they laboured, the distinct noise of an incoming aircraft grew steadily louder from the north-east. It appeared to be headed directly for their position and fears arose that it could be an Italian or even a German aircraft alerted by the earlier presence of the Whitley bombers and arriving to investigate. While the hours of darkness were long during the Italian winter, the small dark shapes of moving men silhouetted against patches of snow could be easily discerned by a vigilant aircrew in the bright moonlight. However, after several heart-pounding minutes the aircraft passed east of the aqueduct and gradually receded. Though the men at the aqueduct were not to know it at the time, Captain Daly and his missing group of sappers were being dropped miles to the north-east moments later. Though the attackers had avoided detection by the enemy, the noise of barking dogs now extended far down the valley towards Calitri itself, prompting anxiety over the possibility of the local military raising their alert level.

Nonetheless, the paratroopers were not deflected from their task and before long the sappers were producing the detonators that each carried in a tins in his battledress pocket. Once enough guncotton had been brought to the aqueduct, Deane-Drummond commandeered a final pair of boxes for his own use. Near the western farmhouses there was a small concrete bridge over the Fosse della Cinestra that connected the unpaved road from Calitri to the farm tracks leading to the aqueducts; it was wide enough to accommodate a truck and looked ripe for destruction, Deane-Drummond reasoning that if it, too, were blown to pieces it would hamper the bringing of men and material to the main target to effect any repairs. Lance-Corporal Watson and Sapper Ross were soon busy placing the two boxes, their detonators and the slow-burning sixty-second fuses beneath the small concrete bridge while a runner was sent to inform Pritchard of the extra bang to be expected.

Not long after midnight all explosives were in place and the Italian captives were herded back into the farmhouse to join the women and children already held within. While most of the sappers and the eastern covering group withdrew to crouch behind a spur of land to the west near the smaller aqueduct, Paterson remained with Pritchard at the site of the explosives. The agreed signal for the fuses to be lit was detonation of a single slab of guncotton and once his men were at a safe distance, Pritchard blew up the small signal slab and prepared to trigger the main explosive. His watch showed 0029 hours. The moment of truth had arrived, and Paterson lit the sixty-second fuse linked to the cordtex and charges on the aqueduct as he and Pritchard ran for cover. Simultaneously Watson lit the fuse to the charges beneath the

A Whitley II bomber, serial number K7232, engaged in parachuting training over Tatton Park.

Left: Soviet paratroopers. The Red Army was the first to see the full potential of massed parachute attacks.

Bottom left: The débâcle of Dunkirk. Beaten from the Continent by the German invasion, the British Army was in some disarray. This provided a fertile recruiting ground for men wanting to 'get back into the fight'.

Below: Bruce Williams, a pre-war circus parachutist and qualified wartime air gunner who joined Louis Strange's training staff. Williams crewed as a rear-gunner during Colossus and was later disciplined for breaching secrecy rules.

BRUCE WILLIAMS PARACHUTIST 1935

Squadron Leader Louis Strange leaving Buckingham Palace with his daughter Susan after receiving a Bar to his DFC, 3 Sept. 1940.

Lt.-Col. Charles Jackson, CO of No.2 (Parachute) Commando, subsequently 11 SAS Battalion.

Gen. Dill inspects 11 SAS Battalion, December 1940, Lt.-Col. Jackson stands second from left, his Royal Tank Regiment insignia visible on his shoulder. Also of interest is the small GQ parachute badge worn by those who are qualified paratroopers before the introduction of cloth wings.

Recruits training on terra firma for jumping through the hole in a Whitley bomber.

Paratrooper showing the rear-gunner perch from which the Whitley 'pull off' method was used, though he would have been facing forward in action.

'Going through the hole' on a Whitley for real.

Italian internment on the Isle of Man, where Fortunato Picchi was recruited by SOE.

Fortunato Picchi.

Raoul Lucovich, alias Ralph Henry Lucky.

'Tag' Pritchard, commanding officer of X Troop, pictured here in pre-war India.

Wally Lashbrook with his DFC ribbon.

The Illustrated London News, 14 December 1940, with an artist's impression of the capture of Prince Olaf of Norway's car during the manoeuvres at Shrewton.

X Troop with a warrant officer instructor. 'Killer' Jowett is immediately recognisable with his bristling moustache.

Flying Officer Adrian 'Warby' Warburton, photographic reconnaissance specialist.

Corporal Ralph Chapman. He was disembarked from his Whitley bomber as it prepared to take off and missed Operation Colossus.

Main image: A Whitley bomber dropping paratroopers; with practice, a stick of eight men could clear the Whitley in less than fifteen seconds.

Bottom: Men of 11 SAS Battalion photographed in front of a Whitley in January 1941 with their Irving parachute systems and leather helmets.

Bottom: X Troop before they left for Malta. Several men are recognisable: Sgt. Lawley is third from left in the front row, with Pilot Officer Lucky to his left. Also in the front row is 2nd Lt. Jowett, showing off his moustache and beloved Highland bonnet, with Sgt. Clements to his left.

The photograph of the Tragino aqueduct used in planning the mission, from published engineering journals. Taken during construction, the foreground buildings were temporary worker accommodation.

The nearest of the scattering of farmhouses to the bridge and aqueduct (photographed here in 2018) has changed little over the decades. Most of them have had an additional upper storey constructed, changing their appearance from 1940.

The smaller aqueduct over the Fosse della Cinestra and the nearby farmhouses, some of them dating from before the raid. The lower buildings of Calitri can be glimpsed in the distance at top left.

A present-day photograph taken from Calitri, showing the Tragino aqueduct, Fosse della Cinestra aqueduct and Deane-Drummond's small bridge. Deane-Drummond's party landed on the sloping field to the left.

Campo 78, Sulmona.

X Troop men photographed by the International Red Cross in their compound in Campo 78.
Four of the five RAF men were the crew of Whitley 'S' that crashed on the night of the operation.
1. L/Cpl. Maher, 2. Sgt. Walker, 3. Sgt. Harry Meddings RAF, 4. L/Cpl. Jones, 5. Cpl. Julian,
6. L/Cpl. Tomlin, 7. Spr. Pryor, 8. L/Cpl. Pexton, 9. Spr. Struthers, 10. Cpl. Grice, 11. Sgt. Lawley,
12. Sgt. Fred Southam RAF, 13. L/Cpl. Henderson, 14. Spr. Davidson, 15. Pvt. James Parker,
16. L/Cpl. Watson, 17. Spr. Ross, 18. RAF Navigator (not on Colossus), 19. Sgt. Durie,
20. Sgt. Clements, 21. Pvt. Samuels, 22. Spr. Phillips, 23. Pvt Humphreys, 24. Sgt Shutt,
25. Cpl. O'Brien, 26. Sgt. Eric Hodges RAF, 27. Sgt. Basil Albon RAF, 28. Pvt. Nastri,
29. Cpl. Fletcher, 30. Spr. Alf Parker.

A photograph taken after members of X Troop had been transferred to Campo di Lavoro 102 in 1942.

1. L/Cpl. Robert Watson, 2. Spr. Owen Phillips, 3. Pvt. Albert Samuels, 4. L/Cpl. Doug Henderson, 5. Pvt. Ernest Humphreys, 6. L/Cpl. Harry Pexton, 7. Spr. Glyn Pryor, 8. L/Cpl. Jim Maher, 9. L/Cpl. Harry Tomlin, 10. Sgt. Edward Durie, 11. Pvt. James Parker, 12. Sgt. John Walker, 13. Cpl. J. Grice, 14. Cpl. Peter O'Brien, 15. Pvt. Nicola Nastri, 16. Spr. R. Davidson.

Haggard and downcast: Fortunato Picchi's mugshot following capture.

58272-PICCHI Fortunato fu Ferdinando

Roll call at Campo 78, Sulmona.

Oflag IX-A/Z, Rotenburg an der Fulda, Hesse, where Captain Christopher Lea ended the war.

Private James Parker in his pre-war Durham Light Infantry uniform.

Private Nicola Nastri after the war. The chevrons on his lower arm denote five years' overseas service.

Christopher Gerald Lea photographed post-war.

Percy Clements, photographed in 1944 as a lieutenant in the 12th (Yorkshire) Battalion, Parachute Regiment.

Arthur Lawley, photographed in 1944–5 while a sergeant-major with 13th (Lancashire) Parachute Battalion.

'Tag' Pritchard (in beret) and liberating Soviet troops, Stalag Luft I, April 1945.

Anthony Deane-Drummond photographed after the war as a lieutenant-colonel.

small bridge near the farmhouses and he and Deane-Drummond raced for shelter behind the nearest building.

The seconds ticked by, stretching to an interminable wait that seemed to have exceeded two full minutes, the damp night air probably causing the safety fuses to burn slower than expected. In their high level of excitement, none of the men had thought to count the seconds and Pritchard and Paterson raised their heads to peer into the darkness towards the main aqueduct. Both men wrestled with the idea that there may have been a faulty fuse before deciding to walk carefully towards the aqueduct to investigate. They had only covered a short distance when, with a sharp ear-splitting crack and blinding flash, the guncotton exploded, its blast wave throwing both men off their feet. This explosion was followed almost immediately by another at Deane-Drummond's little bridge. The latter officer, huddled with Watson, was surprised at the amount of debris that rained down around their ears, large pieces of the concrete bridge blown high into the night sky and landing with seemingly deafening thuds around the two men and across the roofs of the squat farm buildings. In apparent panic, one woman raced from the house with an infant in her arms, obviously believing the roof to be caving in, the anxious cries of the other inhabitants clearly heard by the two paratroopers. They swiftly abandoned their cover and ran across to return the woman to the house and ensure that no damage had been inflicted on either the building or those inside, gradually managing to calm the frightened occupants.

Pritchard and Paterson picked themselves up from the mud as the rubble finally stopped raining about their ears and moved off to investigate the result of the explosion, while the remainder of X Troop gathered in the assembly position to the west. Deane-Drummond and Watson had already returned to the site of their own miniature demolition job and were gratified to see the small concrete bridge blown in half, most of it resting in the sludge of the stream below. Now they awaited the return of 'Tag' and 'Pat' who had disappeared towards the main aqueduct. None of the waiting men could rid themselves of the worry that their efforts might have been in vain. They all knew that they had been desperately short of explosives and that intelligence regarding the aqueduct's construction had been faulty, if not virtually non-existent. After six weeks of arduous training the thought of potential failure now nagged at their minds as they waited anxiously for the two officers to return. Finally, they emerged from the darkness, both men smiling until Pritchard silenced his men's questions with an upraised hand. 'Listen,' he said, and the paratroopers strained their ears before they heard the sound they had hoped for: a huge waterfall where there had previously been nothing.

The cheers that followed from the assembled paratroopers must have been audible for miles, probably alerting anybody within earshot who had not already been awoken by the two blasts. Pritchard allowed them all quickly to survey the damage done to the aqueduct. The single pier that had been girdled with explosives had been completely destroyed and the neighbouring one leaned at a perilous angle to the aqueduct body, which had clearly been severed, water flowing from both ends into the Tragino River below; the western end of the aqueduct was still pumping water from the Apennines, while that at the higher eastern end flowed back through the broken chamber as gravity added its weight to the paratroopers' destruction. The concussion had badly holed other portions of the water chamber and the aqueduct could be considered cut, although the abutment still appeared relatively solid. Nonetheless, Colossus had achieved at least some measure of its purpose and success had been snatched from the jaws of the failure that could have resulted from the unexpected loss Daly's personnel and equipment.

Now, with the incessant barking of farm dogs stretching far down the valley, the raiders immediately felt fingers of cold and fatigue take hold of them as the tension of the past few hours slowly released. They then faced possibly the most daunting challenge of the operation. In a heavily populated enemy country, they needed to make a trek of some sixty miles through a winter landscape that included mountainous terrain and scattered villages along their route before reaching the coast where they would, they hoped, make a rendezvous with their means of escape aboard HMS *Triumph*. While the odds on successfully destroying the aqueduct had been stacked against them following the drop, the odds they now faced must have appeared almost insurmountable. Nevertheless, the now tried and tested paratroopers would give their all, including the two middle-aged translators who, while they may have lacked the peak physical fitness and stamina of their comrades, possessed a raw determination to continue to play the fullest part as men of X Troop.

The attack was over. Now Operation Colossus became a matter of evasion.

Chapter Six

Manhunt

As the men of X Troop gathered around 'Tag' Pritchard, they were finally informed of the nature of the evacuation plan with HMS *Triumph*. He did not sugar-coat the perilous nature of the trek that now faced the raiders: sixty miles over difficult terrain deep in enemy territory where the 'Eyeties' would be fully alert and actively searching for them. The decision had already been taken amongst the officers in Malta that X Troop would divide into separate groups. Obviously, Daly was on his own as he had never made rendezvous at the aqueduct after being dropped so far off course. The remaining twenty-nine men would divide into three parties, each taking a slightly different track towards the coastline, arranged roughly in advance and designed not to intersect, while all retaining as direct a route as was practicable. Though the likelihood of enemy contact was high, Pritchard recommended that all but the minimum arms be jettisoned near the Tragino, each group retaining only their pistols, grenades and knives as well as one Thompson. The Bren guns and all remaining weapons were to be dis-assembled and thrown away as they would need to move fast and therefore as light as possible. All remaining demolition equipment was discarded, but the men were still encumbered by a 30-pound pack that carried five days' supply of food, mess tins and survival equipment necessary for existing in the freezing damp conditions of the mountainous Italian winter countryside. Between them they also carried ten water bottles, ten primus stoves and ten petrol containers.

For Harry Boulter there was to be no escaping. His fractured ankle had settled the matter the minute he had landed. Instructions for all of X Troop were that any man wounded or otherwise injured had to be left behind for the good of the mission; a fact that every man understood and accepted. Though it was a bitter pill to swallow, having been unable to take an active part in the destruction of the aqueduct Boulter had resigned himself to staying behind, insisting that one of the Thompson submachine guns be left with him before the others departed. Pritchard bound and splinted his ankle as best he could and Boulter was made as comfortable as possible and given a quantity of painkillers, a map and a compass in the unlikely event he could evade detection. Boulter also knew of the submarine rendezvous, in the near impossible event that he could make his own way somehow to the coast; more realistically it was understood between them all that if captured he would divulge only his name, rank and serial number. Each man filed past and shook the luckless lance-corporal's hand, leaving cigarettes and chocolate and wishing him the best of luck, while knowing with almost virtual certainty that, before another day was over, he would be an Italian captive.

After breaking apart the weapons that were to be abandoned, pushing the pieces into patches of thick mud and under dense brush thickets, the three groups then prepared to move off. Through Picchi as translator the Italians still ensconced in their farmhouse were informed of the fiction that, although they were not being locked in and most of the raiders were moving off, sentries were being left with orders to shoot on sight any person who emerged from the doorway. It was enough to keep them in place for the hours that stretched until dawn.

Pritchard's party consisted of himself and eleven men and included Deane-Drummond, 'Taff' Lawley, Philip Julian, Doug Jones, Doug Henderson as well as two of the translators, Nicola Nastri and Fortunato Picchi. Nastri had been told by Pritchard while still in Malta to 'stick to me like a limpet, no matter who else gets cut off from me, once we land you are my ears and my only means of communication' and Pritchard relied heavily on the young trooper – more so than Picchi – for what he foresaw as likely encounters with locals. Henderson insisted on keeping his heavy Bren gun despite Pritchard's recommendation to ditch heavy weapons, unwilling to leave the machine gun behind buried in the Italian mud and uncomplaining at the extra twenty-five pounds he had laden himself with. They departed first, falling in single file after Pritchard as they began climbing the mountain behind the aqueduct. From there they intended to follow the ridge until meeting the Sele watershed from which point they would make their way down the north side of the Sele valley and head towards the coastline. However, the theoretical route indicated by the map and aerial photographs did no justice to the monumental struggle the men now faced. As well as thick glutinous mud that sucked at their feet as they traipsed uphill, the terrain was broken by impenetrable thickets of bushes and trees, numerous isolated farmhouses with the inevitable barking dogs, and myriad ravines, some impassable and requiring significant detours to skirt. The going was arduous in the extreme and every three-quarters of an hour Pritchard called a brief halt so that the men could nibble some of their precious chocolate to sustain energy levels and gulp down some water. Occasionally, to maintain the amount of water carried within canteens, men would drink from one of the many streams carrying melted snow downhill, but not only did this chill them but it could also cause painful – though brief – stomach cramps. The weather remained clear but bitterly cold, the date of 8 February, only two nights before, normally marking the coldest average temperature in Calitri and its environs.

At around 0700 hours dawn broke in the eastern sky and the exhausted men settled down into a ravine through which a stream carried melted snow over a jumbled bed of large boulders. Trees sheltered a small clearing and Pritchard ordered his party to hide and rest as best they could. After about three hours of exhausted slumber huddled under shelter, sleep began to prove elusive in the extreme cold, and the smokeless primus stoves were broken out to brew hot, sweet tea which raised morale a little. Some attempted to boil cubes of pemmican into a thick greasy porridge but, despite its warmth and undoubted nutritional properties, it proved almost inedible to the men who preferred to deal with their hunger through an occasional cigarette and piece of hard biscuit or chocolate. Dishearteningly, Pritchard and Deane-Drummond soon established that they were not far from the small village of Pescopagano and although they must have covered about fifteen kilometres of difficult ground, they had only moved six or so closer to the Gulf of Salerno. They would have to at least double the mileage covered to stand any chance of successfully making their rendezvous with HMS *Triumph*, which sailed from Malta that morning in preparation for the rendezvous. The unwelcome appearance of a small reconnaissance aircraft circling near their location for about ten minutes during the morning heightened their anxiety, each man lying still with his face turned away from the searching aircraft, which eventually flew away without appearing to have spotted them. The alarm had obviously been raised, and their intention to make for the coast guessed by the Italian authorities who began to mobilise units of the Blackshirt militia (Milizia Volontaria per la Sicurezza Nazionale, or MVSN), Carabinieri, Bersaglieri troops, and search parties comprised of enterprising local farmers armed with shotguns and farming implements.

Back near the aqueduct, Harry Boulter had seen the rays of dawn pierce the sky from a small shack to which he had painfully hobbled. Not long after the disappearance of the last of the escape groups he had removed the boot from his foot which had begun to swell painfully. After cutting the boot away using his knife, Boulter wrapped his leather helmet packed with snow around his ankle to ease the pain. Managing a few hours of fitful sleep on a small pile of straw within the shack which normally sheltered sheep, evidenced by the presence of wisps of wool caught on the rough wooden planking, Boulter woke with the dawn and saw the first signs of life from the farmhouses below when the Italian soldier who had been incarcerated within cautiously peeked his head out of the door. Detecting no sign of the British troops, the man lost no time in racing to retrieve the station master's bicycle and sped down the road towards Calitri. Boulter raised his Thompson and fired a burst of bullets after the Italian, missing by a wide margin as the man pedalled out of range – and immediately regretting having given his presence away.

Boulter was now acutely aware that he had blown his cover and painfully limped his way uphill to take refuge behind a boulder from where he could still observe the approach road to the aqueduct. Not long afterward, and long before the Italian soldier could have reached Calitri, a pair of cars slowly made their way along the unpaved road leading from the banks of the Ofanto to the farmhouses. Stopping outside, two Carabinieri stepped out of the lead vehicle, followed by several civilian men armed with shotguns from the other. From the farmhouses, they could not see the damage done to the aqueduct, which lay over a small rise and outside of their line of sight, but Deane-Drummond's destroyed bridge and the noise of pouring water was enough to tell them that they had found the source of the explosions heard hours before. While one of the Carabinieri made his way to the Tragino aqueduct, the other talked animatedly with the occupants of the house who had since emerged into the daylight. As the armed civilians drove away, a truck loaded with more Carabinieri arrived and they began a direct ascent towards the small shack in which Boulter had been hidden, several opening fire with rifles at the low building until close enough to rush forward, finding it empty.

From his vantage point Boulter watched the soldiers fan out across the muddy field, deciding to make a stand even if only to occupy this group of soldiers and hopefully buy the others time to get further away. He opened fire with his Thompson, the shots going wide from the submachine gun which, though prized in close combat for its rate of fire and the punch of the .45-calibre bullets, lacked the accuracy of a rifle at greater distances. The Italians dropped to the ground and returned fire, bullets pinging uncomfortably close to the single Briton, sending chips of rock flying.

The outcome was never in any doubt, and after several exchanges of bullets Boulter's ammunition supply was exhausted. Before long the lack of return fire betrayed his predicament to the Italians who warily approached his hiding place, which they soon surrounded, disarming Boulter and knocking him face down into the mud. A Carabinieri NCO handcuffed his hands behind his back and lifted him roughly on to his knees. Amidst much shouting that Boulter could not understand, the Italians tried to prod him to his feet with their rifles, Boulter pointing to his ankle as the pain had reached such a level that he could no longer stand. Instead, the Italians began hitting him with fists and rifle butts, the paratrooper falling sideways and shielding his head from the blows being rained upon him. Apparently, his uniform was torn during this severe treatment, and the corner of the silk escape map revealed. Ultimately, it was this that spared him further injury, as his captors became engrossed in the map which they tore from his battledress.

Pulled painfully to his feet, Boulter was made to limp downhill to the truck, stumbling several times before being hit with a rifle butt to encourage him to continue. Eventually he reached the truck and was unceremoniously dumped in the back with the Carabinieri guarding him as it departed and wound its way uphill to the Carabinieri station in Calitri. He was not there for long, soon bundled into a car and taken to Naples Central Prison, a veritable fortress situated on Via Nuova Poggioreale, where he finally received some medical treatment for his ankle, which was confirmed as fractured. The first of X Troop was now a captive and soon his interrogation would begin.

While Boulter was making his stand against the Italians, Lea and the ten men of his party were resting as best they could after the same nightmarish trek that the other escape parties had experienced, trudging through mud and slush that clung to their battledress trousers like thick treacle. Heading slightly to the north of Pritchard on a roughly parallel course, Lea led a group that included George Paterson, John Walker, Derry Fletcher, Peter O'Brien, 'Mad Bob' Watson, Harry Pexton, Jim Maher and James Parker. Trudging through frequently knee-deep mud, the party took a break every two hours to rest and recover slightly before pushing on like automatons towards their goal. Before dawn had broken, they holed up in a tree-covered ravine, resting at first on a dry river bed before trickling water from snow melting in the higher daytime temperature threatened to wash away their equipment while compounding the misery of already wet uniforms. The same aircraft that had buzzed Pritchard also made its presence known above their position, but again showed no sign of locating the eleven men below. The sound of distant trucks was also heard, probably troops heading to Sant'Andrea di Conza to join the spreading search for the saboteurs.

The last group of seven from the aqueduct – Jowett, Lucky, Clements, Grice, Ross, Crawford and Struthers – travelling furthest to the south, shared the same experiences, recounted three years later by Clements for the official journal of the Leicestershire Regiment:

> My section was commanded by a grand little Scots Canadian, Second Lieutenant Jowett. That first night's travel was something to remember. Although we kept on for over three hours, we covered only about eight kilometres in actual distance owing largely to the hills and the mud, which was well above

the knees for the greater part. All three sections rested for the following day within a radius of about three miles, and at 7.30 p.m. on the 11th we were off again. Dogs barking marked our progress practically the whole way. At midnight we crossed the snow line, and then started down on our journey to the coast. In all, that night from 7.30 p.m. to 2.15 a.m. we covered about twenty-five miles of very broken country, during which our section's interpreter . . . Lucky, RAF, had to drop out with a damaged knee.[1]

As the paratroopers rested in cover after the ordeal of their first night of the trek towards the coast, daylight unfortunately did not permit any RAF aerial reconnaissance of the aqueduct from 69 Squadron due to minor bomb damage suffered during the night by all of the available aircraft. While the Whitley aircrews on Malta were excused duties for the duration of the morning, their aircraft were examined and details of all containers that had failed to release were diligently noted for future study. It was found that the canvas coverings of the wooden framework had sagged considerably during the flight and that this sometimes prevented the bomb bay doors from opening. The development of all-metal containers was subsequently put into high gear to stop this ever happening again. The remaining containers and stores were moved to Lazaretto as the Whitleys were serviced once more for their return to Britain. During the following day, a conference was held with the assembled crews and operational reports taken down. Wing Commander Norman waited only for favourable weather for the return trip, his flight finally departing on the night of 16 February bound for Mildenhall.[2] Not all of the Whitleys were able to depart at the same time, as Wally Lashbrook later recalled in his unpublished memoir:

From the time we first landed at Luqa, the aerodrome had been subjected to increased bombing by both the German and Italian aircraft. After the exercise, the attacks became fiercer than ever, especially at night. The weather reports were continually adverse for the trip back home so after five days we were told we would have to leave the island. If we couldn't go home, there was always Egypt. We packed our bags ready to move out the next day. On arrival at the airfield first thing in the morning, I was dismayed to find that a bomb had exploded just outside my dispersal point safety wall. In doing so, it blasted large rocks over the wall, one going through the port wing, leaving a large hole about two feet across, while the other struck the port rudder and tail fin, causing extensive damage. The rest of the crews took off for the UK leaving behind my crew, with a volunteer replacement tail gunner. Two of my messmates volunteered to let my wife know the reason for my absence. Betty and I were living out in the local village at the time. She heard the Whitleys returning and received one hell of a shock when she answered a knock at the door to find my two mates standing there with my kitbag between them. Her fears were quickly calmed when all was explained. The kitbag was full of 'goodies' – oranges and lemons etc. A welcome change of fruit for one and all!

At the airfield the local riggers and sheet metal workers set about repairing the damage. The rudder was removed and sent to the workshops at Kalafrana (the flying boat base) for their attention. They did a good job, but I finished up with one rectangular rudder and one oval one. The hole in the wing was, I was told, effectively made good by inserting bits from one of three old Gladiators: either Faith, Hope or Charity. Repairs were completed by 21 February. The port rudder was 'squared off' during the repair at Kalafrana and had quite a different profile to its starboard partner. During the 30-minute air test, I found it functioned satisfactorily.

We stood by for a favourable weather forecast and left for UK in the late afternoon of 25th February. We climbed to usual height of around 9,000 feet and entered dense cloud before we were able to sight the coast of Sardinia. Unfortunately, we were unable to break cloud from then on or to obtain loop bearings or see the stars. We had to rely entirely on the Met. Forecast winds and dead reckoning. Wireless silence was a MUST. Our destination was of course Mildenhall, so when our E.T.A. was up, I turned and flew 20 minutes on a westerly course, hoping at least that it would see us clear of the Continent.

I then descended to 1,500 feet on the altimeter. We began to see searchlights weaving towards us then all swinging and pivoting in the same direction. I turned that way and within a few minutes found an aircraft beacon. Further indication by searchlights led us to a flare path. Green Aldis Lamps flashed at us. I decided to land. Once on the airfield the altimeter read 600 feet, quite a change in barometric pressure from Malta. The visibility was below 1,000 yards. After taxiing to near the watch tower, we were all anxious to discover if we really were in the U.K. The first thing I saw was a display board with the message beginning 'Don't Do . . .', what a relief.

On reporting to the tower, I learnt we had landed at Wittering, which happened to be one of the few airfields that was not totally fog bound. We were told we were the only crew airborne that night. Our time in the air was the same as for the outward journey, 10 hours and 45 minutes. We took off for Yorkshire after a couple of hours' rest with the promise that the fog was clearing. Arriving over Dishforth we were unable to get in and diverted to Driffield. Later in the day the fog did lift and we were able to finish the journey. Touching down at home base on the afternoon of 26th February 1941. That was completion of Operation Colossus for Whitley T4165, my crew and myself.[3]

While Lashbrook's aircraft was still being repaired in Malta, reconnaissance photographs of the Tragino aqueduct had finally been taken after Warburton took off once again at 0900 hours on Wednesday 12 February. Though his aircraft carried a 20-inch focal-length lens that provided greater magnification than previously, he nonetheless flew at what was remembered by WO/AG Paddy Moren as 'an almost suicidal low altitude'. The resultant photos, available at 1700 hours that day, initially proved crushingly disappointing, appearing to show both aqueducts completely intact. Close scrutiny under the stereoscope led British intelligence to believe that the smaller western-most aqueduct, which spanned the small tributary rather than the Tragino itself, had perhaps been the target as some trucks were seen parked near the farm buildings and at the roadside nearest to this aqueduct.

Otherwise, no activity was observed, and the officers in Malta had no way of knowing that the trucks were incapable of proceeding further due to Deane-Drummond's unplanned demolition of the small bridge near the farmhouses. Also unbeknownst to the officers in Malta, as they examined the photographs from Warburton's flight, Pritchard, Deane-Drummond and the ten men of the first escape party had finally exhausted their luck and been run to ground by the Italians.

The day of 11 February had passed for the fugitives with agonising slowness. Civilians could be seen working distant fields and the sound of children and barking dogs appeared at one point to be perilously close to the hiding men before receding into the distance. The path that stretched before them looked as difficult as that they had already experienced; a sheer cliff face at first thought to be blocking their way and likely difficult to scale at night, until an Italian shepherd was seen by Sergeant Lawley bringing a small flock of goats along a narrow steep route that traversed the rock face and was almost invisible. The men alternately shivered and dozed until darkness fell once more and they moved off in single file, careful to eliminate any obvious trace of their presence in the ravine. Henderson stubbornly shouldered his heavy Bren gun as the group trudged in single file through knee-deep mud. A swiftly flowing stream was forded with difficulty because, although narrow, it was deep and the boulders available as stepping stones were slick with moss. One man lost his footing and plunged headlong into a deep pool, swiftly recovering his wits but forced to march the remainder of the icy night in soaking wet clothes.

With Pritchard leading, they took the shepherd's path which proved almost as difficult as the cliff face itself as each man heaved his way up the 300-foot steep incline using handholds of thorny scrub and long grass. Finally, they reached the summit and collapsed temporarily exhausted. The going was difficult for the young paratroopers who were all at peak fitness; it must have been torture for Fortunato Picchi, or Pierre Dupont as his identity discs named him. The middle-aged Italian suffered periodically from severe asthma and was well aware that he lacked the same levels of stamina as his comrades. On at least one occasion he requested that the others move on ahead of him lest he burden the party, but the idea was firmly rebuffed. Indeed, Picchi's fortitude was never in any doubt as he showed uncommon determination to match the men around him. It was the elements rather than he that conspired to delay the group as they headed slowly west. Resolutely they pressed on.

> I was leading now and slowly we crept on in single file with ears strained for the slightest sound. We could see a few cottages against the skyline and we assumed that they must be the outskirts of Pescopagano. Dogs could be heard barking all over the village and farther up the valley. Perhaps it was one of the other parties that was causing the disturbance. I kept wondering how they were getting on.
>
> The country looked wilder and more impossible than ever. The moonlight distorted every natural hummock and glade into grotesque and weird shapes. Before us stretched mile upon mile of the roughest country we had ever seen. Few landmarks could be picked out and so we decided to march by compass to a large crossroad near the source of the Sele river. During this night's march we had to cover some twenty miles and then to find hideouts for the following day somewhere along the north side of the Sele valley.[4]

Before long they chanced upon a small road which Pritchard decided to use as a navigation aid; he thought it too risky to march on the road itself but kept it about a quarter of a mile below the paratroopers as a visual guide. Every opportunity to drink from the myriad small streams they were forced to cross was taken, until the decision was made to stop for a while and brew some hot sweet tea as the men teetered on the brink of exhaustion.

Refreshed by the break and the welcome drink, the party moved off with a small measure of renewed vigour. By 0100 hours Pritchard had begun to weigh the pros and cons of actually marching on the relatively smooth road surface instead of blundering through the undergrowth nearby. Undoubtedly, Italian troops were searching for the *Inglesi* and likewise without doubt was the fact that they would be using the roads to move about. The possibility of running headlong into enemy soldiers was always present, but thus far they had not seen or heard anybody using the road. Eventually, with his men exhausted by their efforts, the decision was made, and Pritchard led them onto the road just west of a small bridge across a mountain steam outside of Sant'Andrea di Conza. Once on the road surface of what is now Strada Statale 7 (SS7) they were able to pick up the pace considerably. Given a smooth surface to march on, rather than stumbling over undergrowth in the darkness, soldiers could continue at a good pace for miles with an almost automatic step and Pritchard's decision was a wise move for they had previously made little headway towards their ultimate goal on the coastline. The group's average speed increased dramatically and, after a few hours of solid marching, they reached a crossroads that marked the highest point of their route. From then onwards they would be moving downhill towards the Sele River, their sole priority to make as much distance as possible and secure a hiding place well before dawn.

The sudden sound of hooves nearby jolted the marching men from their reverie as a small pony and cart laden with vegetables and driven by an old woman loomed out of the darkness heading in the opposite direction along their road. With no time to take cover, Pritchard ordered Nastri to take the lead of the file of men, calling out the step in Italian as they marched past and uttering a jaunty 'Buonasera', though to their relief the driver appeared to be asleep as the pony wound its own way to the marketplace for which they were probably bound.

The road departed the hill line shortly thereafter, heading out of the valley towards the north and the twelve men were once again forced to leave it and batter their way through the difficult and wild terrain. The men were very near the end of their tether and Pritchard knew that their only priority now was to find a suitable place to take refuge for the following daylight hours. His map showed a favourable looking wooded area not far from their location, although once the weary men had reached it after climbing above the cloud level, they discovered that it contained an isolated, but inhabited, farmhouse at its centre. Instead, Pritchard elected to aim for another wooded area atop a geographical feature known as la Cresta di Gallo ('the rooster's crest'), a mountain ridge 887 metres above sea level overlooking the town of Teora. Disappointingly, once they reached it they discovered that it had been denuded of the trees indicated on the British map, felled for lumber and firewood. Nonetheless amongst scattered juniper bushes, boulders and one or two small caves, the exhausted men decided to rest and hide themselves as best they could for the looming daylight hours which were beginning to stain the eastern horizon. As Deane-Drummond remembered, 'It was not good, but we were unable to move another step from sheer exhaustion.'[5] He also later ruefully noted that, after covering twenty miles as the crow flies during the night, perhaps they had gone past the point of caring much what happened next or had grown slightly overconfident in their ability to avoid detection, just enough to place them in jeopardy.

Whatever the cause, as dawn approached the men were still tired, freezing cold and miserable. The proximity of Teora had negated any idea of lighting a fire or primus stove to make tea, or even attempt once more to eat some heated pemmican. Most of the men were wet, through a combination of sweat, walking through snow and the winter mist that clung to them as they traversed the valley fringe above the snow and cloud line. Sergeant Lawley was taking the early morning watch when, at about 0630 hours, he heard the distinctive sound of approaching footsteps, a man leading his mule emerging just below the paratroopers' position. Lawley remained as still as he possibly could, and the Italian passed by without having given any indication that he had seen the hidden men though he had glanced once or twice in their direction. However, his apparent nonchalance was, if anything, too evident to Lawley who believed that even if he had not seen the badly concealed men, there was no way he could not have noticed the bold outlines of their footprints in the patchy snow.

Lawley hissed a warning to his comrades and Pritchard quickly weighed up his options. They had obviously been discovered, so he decided to attempt a bold bluff. He quickly ordered Nastri to follow the man and explain that he had nothing to fear as they were a mixed Italian–German group of alpine troops taking a break while on exercise. The small wiry cockney did as he was bid, successfully reaching the Italian peasant and giving him the hastily concocted cover story. The agitated peasant appeared unwilling to engage in conversation and hastened on his way downhill towards Teora, which was beginning to stir into life with the rising sun. Nastri feared that he had not been believed and returned to report as much to Pritchard.

Their available courses of action were limited. With daylight now upon them, the likelihood of slipping away unseen was remote at best. Their concealment had clearly failed, and, at any rate, men with local knowledge would easily be able to comb the area and detect their trail once more. This latter point was made all the clearer with the brief appearance on a ridge above them of Italian civilians Rocco Renna, Nicola Donatiello and Angelo Megaro armed with a shotgun and sharp-edged farm implements. They stood outlined against the sky, impassively looking directly at their location.

Nastri had been correct in his assessment; the man with whom he had spoken had hurried straight to Teora's Carabinieri station and reported the appearance of strangely uniformed men on the hillside, stories of enemy saboteurs at large already having been circulated in the area and helping the locals draw their obvious conclusions. A small group of farmers also armed with shotguns had raced for the hillside to keep the British party under observation, at least two of them the men seen by Pritchard and his group, the remainder staying unnoticed by their quarry.

Teora's Carabinieri mustered a small group of armed personnel before reinforcement from other Carabinieri and Bersaglieri units arrived by truck to assemble in the town square. Although none of this was clearly visible to Pritchard's group, the distinctive sound of military formations being gathered drifted uphill, accompanied by the noise of an increasing number of heavy vehicles. With no clear course of action available, the fugitives adopted a vaguely defensive formation and awaited events. If there remained any opportunity to bluff their way out of trouble, Pritchard had decided to take it. He had two Italian speakers included in his party, though Picchi's guise as a Free French soldier and Nastri's Italian heritage had to be safeguarded to the maximum. Pritchard ordered all maps and photographs burned while his men prepared their grenades and weapons. Aside from Henderson's Bren gun, they possessed a single Thompson and their pistols: not enough to fight their way out of any but the most lightly attacked corner.

To add further complication, spectators had begun to arrive before the paratroopers. At first, individual dogs began nosing cautiously towards them, followed by ragged children who sat at a reasonable distance and stared curiously at the strangers. There soon followed villagers of every description, most of them women in black dresses stained with the mud of labouring in the fields of the Ofanto valley. More men could be seen scattered amongst them, some cradling shotguns, although most the weapons visible appeared older than the paratroopers they faced, but still capable of inflicting a savage wound if close enough. To add a tragi-comic touch to proceedings, a young school teacher, Francesco Freda, who taught local children in a rural school nearby, even used the bugle with which he customarily summoned his students from their nearby farms, to attempt to provide martial music to the gathering of Italians around Pritchard's men.

Before long the sight of uniformed men in the rear was plainly visible to the encircled British as the Carabinieri and Bersaglieri troops formed a loose surrounding cordon about Pritchard's knot of men. The tension was palpable as Picchi attempted to communicate with the Italians, repeating Nastri's previous story but to no effect as an agitated peasant armed with a shotgun waved it threateningly towards him, demanding that all the paratroopers drop their weapons. Pritchard knew, without any doubt, that their position was now hopeless. While they could have thrown their grenades and opened fire, not only were they massively outgunned by the gathering Italian military personnel, but they likely would have killed some women and children with the grenades or in the ensuing crossfire. It was a probability that did not sit well with any of them. In a tired and resigned voice, Pritchard ordered his men to lay down their arms.

> I remember telling Tag that I did not agree with him . . . 'All right Tony', he said, 'you throw a grenade at those people on the right and I will throw mine over there.'
>
> At that moment I realised I could not do it. Women and children and unarmed peasants were everywhere and we would not be able to avoid casualties among them. All we could achieve were a few extra hours of freedom at the price of a particularly odious and inglorious action . . . There was dead silence for a moment and then one man asked in an incredulous voice: 'Aren't we going to make a fight of it sir?'
>
> I had never seen such a look of anguish on anybody's face as on Tag's at that moment.[6]

Pritchard disconsolately told his men to lower their weapons, instructing Picchi to announce their surrender while emphasising that they were doing so due to the presence of so many women and children. Henderson was the only man who moved, dropping his Bren and making a break for freedom as he ran zig-zagging down the hillside where the surrounding crowd appeared thinnest. His dash did not get far as soldiers moved to head him off and farmers fired their shotguns, hitting the paratrooper's outstretched hands with pellets before he stumbled and was quickly subdued. The remainder, biting back their deep feelings of shame that it should come to this, lowered their weapons and surrendered to the gathered crowd of Italian civilians and a section of Bersaglieri who had arrived at the scene. The dispirited paratroopers were herded through the throng of civilians, meeting a unit of Carabinieri climbing uphill towards them, who took charge of their escort. As they did so, a further indignity was heaped on to the captured men. Several of the Carabinieri had arrived with thick chain-link handcuffs, which were unceremoniously put around all the prisoners' wrists except for Pritchard's. The primitive cuffs dug painfully into flesh, every three or four men linked together by more thick chains. While this was being carried out, Pritchard saw that one of his grenades yet to be discarded had a broken split pin which could easily lead to an accidental explosion. He asked Nastri to convey the message to a portly Carabinieri *sergente* but was rewarded with animated shouting from an agitated Italian soldier who then pulled his pistol and pointed it directly at Pritchard's temple, his hand shaking so much that it seemed almost inevitable that the weapon would go off whether by accident or design. Nevertheless, the remaining Italian soldiers gathered the potential danger of the moment and parted the crowd whereupon Pritchard calmly threw the unstable grenade as far as he could away from the assembled people without making any overly vigorous movement. It landed in thick mud and stuck fast.

Gradually, the situation calmed, and the paratroopers were herded through the main square of Teora, amidst cries of *'Viva il Duce!'* and *'Viva il Carabinieri!'* from the civilian throng which jeered and spat at the captured men. Before long they reached the Carabinieri station and were unchained and locked in a small room with whitewashed walls and a red tile floor, damp and cold after the rays of winter sunshine outside. A heavily barred window showed the hillside they had just descended and Pritchard and his men, despite attempting to their utmost to put a brave face on their situation, lapsed into a deep silent depression.

Before long they were lined up and thoroughly searched, most of their hidden escape kit and gold sovereigns being discovered by the Italians, though enough remained to enable the later assembly of a complete set once they finally arrived at a prisoner of war camp. Deane-Drummond demanded, through Nastri, that they be treated according to the Geneva Convention, including the provision of food and water and was rewarded by loaves of bread and some tins of stewed meat being brought into the room and dumped on the floor. Finally, able to eat proper food once again, each of the prisoners immediately felt better with at least some renewed strength and vigour.

> Something then happened which I will never forget. A very small man, not much more than five feet tall and wearing a large hat, came into the room and started shouting. We continued to munch our hunks of bread until Nastri translated that he was a general and expected us to rise when he entered. After a little hesitation Tag told us to get up. He said, with a laugh, that it might get us some more food if we tickled his vanity. The shouting went on and Nastri translated that we were to be treated like soldiers and heroes. All our needs would be granted, he said. The only thing he wanted to know was how many more of us there were, and he received the usual answer 'I can't say.' At this he just shrugged his shoulders and went out. It was quite peaceful when the shouting stopped.
>
> Nastri and Picchi were called out soon after the General's departure and were questioned by a Blackshirt officer. When they came back they said that he had told them that we were all going to be shot at dawn the next day, so that we might as well tell everything. This, of course, received the usual laughing reply which infuriated the Italian who then strode out of the room.[7]

That evening as the sun faded below the horizon, the men were taken from their cell and loaded onto a truck under heavy guard and chained together once again. For thirty minutes the truck lurched its way east to the small Calitri railway station located in the valley below the town's twisting approach road, less than two and a half miles from the shattered aqueduct, which was already being inspected by Italian engineers. There they were confined in a dank waiting room to await transportation to Naples, where they were scheduled to arrive during the following morning. The miles of near-impossible terrain that they had toiled over must have seemed like the ultimate in futility as the paratroopers recognised Calitri on the promontory above the station, their first view of the town having been only two nights previously through the open circular hatches of their Whitley bombers.

That same night, Lea's party were hopelessly tired and hungry after grinding through miles of knee-deep mud. They had spent their second day of freedom hidden in a ravine west of Sant'Andrea di Conza, not far north of Pritchard's group. The young officer's lot had been made considerably worse by the brand new mountain boots that he had purchased on impulse in Malta to replace his ill-fitting military-issue ones. Despite them being well-made, the leather proved stiff and unyielding on his sodden swollen feet and caused him considerable pain until he took his knife to them, 'customising' them to a more comfortable fit. The coastline did not appear to be getting much closer and on their third night of toiling towards the rendezvous point, Lea finally suggested that they too use the nearby road instead of trying to move cross-country. Though perilous, there was no way they would reach their objective in the time given if they continued as before; his subordinate Paterson agreed with the decision as being the lesser of two evils that they faced.

Lea led his exhausted men onto the asphalt surface of the road leading south-west. However, before they had gone more than six miles, their spirits collectively raised by the firm surface on which they could march, they came upon a stone bridge crossing one of the tributaries of the Sele River, the road curving sharply out of sight beyond the bridge end. Lea was instantly wary, later recalling that it was almost too quiet to appear natural, none of the sounds of the Italian night audible to his ears. He ordered his men to take whatever cover they could while he crossed alone, pistol drawn, to reconnoitre the far bank. Peering around the bend, Lea detected nothing amiss and soon waved his men forward. It was at that moment that the watching Italians sprung their trap.

> We were beautifully ambushed. Out of the hedges came this motley crew of Italians: civilians, men and women, soldiers and Carabinieri, variously armed with pitchforks, ancient muskets and rifles. We couldn't attack them without killing civilians and maybe women. One man said, 'Shall I shoot, Sir?', and I replied in the negative. If we'd had a battle, there would have been needless deaths and we'd never have got very far without being picked up by the military. They walked us to a barn.[8]

Lea briefly attempted to bluff his way out of trouble by shouting 'Deutsch, Deutsch!', but to no avail. Like the capture of Pritchard's group, the presence of so many civilians, albeit many carrying weapons of all vintages, negated the chance of any armed resistance. The pain and anguish amongst the highly trained British soldiers at having to surrender to a 'mixed bag of angry, shouting people' was difficult for them to bear, Lea's group were shoved roughly into a nearby barn where they were handcuffed and chained, before being taken by mule carts towards Calitri rail station amidst the jeers and cat-calls of the victorious population.

Initial cries for them to be shot out of hand were silenced by the arrival of an Italian officer, possibly Generale di Brigata Nicola Bellomo, who firmly indicated to his countrymen that the prisoners were now in the hands of the military and therefore subject to, and protected by, military law.

Bellomo, a First World War veteran officer who had been recalled to active duty during the early months of 1941 had been named Commander of the Military Presidium of Bari. To him eventually fell the responsibility of how best to handle the men of X Troop. His decision attracted criticism from local political functionaries, as Bellomo ordered the British troops incarcerated as prisoners of war, with all relevant protections afforded by international conventions, rather than executed as saboteurs. Immediately after the capture of Lea's section, it was Bellomo who prevented civilians from mounting a summary execution of the prisoners in the heat of the moment of capture, though he retained Lea's 1903 Colt revolver as a 'war prize' for himself.

Lea's despondency at having surrendered was lifted somewhat by two of his lance-corporals as the cart jolted its was east. Both men voiced the firm opinion that his decision to surrender had been the best – and only – course of action open to them and, though he himself had no doubt of this, it was comforting for him to know that his men also understood and supported him. Once the mule carts had reached Calitri station during the early morning, Lea's group were unloaded and shoved into the bare waiting room to be reunited with Pritchard's exhausted men who had been sleeping fitfully under Carabinieri guard. Over half of X Troop were now held captive in the small railway station waiting room. However, as Lea's men were being pushed inside and Captain Daly's group of five remained at large, the end of Jowett's escape party of six as well as Lucky's run for freedom was already over.

After a second night pushing on through the mud and snow, Jowett's group had reached the Sele River as dawn began to break. Sergeant Clements recounted what happened next in the pages of the Leicester Regiment journal in 1944:

> We finally halted for a day on a small bushy mud island out in the centre of the Sele River. When dawn came, we were wet and cold and stiff, but had great hopes of pulling through. But at 8.30am first a dog, then an old man saw us hiding. Scores of people were working on the near bank of the river, and we decided to make for the hills again. So, we pushed off and hid again on a hill about 900 feet high with lots of cover. We had been seen, however, and by 11.30 a.m. we were surrounded by about 250 civilians with shotguns and 130 Carabinieri and infantry. Against this we had one tommy gun, seven pistols and three knives.
>
> However, Mister Jowett said he would cover our dash downhill and we would try and burst out of it. After burning our maps, photographs etc, I took the lads out and down. Lieutenant Jowett fired a long burst over the civvies' heads and they scattered about; two ran diagonally towards him and

these he put down with two bursts of rounds, and then he hit an Italian officer who was coming up the hill. By this time the Italians below had opened up, and how we got down the hill I have no recollection. It was a mad scramble, and when we finally took cover in a plantation below, we were still encircled by the 'Eyeties' who continued showing their skill as rapid firers.

Finally, as six of us could not even fire back, we were compelled to surrender. Everything we carried was stolen either by the troops or the civvies, and then they heard for the first time that the two Italians up on the hill were dead. We were marched over to a bare patch where the bodies lay, and a very hysterical civilian with two pistols assumed charge of a firing squad of twelve civilians armed with some very ancient double-and single-barrel shotguns. To us the bores seemed to be a foot in diameter. What saved us was the fact that the hysterical chap liked to hear himself talk, and while he was still raving a warrant officer of the Carabinieri came up and took over. We were marched back to the nearest village and were told that another section had been caught about seven miles away. Our treatment at this time was not too bad and we were moved to another place – Calitri, where we found that every one of the three sections had been caught.[9]

Clements clearly stated in his article that Lucky was left behind by the group due to a knee injury, whereas previously published works have Lucky with the group up until their capture by the Italians. Lucky himself later recalled the damage to his knee in a post-war conversation with his sister Alice and so I feel it is reasonable to follow Clements's account, and presume that Lucky was found independent of Jowett's group by searching Italian troops or civilians. Where he was discovered, and by whom, remains unknown.

The timely intervention of the Carabinieri had saved Jowett and his section from probable execution at the hands of the enraged civilians, who would soon be burying two of their friends who had been killed alongside the Carabinieri officer. The British soldiers had been partially stripped of their uniforms and roughly handled by the frenzied crowd until the arrival of the military, who returned their stolen uniform pieces and provided protection for the Britons from their own countrymen. Italian radio had already labelled the paratroopers as 'desperados', and the danger they faced as 'enemy saboteurs' in a hostile country was extreme. However, despite subsequent empty threats from some members of the fascist Blackshirt militia that they would be shot as spies, their treatment by Italian military personnel was relatively correct, though undeniably harsh particularly the chaining and handcuffing, frequently so tight as to impede blood circulation and cause extreme discomfort and pain. Generale di Brigata Bellomo visited the incarcerated men in Calitri and praised them on their undoubted bravery while ensuring they were adequately fed. He is reputed to have said:

> You were parachuted into the heart of southern Italy and committed an act of sabotage. Your superiors must have known that you would never escape. At worst, you would have been killed trying, at best, you would have been taken as prisoners of war. Being a soldier myself, I appreciate bravery in any man. I will make you my personal responsibility and see that you are treated with honour, as prisoners of war according to international rules.

True to his word, Bellomo steadfastly refused the assistance of the MSVN or any elements of the fascist party in subsequent dealings with the British POWs, though for Picchi, however, there was soon to be no such protection.[10] Thus far Picchi had avoided suspicion of being an Italian citizen, his Free French identity not yet coming under scrutiny, although the other men of X Troop remember him becoming gradually more agitated that his cover story would not hold up to scrutiny. They attempted to reassure him that although he certainly looked European, rather than British, and was obviously older than all but Ralph Lucky, he could quite conceivably pass for French as his Army pay-book showed. Nastri, on the other hand, had distinctive Italian features – particularly evident when in the company of other young Italian soldiers – and was periodically singled out by his captors, Pritchard vociferously, and thus far successfully, defending his British identity at every opportunity.

At about 10 o'clock in the morning the train finally arrived that was to carry them under heavy guard to Naples. The enlisted men were held in a single dining car with a Carabinieri soldier posted at every window, while the officers were divided into pairs, each placed in a six-seater compartment along with four armed soldiers. The Italian soldiers appear to have developed an annoying habit of spitting on the floor, something that the British had noted from their earliest moments as prisoners. During the journey the grating habit finally proved too much for Lieutenant Paterson who swore loudly and artfully at the guards, lacing his stream of articulate profanity with obvious gestures towards the notice on the compartment wall that read: *non sputare*. Apparently, the unexpected outburst from the tall British paratrooper shocked and subdued his Italian guards, who thereafter barely spat once every hour and even occasionally left the compartment to spit on the corridor floor instead of at the feet of the frightening officer.

Arriving at Naples central rail station a little after sunset, the men of X Troop were re-handcuffed, disembarked from the train onto trucks which carried them the one kilometre north to Via Nuova Poggioreale and the Poggioreale prison, a large imposing building with guard towers at each corner of a high wall that was also patrolled by armed sentries. The civilian prison had opened its doors to its first inmates in 1914 and quickly gained a reputation for squalor and brutality. Located in the industrial area of Naples, the prison was surrounded by an artillery barracks, aircraft and locomotive manufacturing facilities and soap and textile plants, and later during 1943, as Allied air attacks on Italy increased, found itself at ground zero for strikes against these other industrial targets.

Once marched through the gates of Poggioreale prison, the men from Calitri were relieved to be reunited with Lance-Corporal Boulter, his fractured ankle now firmly bound by a properly applied bandage. The men were pushed into filthy dimly lit cells, six in each, sharing each malodorous room with an overflowing lavatory in the corner and little by way of bedding: a long stone slab topped with scattered straw damp from condensation and previous use. A small window set high into the wall allowed weak light to filter into each cell during the hours of daylight, but little by night. Uncomfortable, cold and still damp, the men slept sporadically on the hard stone 'beds' or lying huddled together on the flagstone floor. By morning they were still tired and hungry when a guard banged on each cell door, delivering a bowl of ersatz coffee and slice of dried fig for each man. The British soldiers knew that interrogations were soon to begin, and most of their spirits rose slightly as they took some measure of interest in exactly how it would be carried out. Picchi, however, became alternately increasingly agitated and depressed, seemingly resigned to the likelihood that his true identity would be uncovered.

Interrogations began on the morning of Friday 14 February with the prisoners being taken from their cells and held in a passageway outside the small office put aside for the use of the Italian intelligence officers. The men responsible for the interrogations belonged to Colonel Vincenzo Toschi's 'Bonsignore' Section of the Italian Military Intelligence Service, one of the myriad agencies given such responsibility during the Second World War. Like most dictators, Mussolini placed personal ambition above the needs of his country's military hierarchy. While Italian intelligence and counter-intelligence work was of a generally high standard and frequently exceptional, the fascist leader did not deign to unify the various organisation under a single umbrella. The Servizio Informazioni Militare (SIM) was Italy's primary military intelligence service during the Second World War, its seniority probably explaining why it held sway over the interrogation of X Troop. At the time of the Colossus raid, SIM was headed by the capable veteran intelligence officer Colonello Cesare Amè and consisted of three distinct offices: the 'Calderini', concerned with 'offensive' intelligence operations including sabotage beyond Italy's borders; the 'Zuretti', which inherited the 'situation' sections; and the 'Bonsignore', which was concerned with 'defensive counter-intelligence' operations. It was Bonsignore officers who began questioning X Troop.

At Poggioreale prison on the first morning of interrogations, officers were questioned separately from the enlisted men, taken one at a time to face a Bonsignore man dressed in civilian clothes, seated behind a desk and flanked by two black-shirted men of the MSVN who, though denied jurisdiction over the prisoners, exercised their right to supervise the interviews. The interrogations themselves followed a predictable and nearly identical pattern for each man. The interrogator introduced himself as the commandant of the prisoner of war camp they were likely to be sent to, and merely wanted to check details of the prisoners for the International Red Cross. Behind this transparent fiction were attempts to put the captives at ease, asking apparently innocuous details of personal backgrounds and next of kin, before interjecting more specific questions of a military nature. Predictably, none fell on fertile ground and the prisoners declined to answer questions, or, at best, gave misleading answers intended to amuse themselves at the interrogator's expense.

Meanwhile enlisted men were also interrogated singly, probably handled differently by the Italians as they were frequently threatened with summary execution for having waged war on the civilian population, their only hope of salvation being full and frank confessions of their acts and any other information that was asked of them. None of the British soldiers divulged anything of any use to the Italians, also averting potential disaster when asked if they had arrived in Italy in civilian clothes. If so, they could have justifiably been considered spies and shot, but fortunately no man struggled with the truth that they had all worn battledress and carried their accompanying pay books.

While the Britons seemingly shrugged off the interrogation attempts, Lucky was taken from Poggioreale without Pritchard's knowledge and initially much to the Major's consternation as he still failed fully to understand Lucky's role in Colossus. Doubts about the true nature of his mission, which had been harboured by the remainder of the British troops, had no doubt begun to seep into Pritchard's own mind. However, he was forced to shrug off this latest development as his greater immediate concern was for Picchi, who faced his own impending interrogation with growing anxiety. Picchi had confided to Deane-Drummond that he was intending to make a clean breast of everything when confronted by his interrogators. Picchi clung to his certain belief that what he had done by taking part in Operation Colossus was in the best interests of his country. He was a patriot, first and foremost, and harboured hopes that other 'true Italians' would see his actions for what they were: a blow aimed at Mussolini's fascist empire, not the Italy that it currently dominated. Naïve and idealistic such beliefs may have been, but they originated from honesty and an integrity that would be unable to maintain the ruse of his French identity for long under skillful questioning. Somewhat ironically, Picchi was the sole representative of the secretive Special Operations Executive present in Operation Colossus, and yet perhaps the least prepared to counter robust questioning. Deane-Drummond urged him to stick to his cover story, and not deviate beyond name, rank and serial number, which, after all, was all that the interrogator was entitled to receive.

However, by the end of the first day of questioning, Picchi emerged from the interview room despondent, returning to his cell in a state of utter dejection, shivering and staring unseeing at the opposite wall. His cover had crumbled rapidly as Major Giuseppe Dotti, head of the C.S. Section (counter-espionage) of the 'Bonsignore', later attested in a statement provided on 21 August 1944, after the Italian surrender:

> On investigation by the military authorities of the area, the Carabinieri and the police, it was possible to arrest some of the parachutists themselves, among whom there was a certain Peter Dupont. Suspicions were aroused by his perfect Italian and Florentine accent, and on interrogation he confessed that he was an Italian citizen. He was, in fact, identified as Fortunato Picchi, born at Carmignano (Florence).

Picchi had indeed been identified, the Questura (police HQ) of Florence quickly finding his ageing mother, brothers and sisters who all were visited and questioned, and later collectively persecuted by the fascist authorities for the remainder of the war. Letters and photographs of Fortunato were confiscated as evidence, and even former work colleagues at the Grande Albergo Reale in Viareggio were interrogated and shown a mugshot of the dishevelled prisoner, confirming that it was indeed him. A portrait photograph taken of the young Fortunato before his emigration to Britain was forwarded to the special prosecutor's office and submitted as evidence, stamped and certified on 17 February as genuine by the Florence Questura. As night fell, Picchi eventually succumbed to sleep, though shivering and mumbling to himself as if troubled by dreams. Doug Jones remembers him waking, whereupon he attempted to calm the emotionally drained Picchi, the two men sharing the same threadbare blanket until dawn's weak light filtered through the high window.

Meanwhile, at some point on the night of 14 February, Rome had finally issued a War Communiqué that officially released the news of 'Operation Colossus' internationally:

> During the night of February 10th–11th (Monday night) the enemy dropped detachments of parachutists in Calabria and Lucania. They were armed with machine guns, hand grenades, and explosives. Their objects were to destroy our lines of communication and to damage the local hydro-electric power stations. Owing to the vigilance and prompt intervention of our defence units all the parachutists were captured before they were able to cause serious damage. In an engagement which took place one gendarme and one civilian were killed. It has not yet been decided whether to treat these British parachutists as prisoners or spies.[11]

For Picchi, there was no doubt. The next morning, guards came for him and he was escorted from the cell bound for incarceration and trial in Rome. None of his X Troop comrades ever saw him again.

With Picchi unmasked as an Italian citizen, Nastri came under increasing scrutiny, his interrogators convinced he was another Italian member of the party. Though Lucky was also fluent in Italian and obviously of a similar age to Picchi and therefore visibly different from the remaining paratroopers, he was convincingly British, somewhat ironic considering his Balkan origins. For Nastri the game of cat and mouse between interrogator and prisoner was incredibly dangerous. The Italian military authorities are continually derided even to this day as incompetent and lackadaisical, yet it did not take them long to notice and unscramble the rather clumsy anagram of Nastri's cover name 'Tristan' provided before the operation had begun. Equivalent to the Carabinieri was the Polizia di Stato (State Police), which was divided into provincial commands the administrative centre of which was called the Questura, commanded by an official named the Questore. These branches were immediately mobilised to find families of the surname Nastri and attempt to determine whether any of them had living relatives in Great Britain.

The danger for Nastri was that, technically speaking, he was indeed Italian. Nicola Nastri's mother, Trofimena, had been sent from the small fishing village of Minori near Salerno to London in 1908 as her parents disapproved of her suitor at the time, Alfonso Nastri of Ravello, and were determined to separate the pair. Undeterred, Alfonso soon followed to Britain, their courtship lasting seven years until they finally married in November 1915, settling in Myddelton Street, Finsbury. However, the First World War brought Alfonso call-up papers for the Italian Army and the pair and their oldest child, Alfonso Junior, packed their bags and returned to Salerno. There, while Alfosno served in the Italian catering corps, Nicola was born in Ravello, the only one of the family's children to be born in Italy. With the war's end in 1918 they returned to London, renting rooms at 23 Great Bath Street, in what was known as '*Il Quartiere Italiano*'. There Alfonso found good work as a chef in various establishments, including, by coincidence, the Savoy Hotel.

Near Naples, highly efficient officers of the Questura rapidly discovered Alfonso's sister Adele Nastri who, when questioned, admitted that her brother had emigrated to London and that they had several sons who would have been of an age to be in military service. In an attempt to rattle Nicola into confessing his Italian origin, his aunt, was taken to Poggioreale prison, and there the two were brought face to face.

> 'You know this man, don't you? He is a relative of yours.' She answered, 'I have never seen this man before.' 'You know him, he is your nephew, the son of your brother in England,' they insisted. *Zia* [aunt] looked Nicola straight in the eye and announced: 'I have never seen this man before. My nephew in England is a sickly youth, always ill. He is nothing like this man.' The interrogators turned to Nicola. 'You know this woman, she is your father's sister.' He addressed his aunt [whom he had met as a child], 'Never seen you before in my life missus, clear off!' She narrowed her eyes. '*Bastardo*', she hissed. Nicola said later that he had never loved his aunt more than at that moment. His aunt had saved his life by denying him. In later years, whenever Nicola returned to Ravello, he always took his *Zia* Adele a special present.[12]

His aunt's convincing performance fortunately put an end to Italian suspicion of Nicola Nastri, who, from that point onward, was treated in the same way as the other men of X Troop.

Lucky's fate was also soon revealed to the other officers when they were unexpectedly transferred that same evening to the airfield at Capodichino less than a mile to the north and home to an Italian Air Force NCO school as well as fighter and torpedo-bomber squadrons. Due to Lucky's status as an RAF officer, he had been removed and questioned separately from his Army compatriots and housed at the aerodrome. In due course he managed to convince his captors that the other officers would benefit from being assigned the same billet and they were soon taken from the civilian prison and instead housed under guard in rooms on the top floor of the airfield's administration building, reunited with the enigmatic and resourceful Lucky. There they found clean sheets and comfortable beds, two men to each room, and were allowed access to a well-kept wash room at the end of the long corridor. The officers ate plentiful lunches and dinners in the room occupied by Tag Pritchard, accompanied as a matter of course with wine and fruit, and were generously treated by their Italian Air Force guards, commanded by an officer remembered as Colonello Montalba.

This Italian officer staunchly defended the rights of his military prisoners, particularly in one notable event following an attempt by officers of the Questura to photograph and fingerprint the assembled officers. Pritchard vigorously protested through Lucky that they were prisoners of war and therefore not subject to such things that were reserved for civilian prisoners. However, after heated arguing, the Questura men began to take photographs of the angry British officers until the arrival of Montalba, who burst into the room in a towering rage at the temerity of the Questura officers to enter *his* base, without *his* permission and attempt to interfere with *his* prisoners. The Air Force officer smashed every photographic plate he could lay his hands on and had the Questura men forcibly evicted from the base, much to the amusement of the British officers.

Ironically, the enforced idleness of the incarcerated officers and their plentiful supply of food made them begin to gain weight rapidly, breaking out in acne at the unaccustomedly rich diet to which they were treated, rationing not yet being a factor for the Neapolitan military garrison. The routine was only broken after four days at the aerodrome with the arrival of the final X Troop officer. Captain Gerry Daly had at last been caught, ending the freedom of the last of the paratroopers. Ironically, his landing miles from the aqueduct had allowed him and his four accompanying men to slip through the Italian search parties and make it to within a few miles of the coast before capture. Sapper Harold Tomlin later recounted their attempted flight to the Tyrrhenian shore:

> When we started making our way towards the coast we ran into snow and that was waist deep for two days. And you know how easy it is to follow footmarks in the snow don't you, so when we bunked up at night, we used our billy cans to make snow bricks to make a wall around us. Because with night glasses you can pick people up quite easily can't you. We were free for five days after that and we were within five or six miles of the coast.
>
> The last day we were getting a bit desperate food wise and we knew we couldn't make the coast on foot. So, we decided between ourselves and Captain Daly that if we came across a small café we'd risk going inside and see if we could get a taxi and make out we were German airmen that had crashed in the mountains because there were people that spoke German.
>
> We got coffee, and somebody went up to the counter and he had a box of Swan Vestas in his hand and the fella behind the counter was looking at the time and I realised that he'd recognised the English matches. He went around the counter to a small office and he must have rung the police or Carabinieri because all of a sudden there was a screech of brakes and police everywhere. And that was the end of our escapade. There wasn't any resistance because there were women and kids in the café so there was no point in pushing the tables up and making a stand, because we only had pistols, I think we only had one tommy gun between us.

The paratroopers had been caught and were surrounded by Bersaglieri soldiers, though Daly tried his best to bluff their way through. His claim that they were a German bomber crew looking for transport to Naples carried no weight with the Italian officer confronting him. He had never seen such a uniform on any man of the German Heer or Luftwaffe, he informed Daly, before pulling aside Daly's jumping smock and exposing his British rank patches.

> I didn't like being in there to tell you the truth because it was obvious we were going to get caught. I'd rather be out in the open. We hadn't shaved for five days, we hadn't washed. And we were hungry because the food that they'd given us was Pemmican. I don't know if you've ever tasted it, but I wouldn't eat it. I made do with what I could find . . . we had the means of heating it without flames and without smoke, it didn't smell appetising and we had a little taste of it, but God! I couldn't eat it. We had chocolate and things, we couldn't forage for things because we could only move at night, and . . . if you wake up a dog in a village it starts barking and the whole lot start barking.
>
> We were handcuffed and chained, and we were taken to the lorry and our hands were up and the chains took all the skin off our wrists as we tried to climb up. We were taken to Naples military jail, marched through the streets in chains with all the people spitting at us and throwing cabbage leaves as they do.
>
> We were told, though not until we were entrained on the planes going out, that there would be no communication outside of the camp and no letters. So, the first thing my mother and father knew about it was when they got a letter from the War Office telling them that I had not returned to my base and that I was probably a prisoner of war.[13]

Taken to Poggioreale prison by foot during daylight and attracting the ire of passing civilians, Daly and his men were all held in individual cells, mistakenly believing that theirs was the only escaping party that had been caught. Determined still to make the rendezvous with HMS *Triumph* Daly paced his cramped filthy cell looking for possibilities to break out. Before long he focussed his attention on the door and found that the lock was rusted and weak and after applying pressure to it he managed to break it open. Using his Commando training to the utmost, Daly was able to slip past three patrolling sentries in virtual silence and almost miraculously made it on to the street outside unnoticed. He wandered somewhat aimlessly at first before retracing what he believed was the course to the rail yard, hoping to stow away on a train leaving Naples. After establishing an acceptable hiding place in the freight yard, he waited for the right opportunity, wary of patrolling sentries and working railwaymen. Not until the early morning did he find a goods wagon moving slowly enough to attempt to board, running alongside and heaving himself up towards a boxcar door. Unfortunately, at that point his luck deserted him and he lost his footing, falling heavily by the track side and knocking himself cold. When he groggily came to, it was to find an Italian soldier standing over him, pointing his bayonet at his chest and leaving Daly in no uncertain terms that, once again, he was a prisoner. Before long he was returned to Poggioreale and this time his cell was equipped with a more secure locking system. The men were also carefully searched for any escape gear that was concealed in their uniforms.

> They took each of us one at a time in by one door, took all our clothing off us and then we walked out the other door. But we weren't allowed back in to the other until we'd all been through. And by the time we all got back together we'd lost everything. In fact, we never got our jackets back . . . We were all put in solitary confinement and in the jail the cells are about ten foot from front to back and six or seven the other way and they had a board fixed in that wall down at a slope, so if you tried to sleep on it, you slid off.
>
> We were given food and drink and told we were going to be shot in the morning. All of us. And if you're told something long enough and strong enough there's a little bit of doubt comes into your mind, but next morning came and we were still there. But they still said we were spies, or something like that.
>
> The American ambassador came down from Rome and we mentioned this business about being shot and all of that, and he said, take no notice. They don't mean it, because, he told us

Mister Churchill has said that if they take one of us and shoot him then he'd take twenty Italians and shoot them! I have no idea whether that was true or not, but it was a nice thing to hear from him.[14]

The visiting American was also able to provide the first evidence for the British War Office that Colossus had been a success after talking to the men of X Troop. Through diplomatic channels word was finally received in London that seemed to confirm Colossus had at least partially succeeded, though the War Office still desired more concrete evidence.

Before long, Daly was moved to the aerodrome and incarcerated with his fellow X Troop officers. There, the seven men remained comfortably quartered for nearly two weeks, though at times the very privilege of their situation – well fed and no longer subject to overly rigorous interrogation – made them fractious and irritable. Questioning did continue, first at the hands of the Italian military and occasionally by officers of the Wehrmacht – the Luftwaffe were beginning to use the aerodrome as a transit point to North Africa. For the paratroopers, accustomed to an active training regime and freedom of movement, their situation was, ironically, far from ideal. The difference between them and Pilot Officer Lucky also began to manifest itself in unexpected ways. A decorated combat veteran, and volunteer for his second war, there was no doubting Lucky's courage, but the resourcefulness which made him an effective intelligence officer and born survivor sometimes rankled the SAS men:

Lucky was allowed to go down into Naples, under escort, to buy clothes for us, which at the time were very plentiful. I don't think Lucky realised that he was getting more freedom then than at any time afterwards when he was a prisoner ... Lucky rather annoyed us at times. We had a greasy, half-shaved Carabinieri officer who was in charge of our guard, and who occasionally visited us. Lucky used to know-tow to this creature in order to get more privileges, and it sent cold shivers down our spines whenever we saw it going on. However, it did have the great advantage that we obtained a lot of concessions and generally more considerate treatment through it.[15]

By the time that the seven men were moved to a more permanent prison camp they had managed to amass a decent wardrobe of washing kit, shirts, underwear and pyjamas which would stand them in good stead during the months that followed, particularly once conditions for such supply grew steadily worse in wartime Italy.

At Poggioreale prison, the enlisted men of X Troop had also been fingerprinted and photographed by the Questura, with no Italian Air Force officer to intervene, and the results were published in an Italian newspaper:

> I'd love to have got a copy of the paper the next day, because I happened to see a soldier looking at it in Naples, and it had all of us stuck along the top of it with numbers under us, and along the top *'Il Inglesi Desperados.'* You could imagine, we weren't very good looking because we all needed a shave and a wash. I don't know if I would have recognised myself.[16]

Daly's men had eventually been merged with their comrades, each man interrogated seven or eight times before their captors were satisfied. On 27 February, the seven officers at Naples Capodichino aerodrome and their men at Poggioreale prison were given notice that they were being moved to a prisoner of war camp at 0400 the following morning. The officers packed their belongings into some small suitcases that the resourceful Lucky had procured for them, before being taken under Carabinieri guard aboard an ambulance to the train station where they were reunited with their men. Accompanied by a Carabinieri *colonello* and his adjutant as well as one armed guard for each prisoner they boarded a train bound for Campo 78, also known as P.G. 78 (PG = *Prigione di Guerra*), located at Fonte d'Amore, five kilometres outside the town of Sulmona nestled in the hills of the Abruzzo region of central Italy. During the previous war Campo 78 had housed Austrian prisoners captured in the Isonzo and Trentino campaigns and by March 1941 held several hundred Allied prisoners, the majority taken in North Africa. By March 1942, the number had swelled to 2,119 prisoners, many captured by Rommel's Afrika Korps and passed to the Italians for incarceration.

The officers were segregated once more from their men, housed in their own walled compound within the main camp, measuring just thirty yards in length by three yards wide and constantly patrolled by a sentry. They were not allowed to leave this small area under any circumstances; eating, sleeping and exercising in isolation from all about them, nothing visible outside the high walls except sky and the distant mountainside. Once again, the close confinement played havoc with the mental state of the prisoners. Deane-Drummond recalled contracting jaundice not long after arrival and lapsing into something of a depression, harbouring a growing hatred of his Italian captors who attempted to enforce petty rules on the enclosed officers who still felt somehow cheated by the way in which they were captured largely through the presence of civilians. Though they retained a veneer of polite formality, relationships grew strained and unnatural between the British officers. The Scots–Canadian Geoff Jowett grew listless and bored, Gerry Daly ever more insular, retreating into his own mind as he diverted himself by setting maths problems to solve. He also wrote to his brother; the two letters were received during June and immediately passed on to Keyes's office, through Lieutenant-Colonel Rock at Ringway. From that point on, every letter received from any of X Troop was also delivered to the Director of Combined Operations to be combed for hidden messages before being returned, treated in the strictest confidentiality. Meanwhile, Lea and Deane-Drummond chafed against their captivity, dreaming up sometimes outlandish plans for escape, while Pritchard attempted to keep them all in check and occupied, counselling that any opportunity for escape and evasion would only be possible once they were transferred to the main compound, leaving one wall or wire to get over rather than two.

Likewise, the enlisted men were also held within their own secure compound, albeit of slightly larger dimensions:

> For two months we were kept separate from the remainder whilst Rome decided what action to take against us. Eventually we were told that we would join the other prisoners of war. Before this took place, though, we read in the Italian papers that one member of our party had been executed at a place near Rome ... It goes without saying that [Picchi] was an exceptionally brave man to go with us. For us, caught, there was still a chance to live – but for him, none at all.[17]

While the Italian authorities may have been vacillating over how to treat the British paratroopers, they concentrated their full force of vengeance on the one man they believed to have unmasked as a traitor. However, not until 7 April 1941 was the fate of Fortunato Picchi publicly confirmed by an article in the national newspaper *Il Messaggero* published from its Roman office.

> Among the parachutists of the British armed forces who were captured in Calabria, a zone in which they had effected acts of sabotage last February, the Italian citizen Picchi Fortunato, son of Ferdinando of Carsignano, Florence, aged 44, was identified.
>
> Picchi Fortunato was accordingly denounced to the Special Tribunal accused (a) of the crime as per Article 242 P.P.C.P. for having from December 1940 onwards served, although an Italian citizen, in the armed forces of the British state; (b) of the crime as per article 247 C.P. for having during war time, with the aim of favouring the military operations of the enemy to the detriment of the Italian state, helped and collaborated with the British armed forces in accomplishing such operations.
>
> The court case against the traitor was commenced on Saturday [5 April] and it terminated with the sentence of death by shooting in the back. The sentence was executed on Sunday April 6 at dawn in the suburbs of Rome.[18]

Indeed, on the morning of Palm Sunday, Fortunato Picchi was taken from his prison cell in Rome to Fort Bravetta, one of fifteen forts within the city boundary and used as a place of execution of death sentences given by the Tribunale speciale per la difesa dello Stato (Special Court for the Defence of the State). The Special Tribunal had been introduced by the fascist government and operated according to Italian Army penal codes, not subject to any form of appeal. Court President General di Brigata Antonio Tringali Casanuova of the MSVN, a member of the Fascist Grand Council, convened the 'trial', though these were always little more than showpieces, not lasting more than two to three days and frequently as little as a matter of hours, the matter generally already decided. In Rome such sessions were held in the large Hall IV of the Palace of Justice and wore a guise of great solemnity. The President and judges were all clad in the uniform of the MSVN as Picchi was led into the room on Saturday 5 April, climbing from the basement via a stairway on which was written 'Death to traitors! Black shirts will give you lead!' The 'trial' was swift, little defence offered and two uniformed Carabinieri flanking Picchi were equipped with gags should the defendant try to sully the solemnity of the occasion by mouthing his own words in defence – or defiance. Condemned to death, Picchi was taken to Fort Bravetta where he spent his final night. There, before dawn, he was allowed to pen a final letter to his mother.

> My dearest mother,
>
> After so many years you receive a letter from me. I'm sorry, dear mother, for you and for everyone at home for this misfortune and the pain that will cause you. Now all that remains in the world both of pain or pleasure is over for me. I do not care much about death, I only regret my action because I, who always loved my country, must now be recognised as a traitor. Yet in conscience I do not think so. Forgive me, dear mother, and remember me to all. I ask you above all for your forgiveness and your blessing, because I need it so much. Kiss all my brothers and sisters and to you, dear mother, a hug, hoping, with the grace of God, to be reunited with each other in heaven.
>
> With many kisses, your son, Fortunato. Long live Italy!! Sunday, April 6, 1941.[19]

At 7 o'clock that morning, Fortunato was led to the embankment of the fort's firing range and placed on a chair with his back to the assembled firing squad of state policemen, the method reserved for those found guilty of treason. Within minutes he was dead, his the fourth of sixteen such death sentences that were carried out by Italian authorities during that year. Fortunato Picchi's body was taken from Fort Bravetta and buried in an unmarked and unrecorded grave, as an official announcement was made via Rome Radio of the execution, the news being picked up in London, translated and re-broadcast by the BBC as well as written news outlets.

At first, the War Office was uncertain as to the veracity of the report, suspecting that Italian intelligence could possibly be trying to elicit a response from the British and that Picchi might yet be alive. Arrangements had been made for Florence Lantieri, Picchi's landlady at Sussex Gardens, to write to him as he was held a prisoner of war, using his assumed identity of Pierre Dupont. After the letters were cleared by SOE censors, they were to be forwarded to the International Red Cross, but they were all returned to Sussex Gardens without ever having left Britain. Meanwhile, no letters were received from Picchi by anybody. In order to establish the facts, SOE suggested that enquiries could be made through the US Embassy in Rome as to the fate of Pierre Dupont and whether he had in fact been executed. Before long confirmation was received that Picchi was dead.

Amongst those who heard the BBC Home Service wireless report had been Mrs Lantieri. Saddened by the loss of her artistic, sensitive, and good-natured friend, she later left a small tribute of her own in *The Times* newspaper:

> On Palm Sunday, 1941, Fortunato Picchi sacrificed his life for the cause of freedom. Until the day breaks dear – F.
> R.I.P.[20]

Chapter Seven

Aftermath

An unusual aspect in the planning of Operation Colossus was the total lack of communications equipment provided to the men of X Troop. They could neither signal mission completion nor failure. Reliant entirely on aerial reconnaissance to judge the efficacy of the parachute attack – and that itself not possible until the second day after the raid – the results appeared to indicate that Pritchard had been unsuccessful in his attempted destruction of the aqueduct. The intense disappointment felt in Malta at the operation's apparent failure is obvious by the conclusion of the operational report written on behalf of Wing Commander Norman:

> Report on the lessons learned during Tragino raid, February 13th, 1941.
>
> The failure of the operation cannot yet be explained. Although the order and times of dropping were not exactly as planned, the whole of the 'X' troop force was dropped, apparently under good conditions, in the vicinity of the objective. The charges, ladders, and equipment dropped were the full amount required for execution of the complete demolition plan. [This claim is belied by the amount of explosives actually retrieved by the demolition party at Tragino.] The arms containers dropped contained 2 Bren Guns and 7 Tommy Guns and ammunition. While the lack of 7 further Tommy Guns may have been serious, nevertheless the Force could probably give a good account of itself with the arms available and their personal weapons and, in any case, no sign of opposition was observed from the air. The late

arrival of Captain Daly was no doubt a serious handicap, but every member of the demolition party was familiar with the objective as it was thought to exist. If it was in fact the western bridge and not that on the main stream, the party could not have failed to recognise it, since in attacking the adjacent farm, many must have passed close to it, and their rendezvous was in fact within 100 yards of it. It seems impossible that some vital piece of equipment necessary for the demolition was lost or not taken on the operation. The only possibilities that seem to remain are that:-

(i) the details of the operation were known to the enemy, and the party was captured immediately on making the ground.

Or (ii) that the objective was entirely different in construction from anticipated design, and the equipment available was insufficient for its destruction.

It is a significant fact that up to 1930 hours on the night prior to the operation no one concerned had any knowledge of a second bridge within about 230 yards of that over the Tragino. A number of points have emerged having a bearing upon any future operations of a similar nature.

1. It is clear that up to date intelligence supported by air photographs is absolutely essential at the time of planning the operation, and that the parachute party and the Captains and crews of aircraft must have ample time to study and memorise the details of the terrain.

2. The time required for dropping at night on an objective not previously known, even in ideal conditions, is much longer than was thought necessary. After arrival at the rendezvous the Air Attack Commander requires 10 minutes for reconnaissance and to confirm the arrival of other aircraft. Each aircraft should be allowed at least 10 minutes for general reconnaissance of the area before dropping. Approximately 10 minutes is required from giving Zero until dropping begins. 5 minutes must be allowed to each aircraft for making runs over the target. In these circumstances considerable disturbance in the target area seems unavoidable when parachute troops are employed at night.

3. For the actual dropping all available eyes must be employed. In a Whitley, it is desirable that the navigator, in the front turret, should direct the run up. The second pilot, looking downwards, should work the red and green signal lights, the Captain should concern himself primarily with the flying of the aircraft, and the rear gunner must observe the dropping and report to the Captain immediately the last man has gone, so that he can put on engine and get clear, and if necessary, make a second run to release containers that have not fallen. Moreover, up to the time of the first drop, it is essential that the Attack Commander Ground and the Attack Commander Air, be in personal contact, so that decisions regarding the sufficiency of the available force, the timing of the operation and details of the attack can be taken together. It is thought that the Attack Commander Ground should not be a Section Commander but should drop separately on a second run.

4. The present arrangement for container release is not satisfactory. The five-pin plug should be put in and fixed before the flight begins. The container cells should be selected, the distributor timing set and the distributor then set to 'safe'. When 'prepare for action' is given the navigator will then turn the distributor to 'Distributor'; and confirm with the Section Commander that the tell-tale light in the fuselage is on. Alternatively, it is thought that when containers are dropped last, the navigator could very well release them on a signal from the rear gunner that the last man has gone.

5. The present design of container must be entirely revised, and the bomb release gear studied to ascertain that it will function properly with large containers. The new design should incorporate a rigid harness that can be fixed to the bomb rack and firmly stabilised before the container is raised into position. A mechanical means of raising the container to the harness should be provided so that one or two men can fix or lower containers. The dimensions of the container must be such that there is no possibility of jamming in the bomb cell.

6. Army personnel should be given opportunities to become completely familiar with the aircraft used and their bomb release equipment and should have more air experience under operational conditions than was possible in the case of the present operation.[1]

The conclusions drawn by this report, based largely on interviews with the Whitley crews and a certain amount of guesswork, at least included some valuable information for the development of future airborne operations.

In the meantime, Vice-Admiral H. D. Pridham-Wippell, as Flag Officer in Command Malta, exercised the final operational decision on whether the evacuation of X Troop by HMS *Triumph* would proceed as planned, and despite Wotherspoon's aircraft going down at the mouth of the Sele River he nevertheless intended to carry out the evacuation, though he advised Lieutenant-Commander Woods to exercise extreme caution and also requested close air reconnaissance of the withdrawal area to be undertaken by the Royal Air Force.

However, elsewhere, the news that Colossus had apparently misfired provoked decisions which could have had far-reaching consequences for the men of X Troop still heading to what they believed was a rendezvous with HMS *Triumph*. At 1030 hours on 13 February the Chiefs of Staff Committee met in Whitehall: the First Sea Lord Admiral of the Fleet Sir Dudley Pound, Vice-Chief of the Imperial General Staff Lieutenant-General Sir R. H. Haining, Chief of the Air Staff Air Chief Marshal Sir Charles Portal and Major-General Sir Hastings Ismay, from the Office of the Minister of Defence were all present, along with Lieutenant-General Sir Alan Brooke, C-in-C Home Forces.

According to the minutes of the meeting Pound announced that the enemy would now probably be aware of the planned rendezvous for HMS *Triumph* as the message despatched by Wotherspoon's disabled aircraft had been made using a simple code that the Italians would almost certainly be able to decipher in short measure. He therefore considered it wrong to risk the 'probable loss of a valuable submarine and its crew against the possibility of bringing off a few survivors'. Portal confirmed that Warburton's photographs showed no obvious signs of damage to the aqueduct and that, as the operation had apparently miscarried, there was a high probability that most, if not all, of the personnel committed to Colossus had either been killed or captured. After some discussion between the service heads it was agreed that the risk of HMS *Triumph* and its crew could not be justified.

> The Committee agreed with the Admiralty proposal to cancel the despatch of the submarine and instructed the Secretary to inform the Prime Minister of this decision.[2]

Sir Roger Keyes was enraged by what he considered an absolute betrayal of the men of X Troop. In a personal appeal to Churchill, Keyes wrote that he considered 'our failure to make any effort to carry out the salvage arrangements, promised to the parachutists, a clear breach of faith'.[3] Nonetheless, the decision remained unchanged and at 2022 hours HMS *Triumph* received signalled orders to return to Malta, having left for the rendezvous two days previously. After two subsequent failed attacks on sighted Italian and German convoy traffic, *Triumph* entered Malta's Grand Harbour on 16 February. Furthermore, the RAF bombing raids intended to be carried out on the target area to frustrate repairs were never undertaken due to the false impression that Colossus had been unsuccessful. Such attacks, if they had been made promptly, might well have disrupted the temporary repairs that were at that moment being swiftly carried out by Italian engineers.

At Ringway a mixture of pride and sorrow lingered over the men of the Central Landing Establishment. With no confirmation of the success or failure of Colossus the officers and staff threw themselves back into the training regime for the other paratroopers belonging to No. 2 Commando. Despite the Air Ministry continuing to show scant regard for the future of airborne troops, on 23 February Air Chief Marshal Portal sent a personal message to Group Captain Harvey expressing his own feelings regarding Colossus:

> My dear Harvey,
>
> I write to convey my appreciation and thanks to all concerned in the recent parachute operation in Italy, for the care with which this was prepared and the skill and gallantry of the Army and Air Force personnel who took part. The loss of

the parachute force without the certainty of full success having been achieved is a matter for regret, but we must remember that material results are not the only measure of success and that the moral effect of such boldness upon both our friends and enemies must be considerable.[4]

Throughout the Allied nations, Rome's communiqué of 14 February regarding the landing of British paratroopers had been repeated in every major newspaper. In response, London's Ministry of Information issued a brief guarded statement that,

soldiers dressed in recognised military uniforms have recently been dropped by parachute in Southern Italy. Their instructions were to demolish objectives connected with ports in the area in which they were dropped. No statement can be made at present about the results of the operations, but some of the men have not returned to their base.

In the United States, Operation Colossus had already started yielding exactly the kind of propaganda that had been hoped for by the British authorities. The Italian communiqué received considerable coverage, wireless commentators giving credence to the majority of the details revealed by Rome and interpreting the raid as a sign of Britain's aggressive spirit and growing offensive strength. The fact that the Italian communiqué did not specifically say that no damage was inflicted inferred to the American news corps that they must have indeed 'got down to their jobs before capture'.[5] Within five days, the Ministry of Information released an in-depth statement containing background information on British airborne units under training and at last fully revealing the new branch of the armed services. The Air Ministry went as far as to allow interviews with various officers including Louis Strange, heralded as the man who made the 'Sky Army'.

During March the Vatican transmitted a list of names of all the men captured during the Tragino raid eliminating all doubt as to the fate of the British members of X Troop, though the Nastri family only found out after a telegram arrived directly from the Red Cross in Berne, as they had no wireless set in their household. The War Office also sent a telegram to all relatives of the X Troop men, Harry Tomlin's parents receiving theirs that read: '11th Battalion, SAS, Knutsford. I regret to inform you that your son who was chosen for the recent parachute raid in Southern Italy has not returned to his base.'

British intelligence officers were meanwhile facing the difficult task of distilling the confusing news reports that had begun to filter through to Britain during the days after the raid. On 16 February Rome announced a three-day suspension of goods traffic on lines connecting Brindisi, Bari, Taranto, Foggia and Lecce as well as trains to Reggio Calabria (the 'toe' of the Italian boot) due to 'difficulties in the present transport situation'. Although both Italian and German radio broadcasts denied any connection with the landing of enemy parachute troops, in Britain there was speculation that it could be related to the activities of X Troop or at the very least be a precautionary security measure while the manhunt continued for the paratroopers. The transport problems were actually caused by the diversionary raid on the Foggia marshalling yards and the Whitleys' opportunistic bombs that had been dropped at visible railway junctions. Nonetheless, in Rome, American intelligence reported the belief in diplomatic circles that the Italians were 'much disturbed' by the landing of parachutists, rumours abounding among the Italian military that many of the saboteurs were Italian anti-fascist refugees returned to strike a blow against Mussolini's forces.

On 10 March the Yugoslav consul at Bari reported while on leave that the port had been without water for several days due to damage to the aqueduct system. Italian authorities were said to have claimed the capture of 'forty-one parachutists' though also reporting that others might still be at large having caused damage of an 'unknown extent' in Salerno. Brindisi, too, was reported to be suffering water shortages in late February due to damage from an air raid, although there had only been a single raid against Brindisi's aerodrome by four Wellington bombers on the night of 15 February and none at all against Bari.

Four days after the Yugoslavian source's report, a correspondent for the *Chicago Daily News* returned to the United States from Rome after being expelled by the fascist authorities, reporting from his sources that included American diplomatic staff that the Pugliese aqueduct had indeed been blown up, but repaired within two and a half days. He quoted the American Military Attaché, Colonel Norman Fiske, as saying that he had visited the captured British paratroopers at Campo 78, that their morale was 'terrific' and that they had claimed to have destroyed a railway bridge besides damaging the aqueduct. They also informed him that local inhabitants had carried their explosives, under the impression that they were Germans. The paratroopers also boisterously claimed that they collectively intended to escape at the first opportunity.

With its source as the military attaché the American journalist's report was the first firm indication to the War Office that Operation Colossus had yielded some measure of success. Unfortunately for Flight Lieutenant Bruce Williams of the Central Landing Establishment, he was soon cornered by a radio correspondent looking for further information who recorded his impression of the parachute troops' attack, broadcast on 4 April and once again repeated in newspapers worldwide the following morning. Williams's account of the operation included praise for the 'specially selected and trained force' led by 'magnificent officers'. Considering the fact that part of the justification for Colossus in the first instance had been the generation of morale-boosting propaganda at a time when Britain's military star had waned dramatically in northern Europe, Williams's statements could have been used as a bonus, once again without the War Office having officially to supply any information on the raid, its target or result.

However, his interview, which was far from the first lengthy 'official' confirmation of the existence of a British parachute force, led to Bruce Williams being charged with the offence of unlawful disclosure of classified information, and the recommendation from Whitehall that he be dismissed from the Royal Air Force. Louis Strange vigorously defended Williams, considering him to have assisted more than any other man in the pioneering parachute training given to Britain's fledgling airborne forces, but ultimately to no avail. To Strange's fury, Williams was transferred away from Ringway, his skill and expertise with the parachute lost to the Central Landing Establishment. For his part, the former parachutist and air gunner later qualified as a pilot and flew clandestine Lysander missions into occupied territory, earning the Distinguished Flying Cross.

While there was some measure of jubilation in Britain and its Allied nations that paratroopers had taken the fight to the enemy, within

Italy the destruction of the Tragino aqueduct had little effect on the war effort. The large aqueduct had been put temporarily out of action, and it is possible that concussion from either that explosion or the destruction of Anthony Deane-Drummond's small concrete bridge caused some damage to the smaller Ginestra aqueduct. Locals told of water entering their farmhouse following the explosion, unlikely to have originated from the Tragino. At the present day the smaller aqueduct leaks a considerable quantity of water, but then the entire aqueduct system stretching into Puglia leaks nearly 52 per cent of the carried water according to reports produced in the first decade of the twenty-first century. Regardless, the main waterway was quickly repaired, engineers taking two or three days to complete work on a 120 cm diameter auxiliary pipeline, carried on iron beams and scaffolding, that allowed the water to flow once more while more permanent repairs were made to the damaged concrete aqueduct structure. Local reservoirs, even in this most southerly part of the parched Italian landscape, were somewhat swollen by the rains of the wettest part of the year as well as the brief run-off of melting snow from the Murge plateau during winter, so they held enough water to cover any shortfall, despite reports received in Britain to the contrary.

Large contingents of troops were brought from Bari to assist in the reconstruction but did little more than curiously observe the efforts of the few skilled technicians and their labourers who capably handled the resurrection of the water supply to Puglia. The Tragino aqueduct was not fully restored until the following year and, somewhat ironically, suffered further damage by free-ranging American P-38 fighter bombers on 18 September 1943 which caused damage to three of the battered arches. Retreating German forces also damaged several segments of the aqueduct system during their retreat to the north, attempting to achieve exactly the same objective that the British attack had aimed for; they mined the Tredogge and Atella aqueducts on 20–21 September 1943 and then, three days later, the one that spanned the Ginestre within sight of the Tragino and adjacent to the small concrete bridge that Deane-Drummond had gleefully destroyed on the night of the attack. However, damage inflicted by the Wehrmacht engineers was also quickly patched up with temporary water conduits, while more definitive repair was completed by 1945.

After the resumption of water flow along the Pugliese aqueduct only days after X Troop's attack, a series of ostentatious award ceremonies were conducted by local fascist party dignitaries who decorated civilians and troops who had had little part to play in either the capture of X Troop, or the emergency repair work carried out on the aqueduct, though this indeed had been completed in record time. However, despite this bravado and the victorious tone of the official news releases, the psychological effect of the raid was little short of disastrous for Italy's government.

Mussolini's fascist regime, like most of its ilk, relied heavily on strict control of the press and its dissemination of information to the public. There were almost valiant attempts to disguise Italy's string of military defeats from the citizenry, so much so that many had no knowledge that the war was going so badly for their country almost until the end of the North African campaign in 1943. However, though the water supply had not been significantly disrupted, the fact that British paratroopers had been able to penetrate the Italian mainland undetected and commit sabotage provoked great anxiety, not least of all within the halls of the Quirinale in Rome. Word of mouth passed in hushed whispers spoke a mixture of truth and exaggeration: tales of defeated Italian armies abroad, incompetent generals, a fascist party rife with cronyism and corruption, and paratroopers descending in Calabria and Puglia, most of them Italian anti-fascists, with many still at large.

Picchi, the patriot who opposed his country at the known risk of his own life, was held in isolation before his execution, his feelings about the necessity of the destruction of fascism in Italy kept between him and his interrogators. Fear of an ideology such as his resulted in strict instructions issued on 10 March to all Carabinieri stations and MSVN units in the event of capture of further enemy prisoners of war on Italian territory. These included the absolute minimum of questioning to be undertaken by those responsible for making the arrest, and then only regarding what was directly relevant to that event. The prisoners were to be passed as quickly as possible to the Territorial Defence Command in Rome, where full interrogations would be undertaken before transfer to incarceration.[6] The regime feared that men such as Picchi could rationally explain their actions to those that might capture them, escort them or stand guard over them, planting seeds of independent thought in the men who wore the uniforms. For a dictatorship that relied so heavily on censorship, this posed an unacceptable risk.

In Britain Picchi's sacrifice soon became a matter for debate amongst various offices, some keen to use his death as a *cause célèbre* with which to attract other Italians to take up arms or provide a propaganda coup of an Italian anti-fascist willing to risk his life in the cause of freedom. On 24 April Sir Walter Monkton, former Director-General of the Press and Censorship Bureau and recently appointed by Churchill to the post of Director-General of the Ministry of Information and Under Secretary of State for Foreign Affairs, wrote a letter to Gladwyn Jebb, Chief Executive Officer of the Special Operations Executive, recommending that Picchi's story be used as an outright propaganda tool. Within SOE, the idea was greeted with horror, evidenced by this letter written by George Logie, head of SOE's Italian section:

> Surely the most disastrous aspect of the publicity given to the Picchi episode is that any Italians whom we may in future enlist from the Pioneer Corps or Internment Camps at once become marked men among their fellow pioneers or internees. If, for instance, we now recruit a man from the Pioneer Corps the whole of the rest of the Pioneer Corps will assume that he has gone for parachute training; from the Italians of the Pioneer Corps the story will spread through the Italian colony in England, amongst whom, if there are not actually agents of the Italian Government, there are certainly a large number of very noisy gossips. This means that in all probability the Italian government would know the names of Italians being trained by us before they even went out on an operation. I do not think it too much to say that our whole policy of recruiting Italians in England is jeopardised. Surely Sir Walter Monkton must realise that publicity such as this must endanger the lives of other trainees and their families in Italy should they have any.[7]

The news reports of Picchi's death had been repeated around the globe, doing undoubted harm to SOE recruitment of further Italian agents. In return, Jebb pleaded with Monkton to tone down the nature of the reports being issued by the War Office, which were belatedly muted though not before the damage had been done. The number of Italian SOE recruits had reached eight until news of Picchi's death was broken internationally, reducing shortly thereafter to only three willing to return to Italian soil at any point in the future.

The efforts to celebrate Picchi did not stop there, as on 30 May, Ronald Tritton, War Office Publicity Officer, wrote to Lieutenant-Colonel Jackson as Commanding Officer, 11 SAS Battalion in Cheshire. He explained that a film company was anxious to make a picture about Picchi that he considered would be of strong propaganda value, being 'anxious to help as much as possible with its production'. Tritton admitted that very little was known of Picchi as an individual and appealed to anybody who might have known him well to come forward and discuss his personality and life with the film scriptwriter. 'We should', he continued, 'have to make sure of course that the film avoided any possibility of giving valuable information to the enemy.' The letter was immediately passed along the bureaucratic chain, before reaching the RAF's Central Landing Establishment, Ringway, Manchester. The reply was penned by John Rock and sent directly to Major D. M. Grant at the War Office:

> Reference attached correspondence, none of us here knew Picchi well. He was sent us by Brigadier Gubbins, who should be able to provide the information you want. Although Picchi was an idealist, he was also, after all, a traitor to his country and it seems rather difficult to make him out a hero.
>
> I am not at all sure, either, that it is a good thing to publish the fact that we dress Italian civilians up in battle-dress and drop them in Italy in the company of British soldiers. It is the type of ruse of war which we complain about in the enemy.[8]

Certainly Rock, promoted from major to lieutenant-colonel on the eve of Operation Colossus, was writing logically about Picchi in his note to the War Office. A man of action, he had rued the loss of X Troop to probable captivity and Picchi to the fascist firing squad but remained dedicated to continuing his work with the Central Landing Establishment alongside the dynamic Squadron Leader Strange.

The reaction to the initial reports regarding Colossus had been muted within Whitehall. Despite some published accounts to the contrary, Winston Churchill was distinctly unimpressed and even went so far as to deny that he had granted permission for such a risky operation in a memo to General Ismay on 15 February before being tactfully, yet firmly, reminded that he had indeed given his official approval.

Inside the Special Operations Executive there was satisfaction that the mission had apparently succeeded, despite the resultant reduction in Italian recruits. In a report dated 14 March SOE enthused that the raid had 'established that it is possible to land a party of paratroops fully armed and with a considerable quantity of equipment and explosives close to a given point providing no serious ground opposition is encountered'.[9] At Combined Operations, although Keyes remained bitter about the decision not to attempt retrieval of X Troop, Operation Colossus was also deemed a successful employment of the airborne force. Nonetheless it appears that Keyes himself had antagonised the wrong superiors with his plain speaking, finding himself constantly frustrated in future operational preparations as the Chiefs of Staff continually denied him both the resources and permission to undertake his bold schemes. Feeling politically outmanoeuvred, he resigned as Director of Combined Operations on 27 October 1941 and was replaced by Captain Lord Louis Mountbatten, who was promoted to Commodore and his office subtly renamed to 'Advisor Combined Operations', perhaps an attempt to keep the department in its place.

With the supposed effectiveness of the Colossus raid presented to the War Office in as enthusiastic a light as possible, officers of the Central Landing Establishment and Lieutenant-Colonel Jackson of 11 SAS Battalion did their utmost to push for greater means by which to carry on development of a significant airborne force. They also, however, continued to face resistance in the higher echelons of the military hierarchy, not least of all due to the persistent flouting of official regulations by nonconformists like Louis Strange.

Nonetheless, the vacuum left behind in No. 2 (Parachute) Commando by the loss of X Troop was quickly filled with fresh reinforcements from the Commando training centre at Achnacarry. Jackson inspected the latest batch of Commando recruits and selected a group to join 11 SAS, forming L Troop, comprised almost completely of Grenadier Guards. Considerable effort was also being made to expand the Glider Training Unit and in March 1941, twelve Commando glider pupils were transferred to Haddenham where a flight of the Glider Training Squadron had been established, followed by the remainder of the Army glider pupils during April. Five of these glider pilot trainees returned to Ringway during the following month in time for a demonstration before Winston Churchill, planned for 26 April.

When that day arrived, the Central Landing Establishment had prepared a mock attack on the airfield by parachute and glider troops as a demonstration of the potential of British airborne forces. Once the invited dignitaries had been assembled, Wing Commander Norman handed Churchill a radio telephone, inviting him to give the order for the Whitleys to begin the exercise, though the Prime Minister politely declined. Instead, Norman enquired of the Whitley flight leader, Flight Lieutenant Earl Fielden, whether he was ready for take-off. 'No!', the reply came through loudly enough for those nearby to hear, 'I'm not ready to take off! Five of the blighters have fainted!' Following removal of the offending bodies, the demonstration continued though wind had begun to gust up to 35 miles an hour and no doubt images of the final chaotic rehearsal jump made by X Troop before leaving Britain flashed through the minds of the assembled officers of the Central Landing Establishment. However, Strange had an ace already tucked up his sleeve. While five Whitleys carrying forty-four paratroopers and accompanying containers took to the sky and made successful drops, 144 men then rose from the long grass surrounding the aerodrome and went into 'action'. Strange had concealed an extra hundred paratroopers on the ground before the arrival of Churchill's party as his own insurance that the exercise would be as spectacular as possible. A handful of recreational gliders also swept in and landed wingtip-to-wingtip, displaying the potential for this developing airborne service arm.

For Churchill the demonstration was a triumph, though he regretfully noted that the force of 400 paratroopers that he later inspected fell far short of the 5,000 he had originally, and repeatedly, requested. Strange, as always, took the opportunity to speak plainly to the Prime Minister, guiding him by the elbow out of earshot of other officers and lamenting the obstructions placed in the way of building the airborne force by disagreements and delays between the War Office and Air Ministry, and a continual lack of available troops. The structural arrangements of Britain's airborne forces still rested primarily with the Air Ministry, a body inherently hostile to their very existence, and their role remained even less clearly defined than that of the Commandos from which they originated. Strange forcefully argued that the facilities and instructional staff were now on hand to create a sizeable airborne force if fully supported by those in the corridors of power. Churchill was receptive to Strange's plea and soon delivered a demand to Ismay on 28 April for written copies of his original request for 5,000 troops and to be shown where *exactly* he had agreed to reduce this number to 500. The imperturbable Ismay's reply did not stop at this almost petulant instruction and included a detailed and complete description of the entire process that had followed Churchill's original order, accompanied with an explanation of the Air Ministry rationale for limiting the size of the airborne unit. As the Prime Minister silently digested the information, weeks later the German invasion of Crete provided fresh impetus to Churchill's initial bid. Mounted by massed *Fallschirmjäger* drops, the invasion was successful despite appalling casualties that, ironically, prevented the wholesale deployment of the Luftwaffe's airborne troops ever again. On 27 May, as the victorious German Cretan campaign was nearly over, Churchill wrote to General Ismay:

> This is a sad story [about British parachute troops and gliders], and I feel myself greatly to blame for allowing myself to be overborne by the resistances which were offered. One can see how wrongly based these resistances were when we read the Air Staff paper in the light of what is happening in Crete, and may soon be happening in Cyprus and in Syria . . . Thus we are always behind the enemy. We ought to have an Airborne Division on the German model, with any improvements which might suggest themselves from experience. We ought also to have a number of carrier aircraft. These will all be necessary in the Mediterranean fighting of 1942, or earlier if possible.

We shall have to try to retake these islands which are being so easily occupied by the enemy. We may be forced to fight in the wide countries of the East, in Persia or Northern Iraq. A whole year has been lost, and I now invite the Chiefs of Staff, so far as is possible, to repair the misfortune.[10]

Meanwhile the parachute battalion had continued a round of demonstration jumps for dignitaries such as King George VI and other senior military officers, though the endless mock assaults sapped the morale of men who had volunteered for special service to get quickly into action against the enemy. Change had also come swiftly to the Central Landing Establishment. It appears that Louis Strange's direct approach to Winston Churchill had agitated senior officials within the Air Ministry for one final time. Unaccepting of Strange's independent method of 'getting things done' at the expense of official channels, they firmly decided to rid themselves of this maverick officer from the airborne formation. Possibly Strange's methods had rankled even with Group Captain Harvey who never particularly approved of his unorthodox approach, and less still of what he viewed as the barnstorming eccentrics whom Strange had recruited to help train fledgling parachutists. He was likely a major force in the disciplinary procedures that had been taken against Bruce Williams, Strange's right-hand man in teaching the art of parachuting. Wing Commander Norman had warned Strange on several occasions that he was courting problems by his way of circumventing authority. As Strange later recalled himself:

He used to say to me, 'You'd better look out Louis, the job's going well, but I should hate to see the powers that be catch up on you before you've got it really well founded. Don't try to get away with too much at a time. You *will* go at it bald-headed. It attracts too much attention, and you'll find someone taking a pot at you one of these fine days.'[11]

Regardless of where the impetus originated from, two weeks after Churchill's visit, Strange was posted, handing his command over to his deputy, Squadron Leader Jack Benham, the Chief Parachute Instructor at the Central Landing Establishment.[12] Strange was moved to Speke near Liverpool where he became the Chief Flying Instructor of a new unit called the Merchant Ships Fighter Unit. There he perfected the use of catapult-launched Hurricane fighters to be sent to defend convoys from the Luftwaffe.[13] His friend, the recently promoted Group Captain Norman, was also transferred, forming the transport No. 38 Wing on 15 January 1942 and heavily involved in the coordination of airborne operations and SOE drops. Norman was killed on 19 May 1943 when his aircraft, bound for North Africa, crashed on take-off from Portreath.

During June 1941 Leutnant-Colonel Charles Jackson was transferred back to the Royal Tank Regiment and returned to the rank of major. In his place came Lieutenant-Colonel Ernest 'Eric' Down given the task of converting 11 SAS Battalion into a parachute infantry role as he disapproved of their use in small-unit raids and desired to raise an orthodox airborne unit such as those possessed by Germany and desired by Churchill. Until that point, 11 SAS had continued to train in Commando unit operations and tactics for use behind enemy lines. This was soon to change as Major Rock formulated fresh recruiting methods, approved by the War Office, dramatically to increase manpower for the airborne arm. Before long plans were under way to make 11 SAS Battalion one of two battalions belonging to the prospective No. 1 Parachute Brigade, to be commanded by (Temporary) Lieutenant-Colonel Richard N. Gale and conforming to the Prime Minister's original order.

On 25 August 1941, 11 SAS Battalion was reorganised into a conventional headquarters and rifle company structure that conformed to that of an infantry battalion, albeit with lower manning levels, and on 15 September 1941 the unit name changed to the 1st Parachute Battalion of No. 1 Parachute Brigade. This milestone marked the end of the association between parachute forces and the Commandos and the true beginning of what are now recognisable as British Airborne Forces. The term 'Special Air Service' had meanwhile been appropriated by a new unit formed in July 1941 by David Stirling, former Scots Guard and member of No. 8 Commando. Originally titled L Detachment, Special Air Service Brigade, as a means of disinformation to convince the enemy that there existed a paratroop regiment, the organisation originally consisted of five officers and sixty enlisted men who were tasked with operating behind enemy lines in North Africa. This is the genesis of the SAS as it is recognised today; X Troop was never a part of Stirling's service, and its only connection with the Scottish officer had been during training in the Highlands.

With the Central Landing Establishment under new management and settled into its established training regime for new recruits, Rock had begun focusing his attention on the Glider Pilot School and was appointed Commanding Officer of the Glider Pilot Regiment on 21 December 1941, learning to fly them himself by the following September. Tragically, however, this ground-breaking airborne soldier was severely injured in a training accident on 27 September 1942 during a night flight at Shrewton when the towrope of his Hotspur glider broke and it crashed into a telegraph pole in the course of an emergency landing. John Rock, airborne pioneer of the Royal Engineers, died in Tidworth Hospital on 8 October 1942 at the age of thirty-seven.

While the British Army underwent these metamorphoses, Pritchard's original 'guinea pigs' remained for two months inside their specially constructed individual compounds at Campo 78. Though the severe lack of space chipped away at X Troop's collective physical and psychological wellbeing, conditions remained at least tolerable for them all:

> There was a submarine crew from *Oswald* which was captured in the Mediterranean. We were in the same camp, but we were segregated because they considered us *desperados*. Conditions in Sulmona were actually very good. We even had sheets on our beds for about a month, until the Italians got a black eye in the desert, they got pushed back, and they then took our sheets away and cut our rations in half.[14]

On 1 May, the officers and men of X Troop were finally moved from their isolation barracks to the respective officer and enlisted-men areas within Campo 78. Pritchard had made official representations through the American Military Attaché, Colonel Fiske, who had secured visiting rights to monitor the condition of the British Commandos. With the dust of Operation Colossus now settled, Rome had decided to treat all of the paratroopers as conventional prisoners of war, making no distinction between them and the predominantly Royal Air Force and Royal Navy captives they held. Sulmona's Campo 78 was considered extremely secure by the Italians after a previous escape attempt in January 1941 had led to considerable reinforcement of its defences. Three ten-foot-tall rows of barbed wire surrounded the compound, punctuated by sentry boxes every twenty yards or so and floodlit at night. Two roving Carabinieri patrolled the inner compound by day and night and a pair of thirty-foot-high lookout towers had been centrally erected, constantly manned and equipped with powerful searchlights.

While Campo 78 may have seemed impregnable to the Italians, the X Troop officers were determined to make an effort to break out, despite what Deane-Drummond recalled as a distinct lack of enthusiasm for escaping among many other captives. This had included a 'pep-talk' from the senior Allied officer, an Australian lieutenant-colonel captured at Tobruk, that they were not to jeopardise the privileges already granted to the prisoners by making any attempts to escape. The instruction was ignored and on arrival in the main compound Tag Pritchard immediately suggested the formation of an escape committee, using his tact and powers of gentle persuasion eventually to convince many of the other officers, and assembling a dozen of them as part of this committee. All escape material and information obtained was to be pooled centrally, and attempts coordinated properly to allow the greatest chance of success. Flying Officer Lucky (promoted during May) used his position as an official interpreter between the Italian commander and his Allied charges to steal railway timetables from the camp commander's office, while also coaching would-be escapers in useful Italian phrases that could enable them to purchase tickets and the like should they reach the outside world.

Furthermore, both Pritchard and Clements began exchanging information with the War Office using the code taught to them by officers of MI9 in Britain. By this, Pritchard was able to provide the first positive report of the success of Operation Colossus, received in London during October 1941. In the enlisted men's compound, the men of X Troop also hatched various escape plans, the majority involving tunnelling, while at the same time attempting to come to terms with their life behind the wire. Bob Watson became the camp barber, though apparently his skills were at first nothing short of 'useless' according to the recollection of Harry Pexton. He eventually got the hang of it and was able to charge two cigarettes for a short back and sides. Watson also began venturing under guard outside the confines of the camp to use his construction skill doing building work for local people, possibly building new houses or a hospital. As Allied prisoners began to flow into Campo 78, many of X Troop's enlisted men were moved to Campo di Lavoro (Work Camp) 102 during July 1942 where they were used as labourers in the construction of a functional barracks in L'Aquila.

Anthony Deane-Drummond made probably the first X Troop escape plan when he decided to hide in the rubbish-carrying wheelbarrows that were daily taken outside the compound. After studying the routine, he finally named the day on which he would make his attempt after gathering resources he deemed necessary once beyond the wire. However, the same morning that he was due to put his plan into effect, Italian sentries began searching the wheelbarrows for the first time; the cold hard realisation was that there was likely at least one informant among the camp population. During July, Deane-Drummond and approximately twenty other officers began work on a tunnel organised by Commander Brown of the Royal Navy. However, once again, the project was betrayed as news of the tunnel leaked out to other men in the camp and after eight weeks of digging a party of Carabinieri entered the compound and marched straight to the tunnel entrance even though it was well disguised beneath a patch of cracked concrete.

Lea and Deane-Drummond remained absolutely fixated on the idea of escape despite the setbacks suffered thus far. Between them they devised ever more elaborate schemes, before settling on a brazenly simple idea. For brief periods, individual officers were allowed outside the wire under guard to exercise, and Deane-Drummond had observed a potential weakness in the Italian perimeter.

> I had noticed a very small ledge passing across the three rows of wire where the ground changed levels. Searchlights, however, shone on it and a sentry was posted twenty yards away. With

the help of Captain Lea I decided to make use of the ledge. We
made a ladder and decided to leave as Italian electricians.[15]

Using hand-dyed overcoats, the two men planned to disguise
themselves as Italian workmen and bluff their way over the wire.
Such men had been observed in their familiar blue-grey work coats on
several occasions over the previous weeks. Lea and Deane-Drummond
convinced Pritchard and the escape committee of the potential for
their plan and enlisted the aid of Sergeants Clements and Lawley to
coordinate any required cooperation of a small number of men from
the NCO compound. It was there that they planned to assemble
the ladder after passing segments to the two NCOs in the preceding
days. With the lingering threat of betrayal still hanging over all such
attempts, the two officers used the assistance of men they knew to
be completely trustworthy, relying in turn on their judgement for any
additional accomplices enlisted to help. Lucky had already coached
the pair on small bursts of Italian until he had been satisfied with their
pronunciation, and they were given a quantity of survival rations and
Italian lire which had been gathered through bartering with sentries.

The two would-be escapees differed violently on the best method of
reaching the Swiss frontier once out of the camp. Deane-Drummond
favoured using a forged German passport – or at least what the camp
forger, Major Pat 'Sandy' Clayton of the Long Range Desert Group,
believed one to look like – and buying a ticket at Pescara train station,
some thirty-five miles' walk from Sulmona. From there he would
travel to Milan and then onwards to Como, the Swiss border being
within walking distance from that point. His idea was to take refuge
in the anonymity of large numbers of the Italian population going
about their business. Lea, on the other hand, believed this idea to be
bordering on reckless, preferring the more covert method of hopping
goods trains to within sight of the neutral border. Eventually, despite
Lea's reservations being echoed by the escape committee, the two men
had their plan approved, and tacitly agreed to separate once beyond
the wire and make their own ways individually towards safety.

We took the ladder down over the inside walls of the camp to
the Sergeants' compound from which we were due to start.
On the night chosen we dropped over the inside wall of the

camp, and, carrying the ladder, a spare bulb and a coil of wire, we went straight through a corridor in a building in which the Italian guard room and canteen were situated. This let us out into the space between the walls and the wire. We marched straight up to the light which shone on the ledge and, propping the ladder against the pole, unscrewed the bulb. The sentry called out to us, and we shouted back in Italian 'Electricians!' We then sidestepped along the ledge. While we were doing this the sentry became suspicious and fired, hitting Captain Lea in the leg.[16]

The bullet hit Lea in the upper thigh and badly injured the young officer who had unfortunately been shot by a 'Multiple Ball' round (*Cartuccia a mitraglia*). Inside this single round – considered ideal for sentries on night duty – were six cylindrical lead slugs stacked on top of each other that fragmented on exiting the barrel. Designed for short-range shooting, the effect resembles that of a small buckshot charge. One fragment grazed Deane-Drummond's cheek, while others buried themselves in Lea's upper leg, severing an artery and leaving him collapsed on the ground. Lea shouted at Deane-Drummond to run, exclaiming that he was going to make a break in the opposite direction lest his companion give up the escape and return to help him. As Lea lay bleeding on the ground and sirens began to wail Deane-Drummond disappeared into the darkness

Losing consciousness through blood loss, Lea was quickly treated by fellow-prisoner Doctor Patrick Steptoe who had volunteered for the Royal Navy Volunteer Reserve and served as a naval surgeon until his ship had been sunk off Crete in 1941.[17] Once his condition stabilised, Lea was transferred to hospital in Sulmona for his recovery before being returned to the camp where he, somewhat surprisingly, received no reprimand or punitive action for his attempted escape, though the event marked his final bid for freedom.

Meanwhile, Deane-Drummond had made good his escape. Though the bullet fragment had drawn blood from his cheek, he was otherwise relatively uninjured, a minor twist of his ankle not helping him keep up the fast pace that he desired to put miles between himself and any pursuit. He rapidly circled the camp and made for the mountains, battling in the darkness through thick short thorn bushes that tore at his clothes and left him with numerous small holes in his trousers and bloodstains from the myriad scratches. He remained dressed in his blue overcoat that comprised the Italian electrician's disguise, beneath which he had a mackintosh jacket with a swastika pin fastened to its collar to augment his cover story of being a German worker in Italy. His corduroy trousers had, however, been split straight up the rear seam, contributing to a bedraggled and somewhat unsavoury look. Deane-Drummond made for a path just beneath the snow line and spent the remains of his first night huddled beneath juniper bushes, avoiding the thick pine trees nearby as recently felled timber hinted at the presence of woodcutters. He stayed in this refuge during the daylight that followed, only narrowly avoiding detection by a goat herder who spent nearly two hours sitting contentedly only yards from his position. He took to his heels once again as dusk fell, headed to the small town of Popoli.

> My track led straight into the village with high walls of houses on either side. It was smelly but the road went on dropping by steps every six feet or so without any doors opening on to it from the houses. I was determined not to appear a stranger and walked on in as carefree a manner as I could muster. Quite suddenly a window banged open high up in a house over-hanging my road and a bucket full of shit just missed me. Hell! I must be walking through the town's main sewer. With all my pride lost, I retraced my steps and found another way through to the centre of the town without attracting any attention.[18]

He managed to mingle unobtrusively with the Italian population and even passing groups of soldiers, eliciting no response to his presence. Deane-Drummond took the opportunity to drink from wells wherever he found them, using the icy water to wash dried blood from his face and hands where the thorns had pierced his skin and attempting to spruce himself as much as possible for the trials to come.

Within six miles of Pescara, he abandoned his torn overcoat and proceeded into the town towards the railway station, clutching his presumed facsimile of a German passport and hoping the swastika badge would help ease his path. Despite almost being overcome with anxiety, he brazenly approached the ticket counter at Pescara station and muttered the memorised phrase given to him by Lucky in Campo 78: *'Terzo Milano'*. To his relief, although the ticket seller may have wrinkled his nose at the unkempt appearance of the man before him, he accepted the 500-lire note without question and issued Deane-Drummond his ticket.

Once aboard he shared a compartment with two Carabinieri and some overly inquisitive Italian civilians to whom he replied in halting Italian that he was a German construction worker employed at the naval dockyard in Taranto. Apparently, the explanation satisfied their curiosity and Deane-Drummond reached Milan without serious incident, boosted enough by his newfound confidence to order food from a vendor at one of the station platforms they passed through on the way to Milan.

Buoyed by his success, and probably slightly addled by tiredness, once disembarked in Milan he decided to spend the night in a hotel named 'Vittorio' while awaiting the morning train to Como. However, to his horror the receptionist replied to his vacancy enquiry in fluent German, evidently hailing from the Tyrolean region that buffered Austria and Italy.

> I mumbled back something in the schoolboy German I had learnt in prison. His only answer was 'You are no German' in German. My pulse beat a little faster, but I was determined to have my say and told him *'Ich bin ein Sudetener – Heil Hitler.'* This seemed to satisfy him, and he pushed across a card for me to fill in which I did, giving the details from my bogus identity card. He looked at it and shook his head. He had never seen one like that before. I interjected by saying it was only for Sudeteners – of course.[19]

By now terrified, he was shown to his room and took the opportunity to wash quickly before confronting what an error in judgement he had made. He swiftly decided instead to leave the hotel and take his chances in Milan's railway station overnight. He stumbled downstairs, only for the receptionist soon to accuse him of being an Englishman after Deane-Drummond pushed thirty lire at him for the bed he would not sleep in, and he attempted to reply haughtily while making haste from the hotel.

After a night in the Milan station waiting room amidst the anonymity of other sleeping Italian commuters, Deane-Drummond caught the train that he had hoped for and arrived early the next day in Como, which he considered to be his second major mistake. With time to kill in a sparsely populated town he ambled towards the frontier village of Chiasso where he had the misfortune to meet two Italian Alpini troops who immediately apprehended him, suspicious of his appearance and his filthy shoes. Before long he was in a frontier guardhouse in front of a fluent German speaker who immediately identified him as British, and an escaped prisoner from his list of wanted men hanging on the guardhouse wall. It was 13 December 1941, and Anthony Deane-Drummond recalled that it was possibly the most depressing moment of his life as he had come so close to Switzerland but still remained worlds apart from the neutral country.

The writer Eric Newby, who had been an officer in the Black Watch and the Special Boat Service, was captured by the Italians in 1942 during a raid on a Sicilian airfield and later wrote of his experiences, including this illuminating passage that goes some way to explaining Deane-Drummond's recapture:

> It was very difficult to get out of a prison camp in Italy. Italian soldiers might be figures of fun to us, but some of them were extraordinarily observant and very suspicious and far better at guarding prisoners than the Germans were. It was also very difficult to travel in Italy if you did get out. The Italians are fascinated by minutiae of dress and the behaviour of their fellow men, perhaps to a greater degree than any other race in Europe, and the ingenious subterfuges and disguises which escaping prisoners of war habitually resorted to and which were often enough to take in the Germans: the documents, train tickets and ration cards, lovingly fabricated by the camp's staff of expert forgers; the suits made from dyed blankets; the desert boots cut down to look like shoes and the carefully bleached army shirts were hardly ever sufficiently genuine-looking to fool even the most myopic Italian ticket collector and get the

owner past the barrier, let alone survive the scrutiny of the occupants of a compartment on an Italian train. The kind of going over to which an escaping Anglo-Saxon was subjected by other travellers was usually enough to finish him off unless he was a professional actor or spoke fluent Italian. And in Italy before the Armistice, there were no members of the Resistance or railway employees of the Left, as there were in France, to help escaping prisoners out of the country along an organised route.[20]

Deane-Drummond was taken back to Milan's police headquarters and underwent intensive interrogation before being moved to Castello di Montalbo, an old fortress in the Po valley where he was placed in solitary confinement for thirty-five days before being returned to Campo 78 in Sulmona and reunited with his comrades, who had themselves not been idle while he was away.

During Deane-Drummond's absence Lucky had also attempted to go over – and through – the wire using a makeshift ladder and wire cutters. However, despite reaching the outside and starting to run he was swiftly recaptured. Finally having had enough of the escaping officers, the Italian authorities informed Lucky and Deane-Drummond that they were to be transferred to a new camp for 'dangerous prisoners' commanded by Maggiore Massara. As well as the two would-be escapers, 'Tag' Pritchard, Commander Brown, RN, and Lieutenant Paterson were also transferred as the Italian officers at Sulmona were convinced, rightly, that they had helped coordinate the escape attempts. The men were taken by train to Campo 27 in the hamlet of San Romano between Pisa and Florence. There the prisoners – a supposed maximum of forty-nine – were to be held in a few rooms adjacent to the convent of the friars of San Romano. At that point there were only seven British officers held there, alongside fifty-seven Greeks, many of whom had deserted to the Italians during the Albanian war and were therefore treated with the utmost dubiousness by their new co-prisoners. While some of the Greek soldiers had been captured in combat, the majority were deemed untrustworthy and the British officers were warned of their Italian sympathies by those of their brother officers who continued to harbour a deep hatred of the Italians: an enemy they had bested in combat before German intervention.

Rations were deplorably meagre, and the British officers soon lost considerable weight and began feeling listless and lethargic until the arrival of Red Cross parcels restored some vigour. Within a month they began evaluating escape possibilities in earnest, Lucky the first to attempt to break free.

> On approximately 9 January 1942 at Campo 27 I sprinkled mustard powder inside my underwear which I wore for three days and nights. I then had my back scrubbed until the flesh was raw. On approximately 13 January I reported sick and the Italian doctor diagnosed scabies. He sent me under escort to Florence for treatment. I was dressed in an Italian-made RAF uniform which was easily convertible to look like that of an Italian Air Force officer. I also wore a beard. On the journey to Florence I persuaded my escort to take me round to see the sights before we went to the hospital. On arrival I got him to carry my suitcase, which was very heavy. We walked around the city until dusk, and in a crowded main street I spoke to a woman while my escort was momentarily separated from me. I asked this woman to get a taxi and meet me outside a nearby barber's shop. She mistook me for an Italian Air Force officer. A few moments later I escaped from my escort and went to the barber's shop where I had my beard removed. I had only a 500 lire note and the barber had no change. I then said the lady waiting in the taxi would have change and the barber sent his son to her. The woman came to the door of the shop, which was left open, and my escort, who had raised the alarm, happened to pass at that moment and saw me. I was then recaptured.
>
> I was taken to the hospital where I was brought before the Colonel and accused of an attempt to escape. I denied this and stated that as I had been a P.o.W. for two years I only wished to have the company of a woman. The Colonel sympathised with me and said he would send me to another hospital where there were Red Cross nurses. There I made a rope of my sheets and fastened it to my bed placed across the window. I tested

the rope before attempting to lower myself from the window, but the sheets broke as the fabric was rotted with bleaching chemicals. I was not punished for damaging the sheets but a guard was placed in the room until my discharge and return to Campo 27 on approximately 17 January.[21]

Lucky next feigned a strong Catholic faith and requested permission to make his confession with the monks still inhabiting neighbouring parts of the monastery, allowing him gradually to piece together the geography of their position and the layout of the huge building, reporting his findings to Commander Brown as Senior British Officer. Another naval officer in the group, Lieutenant M. J. A. O'Sullivan, a Swordfish pilot of HMS *Ark Royal*'s 810 Squadron who had been captured in February 1941, quickly proved to be a resourceful forger and escape kits were soon assembled. Lucky had realised that one of the men's cells was bordered by a dark corridor that appeared to be unused, and a tunnel through the wall was begun almost immediately. Unfortunately, during a brief rainstorm a monk used the dilapidated corridor for the first time in weeks and reported the digging, bringing Italian guards who ransacked the cells and found escape gear on both Pritchard and Paterson. With Lucky thought to be the instigator of the plan, the three were marched off for twenty-eight days in solitary confinement.

Before long the troublesome inmates were informed that they would be moved yet again, this time to the even more secure Campo 5 that had been established in the Forte di Gavi during June, having a capacity of 200 prisoners deemed the most difficult by Italian authorities. Determined to make one last attempt before they were moved, Deane-Drummond faked extreme pain and deafness, related to mastoiditis that he had suffered as a child. Examined by Italian doctors he was moved immediately to the Careggi Military Hospital, Florence. There, over the course of a month during which time he was treated with great civility and kindness while also managing to improve his Italian and German, he plotted his next escape attempt.

Despite having a permanent Carabinieri guard outside his room, Deane-Drummond successfully used hair oil to loosen the shutter hinges of his window some twenty-five metres above the pavement below. Lowering himself onto a six-inch wide crumbling piece of external decorative moulding, he cautiously worked his way around the building face while overcoming bouts of vertigo that caused his knees to shake and teeth to chatter almost uncontrollably. Climbing in by a lavatory window further down the same corridor, he silently crept past the Carabinieri guards and dropped down into a courtyard which led to the main road.

Free again, Deane-Drummond took a train first to Milan, and then, after spending the day at Milan's teeming station, onward to Varese, a small village on the edge of Lake Lugano about thirteen kilometres from Porto Cerisio on the Swiss border. His initial approach to the Swiss frontier showed a portion that was under heavy guard and he decided to head back towards Porto Cerisio to try a more remote crossing. However, while passing through a small village in the early morning darkness, he was intercepted by an Italian soldier who demanded to see his pass. He had left the hospital with no forged documents and instead tried to bluff his way through, claiming to be headed to Como to collect a pass as he was a shipwrecked German sailor who had lost everything. The Italian vacillated while Deane-Drummond pleaded his case, producing German currency that he had managed to accrue in prison, finally succeeding in convincing the man to let him on his way.

After lying up during daylight he began scrambling up the mountainside above Porto Cerisio to within sight of the barbed wire fence that marked the frontier. Studying the sentry routes, he awaited nightfall and, in light rain, crawled towards the wire fence which was hung with alarm bells. Midway between two sentry boxes, Deane-Drummond pulled out enough of the stakes holding the bottom of the fence to the leafy soil to clear a passage. After ten minutes he began to ease his way through, momentarily getting stuck half-way between Italy and Switzerland and being forced to retreat as the bell above began jingling lightly. After detecting no sign of alarm from the sentries, he tried once more, this time pulling himself through by using a tree root, into the safety of neutral Switzerland.

After walking to Chiasso he surrendered to the authorities and underwent interrogation by officials suspicious that he was a German agent. Finally satisfied of his identity, they moved him to Berne and accommodated him in a hotel before putting him in contact with the British embassy. He wrote a postcard to 'Tag' Pritchard now in Campo 5, from his 'Aunt Agatha' telling his commanding officer that he had 'just come out of a nursing home where I had to spend a month' and was now healthy and recuperating fast. The British Military Attaché, Colonel Cartwright, put Deane-Drummond, along with several RAF escapees, on the escape line 'Pat' which passed through Marseilles. Deane-Drummond eventually boarded a Gibraltar-bound Royal Navy trawler disguised as a Portuguese vessel. From Gibraltar, he spent ten days aboard a ship attached to a small convoy before finally arriving in the Clyde in July 1942. Anthony Deane-Drummond had reached Great Britain, and with him the first eyewitness account of Operation Colossus.

Those left at Sulmona continued to mount escape attempts. Lieutenant 'Killer' Jowett made his try after noticing repairs being carried out in the French compound which meant that its lights were extinguished. Helped by Clements and Lawley, he was boosted over the wall and cut his way through the three lines of wire, making a single train journey towards Switzerland before being apprehended and returned to Sulmona. Harry Tomlin in the enlisted men's compound was also part of a tunnelling plan:

> We were digging a tunnel, which after so many months of work, a bloody farmer went through it before we could get out of it. He had some kind of machine which went through and they found it. Everything was at sixes and sevens for a while.[22]

Over the months of captivity, the war situation in Italy worsened incrementally, mirroring the fortunes of the nation's military. Percy Clements recalled the slide in conditions until things came to a head in September 1943 with the Allied landings in the south of Italy:

> For the first seven months at Sulmona we actually had too much to eat and even had to burn bread, macaroni and potatoes so that the Italians would not cut the ration down; then we lost all fresh fruit, eggs, fish, etc., and we had the other rations cut by 50 per cent. This lasted until September 1942, and then the ration was cut again by 60 per cent. This meant

that each man received 2.5 lb of food every week, and for ten weeks of this period no Red Cross parcels arrived. Luckily, no one died, but towards the end everyone in the camp began to complain of stomach cramp, and another month or six weeks would have just about finished us ... Many attempts were made to escape from Sulmona by different fellows. None succeeded, though, and it has the record for Italian camps, as it was used in the last war for Germans and Austrians, and no one got away from there then ... In August and September of the last year [1943] American Liberators boosted our morale by making two attacks on Sulmona station and the railway and munitions factory nearby. Prisoners stood waving on the roofs and window sills as bombs blasted the targets. What a diversion for us! Then, on 8th September, we got news of the armistice whilst a football match was in progress. At first no one would believe it, and even when the truth sank in, we shook the Italians by keeping quiet about it and carrying on as before ... [23]

On 13 May 1943, Axis forces in North Africa had surrendered to the Allies, who then bombed Rome for the first time three days later. In July they landed on Sicily and Italian politics was in disarray. Mussolini dismissed several high-ranking government figures that he deemed more loyal to King Victor Emmanuel III than his fascist regime, widening an already existing gulf of antagonism between Italian royalists and Mussolini's party. On 25 July Mussolini was deposed, replaced with Marshal Pietro Badoglio, and arrested by the Carabinieri. Two days later the fascist party was dissolved by Badoglio and secret overtures were made to the Allies on the King's behalf; the resulting 'Armistice of Casibile' was signed on 3 September 1943, between the Kingdom of Italy and Allied forces. That same day British forces crossed the Messina Strait and landed in Calabria. On 8 September the treaty was made public and the following day, Allied troops landed at Salerno and Taranto. Unfortunately for the Allied troops in Italian captivity and those condemned to fight the campaign against 'Europe's soft underbelly', the subsequent Allied advance was one marred by lacklustre, indecisive and sluggish leadership.

To compound problems, they faced a skilfully conducted German fighting retreat, aided by Italy's frequently difficult terrain.

On the day that the armistice was announced, the Italian commandant addressed the men in Campo 78 and informed them that, as Italy had now surrendered, they were no longer prisoners of war and could leave if they so wanted. Most of the Italian guards had already deserted the camp, resulting in several of the ex-prisoners breaking into their abandoned barracks where the Red Cross parcels were kept and beginning to collect, and stockpile, supplies sufficient to last two weeks – their plan was to take to the hills and await Allied forces. The Italians had cut the barbed wire fences surrounding the camp and, while the rest prepared, several men took position on the hilltops to observe for German troop movements as the Wehrmacht raced to man a defensive line against the painfully slow Allied advance as well as to begin disarming Italian military units and keeping control of the thousands of Allied prisoners now suddenly liberated by the armistice.

Ironically, it was a British order that doomed as many as 50,000 of these men to further months of confinement. Winston Churchill had demanded that a clause stating that all POWs be immediately released be inserted into the armistice agreement, and Article 3 therefore stated that: 'All prisoners or internees of the United Nations to be immediately turned over to the Allied commander-in-chief and none of these may now or at any time be evacuated to Germany.' These terms were fulfilled by the Italian War Ministry, which instructed camp commandants to remove their guards immediately.

However, in London during the early summer of 1943, MI9, the Military Intelligence office responsible for Allied escape and evasion, reached the bizarre conclusion that it would be 'unhelpful' for thousands of freed Allied prisoners, no doubt somewhat malnourished and unarmed, to be on the loose in Italy, in the belief that the campaign there would be over in relatively short order. Instead, they instructed the 80,000 POWs held in Italian camps to 'stay put' and await Allied forces. Order P/W 87190 was issued on 7 June 1943 and stated that: 'In the event of an Allied invasion of Italy, officers commanding prison camps will ensure that prisoners of war remain within camp. Authority is granted to all officers commanding to take necessary disciplinary action to prevent individual prisoners of war attempting to rejoin their own units.'

A BBC World Service religious programme was used to transmit the coded order, which continued to be broadcast until the actual day of the armistice had arrived. Every Senior British Officer was thought to have received the instruction, and many obeyed to the letter, preventing men from taking to the hills and in some cases even posting their own guards to prevent them doing so. It was a tragic blunder, possibly brought about by mistaken predictions of German intentions, and the knowledge that their military was stretched to the limit by the war in Russia and occupation duties throughout Europe and Scandinavia. Instead, the Wehrmacht quickly secured most of the Italian peninsula and began fighting a dogged retreat that would last until the very final day of the European war. Most prisoner of war camps were swiftly occupied by German units and the transfer of inmates to Austria and Germany began. At Sulmona the first Wehrmacht men arrived on 14 September. Many of the prisoners had ignored the order to remain in their confines, though unfortunately for the mass of Allied prisoners who broke away their flight into the hills was observed and they were swiftly pursued by German troops and many recaptured.

Sapper Alf Parker of X Troop was one of the men who made a break for the hills around Sulmona. Parker had joined No. 2 Commando from 238 Field Company of the Royal Engineers after being evacuated from Dunkirk in 1940. Captured as part of Daly's escaping party, he endured the time at Sulmona while continually looking for ways to escape:

> There had been a cheese issue, 2 oz per man, so George [an unidentified fellow prisoner] and I decided to use some breadcrumbs we had saved to make a concoction of hot cheese and breadcrumbs. We had collected a small store of wood and duly put our very highly efficient little tin stove to use. This stove we had made from Red Cross tins and recirculated the hot gases from the tiny fire so well that we could boil a full billy – about a pint and a half of water on a very small piece of wood. One could hold a finger in the final exhaust without any discomfort. We had got the fire going well and the cheese

was giving off a beautiful aroma, when we heard some bods lower down the compound talking loudly about a giant swarm of bees coming our way, then a few seconds later someone shouted, 'the Planes!' At this George and I walked a few yards to get a view. Certainly, there did appear to be a swarm of bees in the distance up the Sulmona valley. A few seconds later it became obvious that they were planes all flying in a gigantic formation. Suddenly a small Italian fighter plane swept down from the right firing his guns. There was a quick response from the formation and the fighter didn't make another run. By now the actual shape of the planes could be seen and I saw a Flying Fortress for the first time. [On 3 September B-24 Liberators (not Flying Fortresses) of the US Ninth Air Force bombed the Sulmona marshalling yards, losing six aircraft.] There must have been at least a thousand; all apparently heading straight for the prison camp, then suddenly they began to release their bombs. The sky underneath them became absolutely thick with falling bombs, each one adding its own scream to the already fantastic crescendo of terrifying noise. There was nothing we could do to protect ourselves. The guard on the central watchtower provided us a small distraction by first climbing down his access steps then hesitatingly climbing back up. He finally deserted his post completely to the wild cheers of the prisoners. The bombs had at first appeared to be coming directly towards the camp but fortunately when the first bombs actually landed, they were on Sulmona itself and about half a mile away from us. In Sulmona there must have been chaos and also a lot of people killed. It appeared that the railhead must have been the main target but the sheer weight of bombs that fell in a space of not more than three minutes must have been devastating. Our carefully prepared meal was now a burnt offering and completely uneatable, but this time we didn't mind.

The excitement that night was intense and the roving patrols were visibly shaken, it seemed obvious that the Italians wouldn't stand for much more of this, I don't think many prisoners slept much this night. An order came through the next morning that we were all to parade on the football pitch at 12 noon so as to be addressed by the senior British officer (a South African) and there was much conjecture about what was to be said. This was one of the few times we had been allowed outside the high surrounding walls. The parade time arrived, and we all stood before this traitor. He explained that the Italians were in a bad way and after he had given careful thought to the situation, had decided that in view of the fact that some of us may be thinking of escaping, he had decided to issue an order forbidding any attempt to do so. He followed this up with a warning that in the event of anyone escaping and getting back to British lines they would be charged with disobeying orders and Court Martialled immediately. George and I could hardly believe our ears. However, on getting back to our quarters, we both resolved that if an opportunity to escape arose, then we would not hesitate to grasp it. We then quietly checked that our escape kit was still hidden intact in one of the outside walls. The Italian roving patrols were kept going and security was as tight as ever.[24]

Parker and his comrade made a break for freedom as the Italian guards visibly relaxed their vigilance, allowing men to range short distances outside the wire and this was where the two men ran from. As the actual moment of escape had been somewhat impulsively chosen, neither man had his hidden escape kit with him. They opted simply to head south towards Allied lines; German convoys were visible by this point from the mountaintop above Sulmona. Aided by Italian civilians after the Armistice had been announced the two had several close encounters with German troops before their luck ran out within earshot of Bren-gun fire from advancing British troops. Dressed in donated civilian clothes, the two were captured by Wehrmacht troops along with a number of other young military-age Italians among whom they attempted to merge.

When we reached the farmyard, which was hidden from the British line by a large haystack and some outbuildings, we just milled around until a German officer appeared out of the farmhouse. One of his men acting as a very poor interpreter generally questioned the men in the crowd and everything seemed pretty informal and friendly at this time. Then after about five minutes, the officer suddenly brought the proceedings to a stop and ordered us to form up in military fashion. We were all then searched and everything of value taken away. We were then led to what appeared to be an outhouse to the main farm building, but which was a chicken house, liberally covered in droppings and the rickety door was closed on us. George and I by prior arrangement kept away from each other and spoke to no one, only our Italian friends knew that we were English. Looking through the large cracks in the door we could see the Germans struggling to get a very large gun out of its position and hitched to a gigantic tractor. We looked at each other and I thought to myself, it looks as if they are retreating and will leave us locked in here.

After about ten minutes the door was flung open and a tall fine-looking German stepped into the room. He counted the number, then said 'Ah the thirteen apostles' then he pointed two fingers to one of the Italians including George and said '*Prima due*' and signalled them outside. A few seconds later there was a number of revolver shots and it was obvious they had been shot. A feeling of absolute horror overcame me and I looked desperately around the room for a possible way of escape, but to no avail. The Italians were in a frenzy. '*Mama Mia*' they cried, some went down on their knees and prayed to Almighty God. A few seconds later the door was flung open again. The same German came to signal out the next two. I strode up to him and cried 'You can't shoot me, I'm English.' He looked down at me questioningly, '*Eine Englander?*' he said frowning. 'Yes I'm an Englishman' I replied. '*Eine Tommy*' he next asked, to which I blurted 'Yes I'm a Tommy.' With this he took hold of my arm and led me outside to a waiting officer. This officer spoke to me in English with a strong Oxford accent. He asked me who I was and how did I come to be in this situation. I told him my rank and service number and that I was an ex prisoner of war and had escaped from Sulmona Concentration Camp.

While this questioning was in progress, the chicken run was being emptied two men at a time. As they came out of the door, they faced about thirty Germans formed in a semi-circle leading to the entrance to a square large walled-in enclosure with a gateway. As they arrived at the gateway the Germans were shooting them in the back. I watched in horror until they had all been shot and said 'Oh God you've shot my best friend.' The tall German, on hearing this, suddenly looked agitated, pointed to the bodies, *'Eine Englander?'* he asked. Quickly I realised my delicate position and replied, 'No an Italiano.' He looked very relieved. They then turned their attention to me again. They pointed to the other side of the valley and were curious as to how I had managed to get where I was. I told them again that I was an escaping ex-prisoner of war from Sulmona P.G. 78. They seemed to be quite friendly and lots of them came to talk to me to give their English language an airing. I was very impressed by the great numbers who spoke fairly good English. Later I was to find that the standard of education of the average German was better than mine, certainly I had no difficulty in making myself understood.[25]

Parker found himself the captive of a mobile unit of the 1st Fallschirmjäger Division that had conducted a planned – and effective – fighting retreat from Taranto, frequently engaging British paratroopers of the 1st Airborne Division. He finally managed to escape on foot once again and eventually reached Allied forces when he stumbled upon a British Army signals unit and in due course was moved south to Taranto, from where he was transported by ship to Bizerte, by Dakota to Algiers and ship once again to the docks at Liverpool.

Back in Great Britain, after long overdue home leave, he found himself back with the Royal Engineers before volunteering for the Glider Pilot Regiment. He went into action once more on 24 March 1945 when the 6th British Airborne Division made its attempt to secure a bridgehead across the Rhine. During the fighting that followed he and his unit were besieged in a farm house, Parker using a sniper rifle to kill several of the German attackers before being forced to surrender once more. Loaded into a railway goods wagon for transfer to a POW camp, Parker escaped during the journey, reaching the outskirts of Osnabrück where he tried to mingle with civilians fleeing Allied bombing, but was singled out by an alert German officer monitoring the crowds at a fork in the road, only narrowly bluffing his way past arrest as a German deserter. Increasingly desperate, frequently uncomfortably close to Wehrmacht units and caught amidst terrifyingly intense Allied bombardment, Parker found a hole in the ground and lapsed into virtual unconsciousness during the night only to awake with a British soldier standing over him with rifle and bayonet pointed at his chest. In the light of day, he could see destroyed German armour all around him as British infantry combed the area for stragglers and survivors. Once again, Parker had been liberated.

Amongst those that made a successful break for it from Sulmona were Sergeants Clements and Lawley who, along with four others, watched the arrival of German troops from the hill above the town on the morning of 14 September. Two days previously a German reconnaissance plane had passed over the camp, and with the arrival of ground troops imminently expected Clements and Lawley had soon collected another fifty-three leaderless ex-Prisoners of War. Following the Germans' arrival, and the sound of sporadic gunfire, many of the group ebbed away either alone or in pairs to make a run for Allied lines. Eventually deserted by the remainder of the men, for four weeks the two X Troop NCOs dodged constant German military traffic as they headed steadfastly towards Allied lines, Clements keeping a brief diary of his activities and observations as they travelled. Where once Italian civilians had been only too willing to turn in Allied escapees for fear of the Questura and its officers, now they frequently assisted those that they found. However, loyalties were confused in Italy, with many still supporting Mussolini's shadow state – the Italian Social Republic, known as the Salò Republic – that was created on 23 September 1943 after Mussolini had been freed from his captivity by German Luftwaffe and SS troops and taken to Germany before returning to the northern town of Salò. The dangers posed to the escaping paratroopers by fascist Italians still lingered, and they exercised great caution in choosing their route to evade German troop concentrations and the thickening front line. Finally, on 13 October, the exhausted Clements and Lawley reached Allied troops at Casacalenda, in the province of Campobasso thirty miles to the south-east of Sulmona as the crow flies. Both men were returned to Britain and later saw action with the 12th and 13th Parachute Battalions.

Harry Tomlin was also among those who attempted to escape Sulmona before the arrival of the Wehrmacht:

> [After the Italian collapse] they put me in the gash bin and covered me up and wheeled me out to the tip where it was tipped. There were always two Italian soldiers with it, so they tipped me out and they started to walk back, so I covered myself, waited till it was dark and then went off. Eventually there were three or four of us . . . we were on the mountains in Italy until September 43 till we got [sent] into Germany just before Christmas. We were [nearly] recaptured two or three times [before that]. Once we were walking along the mountain-tops and we heard a yell from behind us and there were two fellas standing on top of a peak waving to us. And of course, we hadn't got any binoculars or anything like that. They made their way towards us and I said, 'They're bloody Germans!' We made a run for it, got into some woods and while we were laying there, we could hear bullets thudding into the soil near us, but we just kept quiet and they went away. But it was a close shot. We used to kill a sheep on top of the mountains, skin it, cook it and eat it and then go down into a village and ask for potatoes. We used to sign a note for whoever the sheep belonged to, saying that when the Allied forces got there, they would recompense them for whoever the sheep belonged to. We were making our way down to Campobasso on the Adriatic side and we came to the parting of the ways when two of us wanted to go one way, and two of us another way. I understand that Roy Sherman [of the other pair] got back to England. But we went the other way and we were picked up.
>
> The Germans weren't bad really. I can't say that they were bad at all really. If you behaved yourself and didn't make yourself a nuisance, they wouldn't pick on you. But obviously if you start escaping and you make a nuisance of yourself, then

they make a nuisance of themselves. But it's everybody's duty to try and escape. The Germans took us to the nearest siding where trains were and shoved us in cattle trucks. They took our shoes and boots from us as well, because there were so many getting out of the trains that they knew that once you got into the colder parts of Italy, near December, you're not going to run away from a train without shoes and socks! . . . The train took us to Chemnitz, to a P.o.W. camp nearby, Stalag IV-B.[26]

Tomlin remained in Stalag IV-B until the war's end when he was liberated by Soviet troops. Having taken part in work details in Chemnitz and its surrounds, Tomlin and many of his fellow prisoners had moderated their view of Germans, mixing with civilians who were as hard-pressed as their own families had been back in Britain. Conditions in the camp plummeted with an influx of prisoners either from the Ardennes fighting or evacuated camps to the east. The arrival of the Red Army in 1945 was an enormous shock to the British prisoners, as the Soviet troops embarked on an orgy of rape and pillage, frequently stopping any potential British interference at gunpoint. Sickened, and unwilling to remain in the area, Tomlin was one of many men who marched west, finally reaching American lines.

In Campo 5, Lucky had tried once again to escape, this time using a medical ruse as he rubbed a grease-based anti-lice ointment containing mecury on his face for a week and reported himself as suffering from a sinus condition. The ploy failed, Lucky instead receiving an operation that corrected his 'sinus trouble' before the Italian armistice was announced. The difficult inmates of Campo 5 were immediately taken into German custody and shipped north. Lucky ended up transferred to Stalag XVII south of the town of Wolfsberg, in southern Austria.

On 19 September 43 at Stalag XVII I obtained a French forage cap. At approximately 1200 hours that day I walked through the gate of the camp wearing the cap, battledress trousers, a dark blue pullover and a dark blue raincoat, and I had a false French P.o.W. working pass.

Ralph spent the next two weeks walking and working his way across Austria, tending cows, digging potatoes and eventually cleaning railway carriage windows in Villach. On 3 October he sneaked abroad a train bound for Italy, but again his luck didn't last.

> Some time later the train stopped and filled with German soldiers and civilians. My presence was discovered, and the alarm given. Two SS guards appeared, and I was kicked in the head. I then stated that I was an RAF officer whereupon the guard stood to attention and my treatment afterwards was fair. On 5 October I was escorted to Stalag XVIII.[27]

Before long Lucky was moved on once more, this time to Stalag Luft I (West Compound), a Luftwaffe-operated camp that sat fringed by pine trees at the base of a flat strip of land jutting into the Barther Boden by the Baltic Sea. A Luftwaffe flak school was situated immediately south and the small town of Barth two miles to the south-east. The nearby Barth airfield was used for the re-equipping and conversion of bomber units. The Heinkel firm of Rostock had a production facility at the Barth airfield with thousands of female inmates from Aussenlager Barth, subsidiary of the Ravensbrück concentration camp, toiling away in the converted hangars surrounded by high fences. 'Tag' Pritchard had already been transferred to Stalag Luft I from Gavi and was present on Lucky's arrival. Yet another of the troublesome officers, 2nd Lieutenant George Paterson, had been on the same transport train as Pritchard but managed to escape while in transit and later fought with partisans before embarking on a highly dangerous career as an SOE operative in Italy.

While Pritchard continued his activities as head of a small escape committee, at the behest of Senior British Officer Group Captain N. W. D. Marwood-Elton amongst predominantly RAF and USAAF personnel, Lucky tried once again to escape by medical means.

> At the beginning of November '43 at Stalag Luft I, I decided to put myself in a condition to pass the repatriation medical board. I did not acquaint anyone of my intention. On approximately 23 November I began to smoke cigarettes containing crushed aspirin. A few weeks later I was taken into the camp sick quarters suffering from palpitations and a murmur of the heart. During the time I was in sick-quarters I stole a small

quantity of Benzedrine tablets and two caffeine capsules, which I kept for use prior to the electro-cardiogram test, which I heard to be the basis of the heart trouble diagnosis.

In January 1944 I was taken by ambulance to hospital for the test. Several hours before the test ensued, I consumed six half-grain Benzedrine tablets, and in a few minutes before the test I crushed one of the caffeine capsules in my handkerchief and swallowed the contents. The electro-cardiogram test showed that I suffered from myocarditis.[28]

Flying Officer Ralph Henry Lucky was repatriated to Great Britain on medical grounds on 13 September 1944. On arrival he was examined by a heart specialist, who detected no trace of myocarditis, though the effect of Lucky's unorthodox drug intake took several weeks to pass as he convalesced in Northampton. For Pritchard, there was no escape and the advance of the Red Army finally liberated him on 1 May 1945.

Chapter Eight

The Reckoning

What exactly had Operation Colossus achieved? It is true that the objective had been at least partially destroyed, but even the choice of that aqueduct as the primary target seems somewhat strange. The Pugliese aqueduct system was largely underground but required some major river crossings. While the Tragino torrent was one such crossing, it was a relatively small structure, neither too high nor too long to be out of commission for an extended period unless completely destroyed end to end. Considering the fact that Captain Daly, four sappers and much of the explosives were not available for the actual demolition, there was no way that the entire span could be wrecked, though Paterson's performance achieved the absolute best result possible. However, targeting larger aqueducts such as the one that straddled the Atella River (417 metres long and consisting of 29 arches) south of Mount Vulture, or the Bradano (210 metres long and of 14 arches) further south-east again, could well have had greater effect. The two aqueducts were in relatively unpopulated areas, or at least no more or less so than the Tragino crossing and would have added relatively little to an already impossible escape route to the Tyrrhenian coast. Both structures were longer and higher, gravity perhaps assisting in the destructive force created by explosives and bringing larger sections crashing into the river below. Additionally, the fact that the rivers themselves were more imposing could quite conceivably have complicated reconstruction attempts significantly and Colossus would have stood a greater chance of actually inflicting genuine hardship on the population and military ports of Puglia. Of course, these alternative targets were not without their drawbacks: the Bradano aqueduct had actually been considered by British planners in the early stages of the operation's development but was deemed too difficult to damage effectively due to the sheer size of the pylons and limited amount of explosives that could be dropped.

The choice of the Tragino aqueduct appears somewhat arbitrary. The fact that Mr Ardley of George Kent and Sons had drawn it to the attention of the Air Ministry planners is not enough reason for them to have abandoned any further research into the target area. However, British intelligence and information-gathering shows a shocking lack of thoroughness in this respect. To illustrate this point perfectly is the fact that the construction of the Pugliese aqueduct system was seen as a genuine engineering feat at the time of its instigation, and numerous worldwide engineering journals boasted accounts of its building accompanied by many technical drawings and specifications. One detailing the Tragino aqueduct shows a transverse section of the main water conduit but no firm information regarding the pylon construction material. Other aqueduct drawings, however, show an external brick skin over a concrete core. By this rationale it seems that the safest assumption – and a worst-case scenario – to be made by those planning the raid would have been that the main building material of the Tragino aqueduct could be concrete. This assumption was never made, rather the decision taken to embrace the fairly major supposition that the entire structure was constructed of masonry and calculations regarding the quantity of explosives required adjusted accordingly.

The slipshod nature of investigation into the target is further emphasised by the fact that British planners were not even aware that there was a second smaller aqueduct over the brow of the low sloping hill to the west. This oversight once again illustrates the lack of attention paid to full research by those in military intelligence. It was not the last time that British airborne operations were torn apart by such lapses in reasoning, the most disastrous of course being in September 1944 when paratroopers were dropped miles from the Arnhem bridge in the middle of the resting area of two SS panzer divisions and numerous other potent German forces. Fortunately for those involved in Colossus, there was no such enemy presence.

It remains testament to Paterson's skill as a Royal Engineer, and his accompanying sappers, that he was able to wreak as much havoc on the structure as he did. Nonetheless, the Italian reconstruction effort was equally effective, and the water flow towards Puglia resumed within three days of the explosion. The period occupied by reconstruction would also appear to have been an ideal time to attempt aerial bombing of the same target, but, of course, there was considerable uncertainty as to whether the paratroopers had succeeded at all. Despite Adrian Warburton's superb photo reconnaissance, strong doubts persisted that the aqueduct had been damaged and, with no means of communication between the paratroopers and any other Allied force, the uncertainty remained.

It seems in hindsight that Operation Colossus was mounted by the British primarily to use their recently created airborne force in action. The high morale attained by the men selected for 'Special Service' had ebbed away after countless demonstration jumps and months of intense training but no actual operations. Once the soldiers had reached a physical peak and mastered the art of jumping into an imitation combat scenario, they became a solution looking for a problem. The sabotage of the Tragino aqueduct became the first 'problem' that drew the attention of the Chiefs of Staff.

As well as the potential military benefit, a corresponding propaganda victory was also hoped for as the British people tired of an apparent inability to strike back at Axis forces which had reached the French coast and relentlessly bombed and shelled the British mainland for seven months. Military success in North Africa appeared remote to all but those either directly involved or connected via a loved one to the fighting in the desert. The aggressive nature of a parachute attack on enemy soil was believed to be exactly the image of an undaunted nation that Winston Churchill hoped to portray. However, once again, by very virtue of this fact, one cannot help but wonder whether it would not have been better to select a target from which there was a greater chance of recovering the men involved. Clearly there had been little thought given to the escape of X Troop from the area of the Tragino river. The idea that thirty-five men could pass through the frequently inhospitable Italian countryside without being seen by a population alerted to the attack is ludicrous. Assuming that HMS *Triumph* had indeed made the rendezvous point in the Gulf of Salerno, and successfully remained undetected, the likelihood of Pritchard's men achieving their evacuation timetable was extremely slim. Italy's militarised police were not as inefficient as Allied propaganda suggested and the region also hosted numerous infantry units in garrison and training. Coupled with a potentially outraged civilian population, the odds stacked against X Troop were appallingly high. What effective propaganda was created in Britain and Allied nations by the attack itself was somewhat marred by the swift capture of all the men involved, and the execution of Fortunato Picchi. Subsequent difficulties encountered by the Special Operations Executive in recruiting future Italian operatives willing to return to their fascist homeland remain testimony to that fact.

Nonetheless, there was at least some 'positive press' generated by Colossus and most certainly a reciprocal negative impression on the Italian psyche as a whole. The fact that Allied paratroopers had landed and committed this brazen act of sabotage shocked many among the Italian citizenry. The presence of at least one anti-fascist countryman meant that the effect was magnified considerably. Allied propaganda had already been heavily directed at the Italian population, attempting to cause panic and mistrust of their own government. Leaflets had been dropped on Italian cities at the beginning of 1941 entitled *La Verità* ('The Truth') which informed the population that Mussolini and his fascists had abandoned the Italian empire in Africa, that Italian troops were losing the battle in Greece and that public demonstrations against the presence of German soldiers had taken place in Rome and Milan. The ideology of the Allies was spelled out as a love of freedom and the right to free speech and a free press. Although faith in the Duce's decision-making had remained high at the outbreak of war, even in the poverty-stricken south of Italy, it eroded quickly.

Within the halls of the Quirinale there was great concern at the negative impact of the raid at a time when Italy's military lustre was already severely tarnished by defeat or checkmate in Africa and Albania. Much was made in the state-controlled press about the successful capture of all the enemy saboteurs, and the relatively minor damage that had been inflicted, though concern ran deep about the cracks showing in a country that had never truly wanted to join Hitler's European war. Considerable military reinforcement was made to Italy's infrastructure with troops that could have better used elsewhere along the crumbling combat fronts. Instead they were redirected to guarding important bridges, aqueducts, and other industrial installations thought vulnerable to any repeat attack. Cumbersome camouflage covers held in place by thick steel cables were erected over some of the more important bridges and aqueducts, and anti-aircraft batteries installed. The complex air raid precautionary measures and blackout regulations that appeared to fox the majority of the population received a temporary boost, and enforcement measures were more rigorously applied than previously, though they never reached the level of effectiveness attained by Britain and Germany.

In Britain, lessons gleaned from Operation Colossus were soon put into effect. Equipment concerns such as jumping helmets, uniform details and weapons containers were addressed and quickly updated. The somewhat archaic leather flying helmets worn by X Troop were no more, replaced by the rubber 'Sorbo' headgear and eventually the rounded airborne steel helmet with chin strap. Although the Whitley remained a poor option for the dropping of paratroopers, the 'hole' through which they exited at least had a vertical curved windshield fitted to its leading edge, protruding about two feet beneath the fuselage. This was intended to reduce the effect of slipstream on a parachutist's legs, which, as has been seen, could result in him being whipped backwards and the hapless man performing a 'Whitley Kiss'. By mid-1942 the vastly superior Dakota had become the workhorse aircraft provided for dropping parachute troops.

The control arrangements for Operation Colossus had also been mired in some measure of confusion, Keyes informing the Air Ministry in the aftermath that responsibility for future air preparations and execution must be more clearly defined if they were to function smoothly. In the case of X Troop's attack, he stated that 'It was not clear whether the operation was being undertaken under the Director of Combined Operations or the Air Ministry.'[1] As a result, control of airborne operations was from that point onwards divided to be handled by the respective service heads. On 26 April 1941, the Air Ministry informed Combined Operations Headquarters that it had reached agreement with the War Office that the conduct of future airborne operations would be its responsibility until the troops had actually landed. While this did not solve potential future confusion – a notable example being the planning of Operation Market Garden's

Arnhem drop and resupply – it at least delineated the sphere of duties for each branch of service – and the airborne troops were later entirely removed from Combined Operations remit anyway.

The next airborne operation mounted by the British was not until a year after Colossus, when Major John Frost led C Company, 2nd Parachute Battalion, against a Freya radar station on a coastal clifftop immediately north of the village of Bruneval, France. This mission – code-named Operation Biting – was deemed a complete success; casualties were two men killed, six wounded and six captured but the remainder were evacuated by the Royal Navy with enough captured radar components to enable effective British jamming measures and provide ideas for more streamlined radar construction on the British side. The propaganda coup that accompanied Biting featured prominently in the British press for weeks that followed.

What became of the men involved in Operation Colossus? The fate of Fortunato Picchi has been documented, though he seldom receives the attention for his selfless sacrifice that he deserves, his death lost amidst the hundreds executed by the Axis for supposed or genuine treason. Of course, Fortunato was not the only Picchi to suffer the consequences of his capture. The entire Picchi family was later subject to constant harassment by the fascist regime. Three of Fortunato's brothers – Cleto, Francesco and Giorgio – were soon released from their jobs with the Lanificio Franchi company due to their family relationship to a 'traitor to Italy'.

Another brother, Giovanni Rolando had enlisted as a Bersagliere in 1940. As Fortunato's great-niece Fabiana recalled, 'He was very slim but the hardest man of the family.' Giovanni Rolando fought in the Yugoslavian campaign in 1941 and after being allowed to return home was forced to leave once again for Russia with the Italian Expeditionary Corps (Corpo di Spedizione Italiano), though fortunate to return once more in 1942. The following year he was called to active duty again and only demobilised in 1945. A fifth brother, Luigi, had served in the Italian Army during 1936 in Eritrea and in Albania during 1939. He remained in the Social Fascist Republic Army until 1944, now a *sergente maggiore* and working as a telegraphist in Florence, until suddenly he was deported to Mauthausen concentration camp after being denounced to the

Germans as the brother of a traitor. He survived and returned to Italy following the camp's liberation by American troops in 1945.

During 1946 Fortunato's mother, Jacopina Pazzi Picchi, requested that the authorities of the newly established Italian Republic – the monarchy having been abolished following a constitutional referendum – officially recognise Fortunato as an Italian patriot or partisan fighter rather than his existing status as an executed traitor. Unfortunately, Italian bureaucracy required a plethora of paperwork to register such a request, and this was shuffled from one petty official to another within the labyrinthine maze of Italian officialdom. After over a year of such interdepartmental time-wasting she received her reply.

> It does not appear from the papers attached that the aforesaid carried out continuous political activity against Nazi–fascism. Having attempted acts of sabotage in the first years of the war as a paratrooper of the British army, he cannot be considered as a military fighter in the service of the aforementioned [partisan] army.[2]

Indeed, it appears that Fortunato did not fit the requirements of a 'patriotic hero'. He had had the misfortune to make a visible stand against Italy's fascist regime nearly three years too early, the majority of 'anti-fascists' miraculously only emerging after 8 September 1943 when Italy had been beaten into submission.

Deploring the lack of support given to her son by his own country, on 8 July 1947, Fortunato's mother wrote a letter to the British War Office to try and make sense of whether his son's death was remembered or whether he had been forgotten amongst so many other deaths.

> I am a poor old woman who cannot hope to live much longer, but before dying, I would like to know something about my son: to know whether, before leaving on that mission which was to cost him his life, he had left some kind of message or souvenir for his mother far away. In the newspaper 'Il Corriere del Sabato' [Saturday Post] which was printed in London by the interned Italians on the third anniversary of my son's death, they published a photograph of him and an article

which stated, among other things, that a ward in the Queen Elizabeth Hospital at Stepney, London, had been named after him, and that he had been acclaimed in England as the first martyr of Italy's second resurrection. If this is not true, why have they tried to make me believe it? And if it is true, why has nobody thought of the mother of this martyr? I have hopes that news will reach me from you, which nobody else has given me as yet, and which will bring some solace to my poor heart.[3]

She received her answer from the office of MO 1 (SP) – 'Military Operations 1 (Special Projects)', a cover name for the Special Operations Executive – written on 1 August. Amongst the typewritten words was at least some measure of humanity sorely lacking from the Italian government's response:

Fortunato Picchi was the first Italian to volunteer to return to Italy in the cause of her liberation, and his heroic death made a great impression on the Italians in this country. A Fund was started to raise money to endow a cot in his memory in a Children's Hospital. Your son did not give us your name and address before he left this country, knowing that in any case it would not be possible to communicate with you at that time. In a will written before he left on his mission your son left everything of which he died possessed to Mrs Florence Lantieri . . . a friend of your son's, and he had lived with her family for many years . . . Please accept our sympathy in the loss of your son who was very much respected in this country.[4]

Jacopina Pazzi Picchi died in 1954. For her son Fortunato there remains little commemoration. At La Briglia, part of the Tuscan commune of Vaiano to which the Picchi family moved during the war years, a small bridge has been named 'Ponte Fortunato Picchi' in his honour, though the metal plaque attached to the concrete structure bears no description of the man beyond his name. In Britain, there is less. A memorial established in 2016 at Brookwood's Commonwealth War Graves Cemetery in Surrey, south-west England, commemorates twenty-three Jewish members of the Palmach – the fighting force of the Haganah in Palestine – missing in action with their British liaison officer Major Anthony Palmer during Operation Boatswain, a 1941 SOE mission to sabotage Vichy French oil installations at Tripoli, Lebanon. This operation in itself has been largely ignored or forgotten by history, and the men whose names are listed there deserve such recognition. However, there is one extra name on the small memorial that does not belong with those of Operation Boatswain: 'Picchi, F.' Rather than providing a separate memorial to the first Italian SOE man ever to go into action with the most disastrous result for him, his name was added to the same granite surface. Almost as an afterthought.

It has proved difficult to account for the eventual fates of all of the remainder of X Troop, but some at least are traceable. The promoted Flight Lieutenant (temporary) Ralph Henry Lucky's eventual fate remains somewhat mysterious as almost befits his apparently mercurial character. What is certain is that on 1 June 1945, Flight Lieutenant Ralph Henry Lucky, MC (serial number 79272), Royal Air Force Volunteer Reserve, was awarded the MBE in recognition of his wartime service.[5] Although the citation itself has proved highly elusive in pinning down, the likelihood is that the award was prompted by MI9 and due to Lucky's extremely important role in escape plans hatched in the camps in which he was incarcerated. He provided valuable linguistic knowledge to would-be escapers and proved virtually indefatigable in his own attempts to break out, one of which was finally successful. The award of the MBE also raises once again the question of exactly why Lucky was attached to Operation Colossus. Though his mastery of languages is beyond doubt, he was somewhat older than all but Picchi and originated from the RAF which had been relatively ambivalent about the entire scheme of parachute troops since its inception. Post-war, the Special Operations Executive claimed no control over Lucky at all, though he certainly appears to have been acquainted with Admiral Sir Roger Keyes.

Could part of his mission have been the preparation of evasion lines at the behest of MI9? With the likely escalation of Allied bombing of Italian targets would come an increase in the number of men forced to bail out over enemy territory. Lucky's ingratiating himself with the Italian prison authorities in Naples that so annoyed Anthony Deane-Drummond and his fellow paratroopers may well have provided exactly the opportunity to get beyond the bars of his prison and contact any known or potential anti-fascist cells in Italian territory. This theory remains just that – a theory – and no more. However, it does seem at least plausible and not beyond possibility, Lucky having repeatedly proved himself capable of great personal secrecy and complete independence of action.

Since his days as a precocious youth, Lucky always trod his own path and was relatively aloof from the remainder of his family. He did, however, remain in contact with his sister Alice-Henriette following the end of the Second World War while recovering in Northampton from the self-induced sickness that had liberated him from German captivity. His relationship with his other sister Anne-Marie-Paule, could only charitably be described as 'distant', while he appears to have been slightly overbearing to his brother André, who had also spent years in an Italian POW camp and who Ralph insisted change his surname to Lucky on the grounds that brothers must share the same last name.

Following his recovery, Ralph apparently married a Danish woman named Betty. The couple briefly moved to South Africa, before returning to Denmark during the 1950s when Betty fell ill and died, possibly through cancer of the jaw. On 27 July 1954 the Air Ministry published in the *London Gazette* that reserve officers named on their 'Emergency List' were to relinquish their commissions under the provisions of the Navy, Army and Air Force Reserve Act 1954. Flight Lieutenant Lucky was granted permission to retain the rank and benefits of a squadron leader with effect from 10 February 1954. Following an absence of contact between him and his siblings, his brother André attempted to get in touch, but his letters remained unanswered. As a last resort he registered an enquiry through the British Consul in Denmark that finally drew a response; a letter stating that Ralph did not want to keep in touch with his family and so would 'he kindly stop pestering him'. From there, the enigmatic Ralph Lucky, MC, MBE, disappears from public view and it is unknown exactly when, or where, he finally passed away.

Trevor Allan Gordon Pritchard (serial number 49939) was awarded the Distinguished Service Order on 25 November 1941. Captain (at that time temporary Major) Pritchard, Royal Welch Fusiliers, was recommended by Roger Keyes for the DSO – the second highest British military award for valour, at that time given only to officers – that his 'award may be treated as an immediate one, as an encouragement to other paratroops'. The citation reads as follows:

> Major Pritchard commanded the expedition of paratroops which landed in Italy on the 10th February 1941. He organised the expedition and trained the personnel, who reached a high standard of efficiency. The success of the operation, as a result of which the aqueduct to Brindisi was blown up, the bankseats and one column destroyed, and the town cut off for ten days, was due to his leadership and inspiration. Major Pritchard had a reasonable chance to escape if arrangements had gone according to plan. The fact that they did not and that he was captured, was due to no error of judgement on his part.[6]

Following his liberation by Soviet troops and return to Britain, 'Tag' was eventually awarded an MBE in August 1946. The recommendation, written during the previous April, originated from MI9:

> Major Pritchard was captured in Southern Italy on 12 February 1941 and after serving several months imprisonment at Sulmona he was sent to San Romano (near Pisa). Appointed senior British officer he led an unsuccessful escape attempt to break out through an adjoining church.
>
> In June he was sent to Gavi, and even though this old fortress was reputed to be escape proof, Major Pritchard did everything in his power to foster escape activities. After the Italian capitulation when the Germans were evacuating all prisoners from Gavi, Major Pritchard hid only to be discovered and transferred with his companions to Germany.
>
> Throughout his captivity Major Pritchard sent important information to the War Office by secret means, and after reaching Stalag Luft I in January 1944 he completely reorganised this side of the Intelligence work, with excellent results.
>
> The Senior British Officer who praised him highly for this work, also commended Major Pritchard for his valuable

contribution to the building of the camp morale through his keen interest in sport and P.T. Major Pritchard made his presence felt in every camp to which he was sent, and no less than eight officers have praised his Escape Committee work and a further seven his Intelligence activities.[7]

During the four years that Pritchard had spent as a prisoner of war, his fiancée called off their engagement, something that his subordinate, and friend, Anthony Deane-Drummond recalled as having the effect of a 'personal tragedy'. Promoted to lieutenant-colonel after the war and assigned to the Royal Military Academy at Sandhurst, Pritchard married hastily and unhappily to a woman who detested the Army and did her best to persuade him to leave. Though he refused to be coerced into doing this, Pritchard sadly developed tuberculosis and, after periods of time spent at the Midhurst Sanatorium was invalided out of the Army, retiring on account of disability on 20 May 1953. Once again, Anthony Deane-Drummond recalled meeting his former commander but left with an overwhelming sense of sadness to see such a strong man 'so wasted in body and spirit'. However, following a divorce, Pritchard later remarried and lived apparently contentedly in London until his death in 1982.

The Military Cross was Britain's third highest military award for officers during World War II. (It can now be awarded to all ranks.) Deane-Drummond was decorated for his part in Operation Colossus, awarded the Military Cross on 29 September 1942. The citation for Lieutenant Anthony J. Deane-Drummond, Royal Corps of Signals, reads:

> This officer was one of a party of paratroops who landed near Calabria in Southern Italy on 10 February, 41. Two days later he was captured and taken to Naples aerodrome from where after interrogation he was later removed to the camp at Sulmona. On 15 June 1941, Lieutenant Deane-Drummond had made plans to get out of the camp in a garbage wheel-barrow, but had to abandon the idea, as the guards had been warned. In July he again attempted to escape, together with about twenty others, by digging a tunnel, but the scheme was discovered before the tunnel had been completed.

Lieutenant Deane-Drummond made a further attempt to escape in December 1941, accompanied by another officer who was, however, hit by the guard who fired when he saw them climbing over the wire which surrounded the camp. Lieutenant Deane-Drummond got away and managed to travel as far as Ponte Chiasso before he was detained by soldiers who took him to the frontier post to be searched. Later he was again transferred back to Sulmona, but after a month was moved to the camp at San Romana. Here another plot to escape was discovered and all the English officers were moved to a special camp south of Naples. Lieutenant Deane-Drummond, however, had managed to be sent to hospital at Florence a few days before the party left. Here he was left locked in a room on the fourth floor with a guard outside the door. On 15 June 1942, he escaped from the room by sidestepping along the ledge outside his window, entering another room some distance away, and going downstairs and out through a window on the ground floor. Dressed in battle-dress, trousers and a navy-blue sweater he travelled by train to Varese, changing at Milan, and walked towards the frontier. After seeing what he thought were sentry boxes, he decided to return to Varese and travel on towards Como. He was stopped by a Mareschallo (Regimental-Sergeant-Major) while passing through a village but was allowed to proceed. He reached Ponte Chiasso and at night on 19 June he managed to scoop enough earth to allow him to get under the frontier wire.

He intended to try to get to Berne without giving himself up, but at Chiasso he was stopped by a Swiss policeman and after questioning, he admitted that he was an escaped British prisoner. He was taken to Berne on the same day and after further questioning was handed over to the British authorities for repatriation.[8]

By 1944, the 27-year-old Deane-Drummond had reached the rank of major and was second in command of the 1st Airborne Divisional Signals, which played such an important role in Operation Market

Garden and his unit's attack on the Arnhem road bridge. He and his fellow signals officers expressed great concern at the distance between the British drop zones and the target bridge, but the determination to get into action almost at any cost outweighed more pragmatic thoughts. The much-storied battle at Arnhem was a disaster for 1st Airborne, the attack carried out despite intelligence concerns regarding the potential enemy strength and major difficulties involved in the British drop. Major Deane-Drummond was taken prisoner once again and managed to escape in an extraordinary escapade detailed fully in his book *Return Ticket* that involved thirteen days standing concealed in a cupboard inside a building occupied by German troops, before crossing the Rhine back to Allied lines. For his role in Market Garden he was Mentioned in Despatches and awarded a Bar to his Military Cross.

Post-war, Deane-Drummond continued to serve in the armed forces, commanding 22nd SAS as a lieutenant-colonel during the Malaya Emergency, penetrating deep into the jungle and operating against communist guerrillas. He later commanded the SAS Regiment in Oman, for which he received the Distinguished Service Order after fighting against rebels holding the Jebel Akhdar mountain range. He was promoted to brigadier and later took over command of 44th Parachute Brigade (TA), ending his military career as a major-general. Anthony Deane-Drummond died on 4 December 2012.

On 1 March 1945, Second Lieutenant George Robert Paterson (serial number 130870) Corps of Royal Engineers, No. 11 Special Air Service Battalion, was awarded the Military Cross.

> Lieutenant Paterson was captured on 12 February 1941 at Calabria, Italy, when returning from a special mission. Subsequently he was imprisoned at Sulmona, Pisa, Padua and Gavi (Camp 5). In May 1941 Lieut. Paterson was one of eight officers who escaped from an organised walk; he was, however, recaptured the same day. Almost a year later, at Pisa, he participated in an attempt to break through into an adjacent church; this project was discovered before the officers emerged. Throughout his imprisonment in Italy, Lieutenant Paterson was in secret communication with the War Office.

When the Germans took over Gavi Camp at the time of the Italian armistice, they transferred all PoWs to Germany. Immediately they had been locked in the train, Lieut. Paterson and his companion began to break a hole in the side of the carriage. Lieut. Paterson was the fifth to jump, and, although the sentries fired, he was not hit. After swimming a river, he continued for another three days until he was exhausted. Friendly Italians then cared for him, and upon his recovery, sent him to a partisan band near Brescia. Captured by fascists early in January 1944, he was handed over to German custody. Although for three months escape was impossible because he was isolated, ultimately he was allowed to work in the prison itself (San Vittore). He and four other PoWs bribed one of the guards to loan them the key of the side door; a duplicate key was made, and they escaped on 8 July 1944. Lieut. Paterson made his way to friends, who arranged for his journey to Switzerland.[9]

Indeed, Paterson had escaped from the crowded boxcar carrying prisoners to Germany and made his way to Switzerland where he was recruited by SOE for a return to Italy in order to assist other Allied prisoners using the escape lines. Posing as a POW he was recaptured, spending three months in solitary confinement in the wing of Milan's San Vittore prison controlled by Hauptsturmführer Theo Saevecke, head of the Gestapo and fascist police in Milan. From there he escaped a second time and made his way back to Berne where SOE briefed him for another Italian mission. The 25-year-old Canadian crossed back into Italy during September 1944, moving into the Piedmont region where the city of Domodossola had staged an uprising against the German and Italian fascist authorities and declared itself a free partisan republic. Paterson had been charged with providing whatever assistance he could to the partisans, including the coordination of air-dropped supplies. The Wehrmacht's own supply lines in Italy could be severely disrupted by wholesale revolt against fascist rule in the north, and SOE intended to do as much as possible to foment such a rebellion while attempting to prevent communist and royalist factions from clashing in a virtual civil war.

Paterson's attempts at mediating between neighbouring partisan bands were frequently undermined by political friction. His efforts to create a unified military command structure eventually bore some fruit, but to little real effect as 'local party politics, distrust and jealousy' generally derailed any meaningful cooperation. On 8 October, the predicted German retaliatory attack on Domodossola opened and Paterson was captured once more and transferred back to SS control at San Vittore. There he remained until liberated by partisan forces and advancing Allied troops in April 1945 whereupon he resumed assisting SOE in the city for nearly another full year before finally returning to his forestry studies in Scotland. Due to his outstanding valour, he was awarded a Bar to his Military Cross on 4 October 1945 and a second Bar on 20 June 1946.

At the same time, both Arthur Geoffrey Jowett (P/130598), Highland Light Infantry, and Christopher Gerald Lea (serial number 73126) Lancashire Fusiliers, were also awarded the Military Cross, announced in the *London Gazette* for 20 June 1946. Both were furthermore Mentioned in Despatches, Jowett on 4 January 1946, and Lea on 14 February 1947:

> Lieutenant Arthur Geoffrey Jowett (P/130598), 1st British Parachutists ('J' Troop, 11 SAS Btn).
>
> Dropped in Southern Italy on 12 February 1941, Lieutenant Jowett was subsequently imprisoned in various camps in Italy and Germany. Whilst at P.G. 78 (Sulmona) he took part in two tunnel digging operations, but both were discovered before completion. In November 1941 he succeeded in getting out of the Camp and made for the Swiss frontier but was recaptured a few hours later. Transferred to P.G. 17 which was an old convent, Lieutenant Jowett and two comrades attempted to get into those quarters still occupied by Nuns and so escape. They succeeded in entering the attic directly above the Nuns' quarters but were discovered by guards and put in cells.
>
> Transferred to Germany, he assisted in digging a tunnel from Oflag VIII-F, but he was moved to Stalag Luft III (Sagan) before it was completed. Whilst in Italy between June 1941 and September 1943, Lieutenant Jowett on many occasions passed

valuable information to the War Office by secret means. He was liberated by Allied forces in May 1945.[10]

Jowett had been moved to Oflag 79 at Waggum near Brunswick in Germany which had been created in a three-story brick building previously used as a barracks for a *Fallschirmjäger* training battalion. It was there that the US Ninth Army liberated him on 12 April 1945.

> Captain Christopher Gerald Lea (serial number 73126), Lancashire Fusiliers/11 SAS Btn.
>
> Captain Lea was captured near Calitri Italy on 12 Feb. 41. In Dec. of the same year he and another officer made an attempt to leave Sulmona disguised as electricians. They had climbed over the inside wall and had entered the Italian section of the camp when a sentry became suspicious and fired, hitting Captain Lea in the leg. His companion, however, reached Como before he was arrested.
>
> Throughout his captivity Captain Lea participated in numerous tunnel schemes, none of which were successful. He also communicated secretly with the War Office.[11]

Lea was moved to German captivity following the Italian armistice, held in the officer's camp in Oflag IX-A/Z, Rotenburg an der Fulda, Hesse, central Germany. Following liberation by Allied forces and fully recovered from his wound from the abortive escape attempt with Anthony Deane-Drummond, Lea served post-war in the Indonesian campaign and in Austria before leaving the Army with a Mention in Despatches during 1948. During his time as a prisoner of war, Lea studied law and was called to the Bar by the Inner Temple as soon as he had left military service. Married in 1952, he practised as a barrister before becoming a Metropolitan Magistrate and then Circuit Judge. On his retirement in 1992, Lea was then ordained as a priest and became the assistant curate at Stratfield Mortimer, Berkshire. He passed away on 1 June 2006 at the age of eighty-eight.

For the non-commissioned officers and men of the British Army, the second-highest award during World War II for 'distinguished, gallant and good conduct in the field' after the Victoria Cross was the Distinguished Conduct Medal. On 2 March 1944, Sergeant Percy

Priestly Clements (serial number 2564415), Leicestershire Regiment, was awarded this medal for his part in Operation Colossus and exploits thereafter. The recommendation for his medal, given by officers of MI9, reads:

> Sergeant Clements was a member of a party of parachutists dropped in Calabria in February 1941 to blow up an aqueduct, who were subsequently captured by the Italians. Shortly after capture they were taken to Camp 78 Sulmona, where Officers and Other Ranks were placed in separate compounds, no communication between them being allowed. Despite this regulation Sergeant Clements, who took charge of the most secret communications in the Other Ranks compound, managed to maintain clandestine communication with the Officers, and exchanged with them the particulars of all secret messages received from the War Office. He also arranged the despatch of similar messages to the War Office in selected Other Ranks letters and later, as the Officers were moved to another camp, was responsible for maintaining all communication between the Camp and the War Office.
>
> On 12 September, following the Italian armistice, when all attempts to escape were strictly forbidden, Sergeant Clements escaped to the hills. From there, on 14 September 1943, he watched the Germans enter the camp, and he then made up a party with Sergeant Lawley and Private Rae, both of the Parachute Regiment and started walking South. Private Rae was unable to keep up and fell out at an early stage of the journey, but Sergeant Clements and Sergeant Lawley continued walking as far as Morrone, their journey lasting twenty-two days. At Morrone they hid up for a week and they were able to join the British forces at Casacalenda on 13 October 1943. Throughout their escape Sergeant Clements was in charge.
>
> In view of the fine work of a secret nature which this NCO rendered, in addition to his initiative in making his escape, I strongly recommend him for the award of the DCM.[12]

While the DCM had been awarded mainly due to his important work that benefitted MI9 as a prisoner and escaper, he would also be belatedly awarded the Military Medal – the third-highest other ranks' award for valour – for his active part in Operation Colossus, his citation given on 20 June 1946 reading:

> Sergeant Percy Priestly Clements (serial number 2564415) Leicestershire Regiment (since commissioned in Army Air Corps).
>
> On the night of 10/11 February 1941, Sergeant Clements was Second-in-Command of a Section of Parachutists which with three other (of the six) Sections successfully landed near the aqueduct. Despite the Royal Engineer Section being missing, along with all the arms containers, the remainder of the Force with a reduced quantity of explosives successfully destroyed the aqueduct. The party then set out in small groups to cross the mountainous terrain to an RV fifty miles away at the mouth of the River Sele, to be collected by a submarine. After two days and nights exposed to the winter elements, when within about ten miles of the RV, Sergeant Clements' group was surrounded by a far superior force of armed civilians and of Italian carabinieri and infantry. After a short fire-fight in which the group, armed only with one SMG, seven pistols and three knives, was entirely outgunned, it was forced to surrender, and all were taken P.o.W.

Following his return to British lines and subsequent transport to Britain, Clements was commissioned as a lieutenant in the 12th (Yorkshire) Battalion, Parachute Regiment, on 19 August 1944 and attended a refresher parachute training course (No. 134) at RAF Ringway in September 1944. Clements and the battalion were posted to the River Meuse in December 1944 as part of 6th British Airborne Division to help counter the German Ardennes offensive. On 5 January 1945, Clements's platoon was part of the parachute force, supported by Sherman tanks of the Fife and Forfar Yeomanry detached from the 11th Armoured Division, ordered to occupy the Belgian town of Bure. During the battle they clashed violently with defending troops of the *Panzer Lehr* Division, including a small number of Tiger tanks.

During the heavy close-quarter fighting, Clements directed supporting artillery fire, but he and his men were soon surrounded and forced to fight their way out. In this close-quarter fighting he was wounded in the stomach. Unable to move, and in bitterly cold snow, he continued to coordinate his troops' movements with the incoming artillery fire and successfully extricated his men. He himself was also evacuated by stretcher, now severely wounded in the arm and leg as well, and both of his stretcher bearers were killed by intense enemy fire. Clements lapsed into unconsciousness and did not wake until in an officer's hospital in Gleneagles, Scotland. For his outstanding leadership and determination during the battle at Bure he was awarded the Military Cross. Due to the severity of his wounds, Clements was invalided out of the Army and a civil service position was found for him in the Ministry of Defence, which he held until his retirement. Clements, one of the most highly decorated British paratroopers and one of the service's pioneers, passed away in 1998.

Clements's fellow escapee and X Troop NCO, WOII 'Taff' Lawley, was also awarded the Military Medal on 18 June 1946, though the original citation was given to 'WOII Arthur William Albert Lolley (serial number 3952374) 11th SAS Regiment/Army Air Corps.' Following his return to Britain, Sergeant Lawley joined A Company of the 13th (Lancashire) Parachute Battalion in May 1944 and took part in Operation Tonga, dropped into Normandy six hours before the seaborne landings of Operation Overlord on 6 June 1944. Lawley was promoted to Company Sergeant-Major of C Company and later received a signed certificate from Field Marshal Montgomery for 'outstanding good service and devotion to duty'.

Lawley and his battalion later took part in the same Ardennes fighting as Clements, and subsequently Operation Varsity – the crossing of the Rhine and the last British parachute drop of the war – during which he was Mentioned in Despatches. Lawley's unit advance into Germany behind the 15th (Scottish) Infantry Division. On 30 April they were ordered to make for Wismar on the Baltic Sea and arrived just before the lead units of the Red Army. 'Taff' Lawley died in 1982.

The Military Medal was also awarded to Sergeant Edward William Durie (serial number 1881068), Corps of Royal Engineers, on 20 June 1946, who had been held prisoner in Stalag VII-A, Moosburg, after the Italian collapse, his POW number listed as 127102. On 21 February 1946, Lance-Corporal Robert Brimer Watson (serial number 1888304) Royal Engineers (attached 11 Special Air Service Regiment) also received the Military Medal.

> Watson was captured on 13 February 1941 at Avellino after being dropped by parachute to carry out a special mission. As a result, he was imprisoned in Naples, Sulmona and Aquila. Watson served as a member of the Escape Committee and sent valuable information to the War Office by secret means.
>
> Released on 11 September 1943, he found a shelter at Coppito until his recapture on 6 December 1943. Six days later he escaped from the Germans and returned to Coppito. On 27 December 1943 he went with a companion to Aquila. At the beginning of May 1944, when attempting to reach Allied lines, Watson was caught. Imprisonment at Aquila and Laterina followed. Entrained for Germany on 23 June 1944, he and two others escaped through a hole they made in the floor of the truck. Travelling North to Switzerland on foot, they crossed the border on 13 July 1944.[13]

'Mad Bob' Watson – who was also Mentioned in Despatches on 20 June 1946 – was demobilised in October 1945 and returned to Northampton and his building firm. Unfortunately, the severe winter of 1947 curtailed work and his small firm went bust. He soon left Great Britain, though his whereabouts are now unclear – family members remember him saying he was going to Burma to help construct oil rigs. All that is known is that he later returned to his native Newcastle, where he died aged only fifty-three on 25 June 1962.

On 15 June 1944, both Parkers of X Troop received awards. Sapper Alf Parker (serial number 1877817) was Mentioned in Despatches after his extraordinary escape from first Sulmona and then German forces, while Sapper James Parker (serial number 4447110), Corps of Royal Engineers/11 SAS Battalion, was awarded the Military Medal. James Parker had originally enlisted in the Durham Light Infantry at Newcastle-on-Tyne on 6 October 1928 but left the Army in 1935. Recalled to active service on 6 September 1939, he transferred to the

Royal Engineers and saw service as part of the British Expeditionary Force before the Dunkirk evacuation. Immediately upon hearing the call for Special Service volunteers, he had put himself forward and was accepted into No. 2 Commando. After capture he was taken to Campo 102 Aquila. On the Italian capitulation in September 1943, the camp gates were opened, and most of the prisoners headed for the hills, but were recaptured by German *Fallschirmjäger* and placed on a transport train to Germany on 3 October. Parker and fellow prisoner R. K. Quinlan then escaped the train on a slow bend, though Quinlan broke his legs during the fall and Parker carried him all the way to a farm in Cocullo, where a woman called Agata di Cesare nursed him back to health. On 13 November 1943, Parker and Quinlan finally reached American lines. Parker was transferred to the Royal Engineers on 16 February 1944, becoming a sapper in 874 Mechanical Equipment Company and 70 Mechanical Equipment Platoon. He served in Burma before being moved to the Army Reserve at the war's end and his final discharge on 28 April 1955.

On 28 September 1944, Lance-Corporal Harry Boulter (serial number 5047114), 11 SAS/North Staffordshire Regiment, who had been incapacitated at the beginning of the aqueduct attack, was awarded the Military Medal for his actions after capture.

> Boulter was captured in the vicinity of Naples on 10 February 41, after fracturing his ankle when being landed for sabotage work. He was sent via Sulmona, Vetralla and Rome to Fara Nel Sabina (Camp 54). During his imprisonment he was in secret communication with the War Office. Whilst at Sulmona he participated in an unsuccessful tunnel scheme; on two other occasions he made plans for escape, but both were frustrated by camp restrictions imposed at the last moment.
>
> When Fara Nel Sabina was evacuated on 11 September 43 under the direction of the Senior British Officer, Boulter stayed in the vicinity for a month. In an attempt to reach Allied hands, he travelled to Carsoli before discouraging reports deterred him from proceeding further. Because of Fascist activity he moved to Canneto where, on 9 Jan 44, he was recaptured and sent back to Fara Nel Sabina. En route for

Germany on 26 January, the train was bombed in the vicinity of Orvieto and although the guards had removed all the P.o.W.'s boots, Boulter braved their fire and escaped.

After reaching Canneto, he and two other escapers were arrested by the Germans. Later, left with one guard only, they overpowered him, seized his rifle and returned to Toffia. They persuaded the Italians that the Germans had gone and, after obtaining rifles and ammunition, led a party of twelve Italians which ambushed a German staff car. Although the officer got away, they secured all his documents and handed them to advancing Allied troops on 10 June 1944.[14]

Also Mentioned in Despatches on 20 June 1946 were Captain Gerrard Francis Kirkpatrick Daly (serial number 69066), Royal Engineers, attached 11 Special Air Service Battalion, Lance-Corporal J. E. Maher (serial number 1888254), Corps of Royal Engineers and Private Nicola Nastri (serial number 5340622), Oxfordshire & Buckinghamshire Light Infantry.

Captain Daly was captured in Italy near Salerno on 13 February 1941. On 15 February, Captain Daly broke out of the Carabinieri barracks in Naples, the place being very badly guarded. He was caught, however, the following morning by Italian police when trying to board a train.

With two companions he escaped from the Padua Camp by walking out through a deserted part of the building. The three men were arrested the next night by a road patrol.

In June 1943 at Gavi, Captain Daly and nine other PoWs tunnelled through a disused water system discovered by them underneath the castle. The outer wall of the castle was scaled by means of a rope, which broke, however, before all the men were able to get away. The guard was aroused and all the escapers were rounded up. Captain Daly was liberated near Mulhausen on 10 March 1945 by the US Army. In addition to attempting to escape, Captain Daly sent valuable information to the War Office by secret means over a period of three years.[15]

Daly married in January 1948 and eventually gained the rank of lieutenant-colonel in the Royal Engineers during 1957 before retiring from the Army on 16 April 1960.

The only other Italian beside Picchi to take part in Operation Colossus, Private Nicola Nastri, was among those who took to the hills after the departure of their Italian guards. There he joined a local partisan band, his Commando training and knowledge of the local dialect soon helping make him one of their leaders. Harassing German transport convoys became their main task and it was during one such ambush that Nastri was recaptured, attempts to outrun pursuit coming to nothing amid a hail of German gunfire. Nastri was sent to a POW camp near Innsbruck, Austria, and then Stalag XI-B at Fallingbostel, Lower Saxony, where he spent the remainder of the war. There, on Christmas Day 1944, after refusing to work, he was struck on the head by a guard with his rifle butt and injured with enough severity to require an operation and insertion of a metal plate into his skull. In 1976, Nicola suffered a fatal stroke at the age of fifty-nine.

For the remainder of X Troop not already mentioned above, the rest of the war was spent in German prisoner of war camps. Sergeant John 'Big Jock' Walker, Sergeant Joe Shutt, Corporal Peter O'Brien, Corporal Derry Fletcher, Private Ernest Humphrey, Sapper Alan B. Ross and Sapper David L. Struthers were all confined in Stalag VIII-B – later renamed Stalag 344 – near Lamsdorf, Silesia, until liberated by Soviet troops. Lance-Corporal Doug E. Jones was held in Stalag IV-D, Torgau, Saxony, assigned to work camps until liberated when American and Soviet forces met on the Elbe River nearby in late April 1945. Lance-Corporal Doug Henderson was kept at Stalag VII-A – Germany's largest prisoner of war camp – at Moosburg an der Isar, Bavaria, until liberated on 29 April 1945 by Combat Command A of the US Army's 14th Armored Division. Corporal Philip Julian, Private Albert Samuels, Sapper R. Davidson and Sapper Owen D. J. Phillips were all held in Stalag IV-B, Mühlberg, Elbe, Brandenburg, until the arrival of the Red Army on 23 April 1945. Corporal J. E. Grice was a prisoner in Stalag VIII-A, Görlitz, Saxony, though I do not know if he was among the majority of the inmates that were forced to undertake one of the numerous 'long marches' of 1945 in freezing conditions as they were evacuated away from the advancing Red Army. Lance-

Corporal Jim E. Maher was liberated by British troops from Stalag 357, established on the site of the former Stalag XI-D at Oerbke, Lower Saxony. Lance-Corporal Harry Pexton was held in Stalag XI-A at Altengrabow, Saxony-Anhalt; Sapper 'Jock' W. Crawford, was an officer's orderly at Oflag XII-B, Hadamar, Hesse, and Driver Glyn Pryor, of the Corps of Royal Engineers, was held in Stalag XI-B at Fallingbostel, Lower Saxony, until the war's end.

From the captured crew of Pilot Officer Jack Wotherspoon's Whitley which had come down near the mouth of the Sele River on the night of the parachute drop, two men escaped back to Allied lines: Sergeant Frederick A. Southam (serial number 967920), who escaped from Campo 102, Aquila, following the Italian Armistice, reaching Allied Lines in October 1943, and W/O (formerly Sergeant) Henry J. Meddings, who likewise escaped from Campo 78 (Sulmona) following the September 1943 Italian surrender. Their pilot, Jack Wotherspoon (serial number 83283), was moved to Stalag Luft III near Sagan, Lower Silesia, during 1943 and remained there until the war's end.

Navigator aboard Hoad's Whitley, Acting Pilot Officer James Thomas Houghton (RAFVR no. 81685) was awarded the Distinguished Flying Cross on 23 September 1941, largely for his part in Operation Colossus. Houghton had joined the RAFVR on 30 June 1940 as a leading aircraftman before rising to acting pilot officer, the promotion to pilot officer being made substantive on 30 June 1941.

Flying Officer Alfred Denys Webb (serial number 43463), qualified gunnery leader of 78 Squadron, was awarded the Distinguished Flying Cross, announced in the *London Gazette* on 22 August 1941.

> Flying Officer Webb has completed twenty-six sorties, including the Colossus operation. Throughout this period, he has shown an outstanding desire to come to grips with the enemy by his keenness and willingness to take part in operations on every possible occasion. His skill as an Air Gunner and his example and leadership to his fellow Air Gunners have been of the utmost value.

Webb ended the war a squadron leader with a Bar to his DFC.

'Willie' Tait was awarded the DSO for his part in Operation Colossus. After the mission he joined 35 Squadron, flying Halifaxes and receiving further awards for valour before taking command of 78 Squadron and eventually the famous 617 Squadron, the Dambusters. It was Tait who led the raid that finally sank the German battleship *Tirpitz* in Operation Catechism on 12 November 1944. Tait had been made a temporary wing commander on 1 June 1942, made substantive on 1 March 1944. By the war's end, Wing Commander Tait had a third Bar to his DSO, the only RAF officer to be so decorated, and the DFC and Bar and two Mentions in Despatches. Tait died on 31 August 2007.

Another of the notable RAF officers connected with Operation Colossus was the reconnaissance specialist Adrian Warburton. By the beginning of 1944, despite his disregard for military formality and somewhat introverted nature, he had been promoted to the rank of wing commander and already awarded the Distinguished Service Order and Bar, the Distinguished Flying Cross and two Bars and an American Distinguished Flying Cross. He had, by that time, flown nearly 400 operations and claimed the destruction of nine enemy aircraft. On 1 April 1944, he was posted as the RAF Liaison Officer to the 7th Photographic Reconnaissance Group, US Eighth Army Air Force, at RAF Mount Farm in Oxfordshire. Eleven days later, he piloted one of two Lockheed F-5B photo-reconnaissance aircraft scheduled to photograph bombing targets near Munich, Germany. Although strictly speaking Warburton should not have been flying operations as he was the station liaison officer, he had been granted permission by the USAAF base commander, Lieutenant-Colonel Elliott Roosevelt, son of the President of the United States of America. The two aircraft separated approximately 100 miles north of Munich, planning to rendezvous after their respective tasks were complete and then proceed to Sardinia. Warburton never made the rendezvous and was posted as missing in action shortly thereafter.

Speculation about his fate was not resolved until 2002, when his remains were found in the cockpit of his aircraft buried nearly two metres below ground in a field near the Bavarian village of Egling an der Paar, thirty-four miles west of Munich. The aircraft remains showed bullet holes, suggesting that he had been shot down by a German fighter. Originally, Warburton's remains were assumed to be those of an American airman and he was buried in the Kaufering town cemetery, marked 'Unknown American Airman'. On 14 May 2003 he was reburied at the Dürnbach Commonwealth Military Cemetery.

The last of the veterans of Operation Colossus, Harry Pexton, passed away on 15 July 2016 at the age of ninety-nine. Harry had been a painter and decorator by trade before being called up into the North Staffordshire Regiment in March 1940 and soon volunteering for Special Services. Harry was imprisoned with his X Troop comrades in Campo 78 before being moved to Stalag XI-A east of the village of Altengrabow in Germany following the Italian armistice. There he spent the rest of the war until liberated in 1945 by an almost disastrous airborne mission. In fact, the drop that began the process of Pexton's liberation was, somewhat fittingly for a man who had taken part in the first British parachute raid of the war, the final Allied parachute drop in the European Theatre of Operations. Major Philip A. Worrall led six three-man teams of British, Commonwealth, French and United States paratroopers (designated the Eraser Group) on Operation Violet, designed to assure the protection of prisoners held in Stalag XI-A. Dropping on 25 April 1945, the men were part of the short-lived Special Allied Airborne Reconnaissance Force (SAARF) of experienced paratroopers, SOE operatives and Special Forces men which had been given the mandate of securing the safety of Allied prisoners of war in Germany. As the Third Reich collapsed there were fears of random or organised violence directed towards such prisoners by military units or civilians, as well as the prospect of starvation and disease if they were abandoned by the camp staff. The SAARF teams were charged with dropping near the camps to reconnoitre the situation, though Operation Violet was the only such parachute drop made.

The six teams were badly scattered during the drop and all members soon captured and interned within Stalag XI-A. However, Worrall still successfully negotiated the evacuation of prisoners with camp commandant Oberst Theodor Ochernal and his staff, and American trucks arrived on 3 May to begin taking prisoners away.

Harry Pexton returned to Britain and was demobilised in 1946 whereupon he returned to Manchester and continued his previous career as a painter and decorator. Happily married and with four children, he attended reunions of the veterans of Operation Colossus until he became the final survivor.

*

Although the military rationale for the operation remains a subject of some debate, the fact of the matter is that 'Colossus' provided the impetus for the continued development of Britain's parachute force and proof positive of its possible applications. Overshadowed by subsequent European operations by British paratroopers in such places as Sicily, Italy, Normandy, Arnhem and Germany, it remains something of a 'forgotten mission', not alone in this distinction, but unfairly ignored in the pantheon of British military expeditions of the Second World War. In truth it was an accumulation of ad hoc and inventive training instigated by an assortment of officers and men who were almost quintessentially British in their mix of maverick freethinkers and the more traditionally militarily orthodox. Operation Colossus did what it was supposed to do, and the small group of men who carried it out continued to show the fortitude in the face of adversity that had led them to X Troop in the first place – both those who escaped and fought again and those who spent over four long years behind Italian, and then German, barbed wire.

Appendix

X Troop

The men of X Troop, No. 11 SAS Battalion, who dropped into Italy on the night of 10 February 1941.

Major Trevor Allan Gordon 'Tag' Pritchard, Royal Welch Fusiliers
Captain Christopher Gerald Lea, Lancashire Fusiliers
Captain Gerrard Daly, Royal Engineers
Lieutenant Anthony Deane-Drummond, Royal Signals
2nd Lieutenant George Robert Paterson, Royal Engineers
2nd Lieutenant Arthur Geoffrey Jowett, Highland Light Infantry
Pilot Officer Ralph Henry Lucky, Royal Air Force Volunteer Reserve
Warrant Officer II Arthur William Albert 'Taff' Lawley, Royal Army
   Service Corps
Sergeant Percy Priestly Clements, Leicestershire Regiment
Sergeant Edward William 'Little Jock' Durie, Royal Engineers
Sergeant Joe Shutt, Leicestershire Regiment
Sergeant John 'Big Jock' Walker, Royal Signals
Corporal C. E. McD. 'Derry' Fletcher, Sherwood Foresters
   (Nottinghamshire and Derbyshire Regiment)
Corporal J. E. Grice, North Staffordshire Regiment
Corporal Philip Julian, Royal Engineers
Corporal Peter O'Brien, Royal Engineers
Lance-Corporal Harry Boulter, North Staffordshire Regiment
Lance-Corporal Douglas 'Flash' Henderson, Coldstream Guards
Lance-Corporal Doug E. Jones, Royal Engineers
Lance-Corporal Jim E. Maher, Royal Engineers
Lance-Corporal Harry Pexton, South Staffordshire Regiment
Lance-Corporal Harry Tomlin, Royal Engineers

Lance-Corporal Robert Brimer 'Mad Bob' Watson, Royal Engineers

Private Ernest Humphrey, Royal East Kent Regiment

Private Nicola Nastri (using the pseudonym John Tristan),
   Oxfordshire and Buckinghamshire Light Infantry

Private Albert Samuels, East Lancashire Regiment

Sapper 'Jock' W. Crawford, Royal Engineers

Sapper R. Davidson, Royal Engineers

Sapper Alf Parker, Royal Engineers

Sapper James Parker, Royal Engineers

Sapper Owen D. J. Phillips, Royal Engineers

Driver Glyn Pryor, Royal Engineers

Sapper Alan B. Ross, Royal Engineers

Sapper David L. Struthers, Royal Engineers

Fortunato Picchi (using the pseudonym Private Pierre Dupont),
   Special Operations Executive

Notes

Chapter One: 'We ought to have ... 5,000 parachute troops'

1. Prime Minister to General Ismay, 6 June 1940. Winston Churchill, *The Second World War*, Vol. II, p. 217.
2. The Independent Companies are frequently confused with the later 'Auxiliary Units', also formed and commanded by Gubbins to operate as 'stay behind' guerrilla units for resistance-style warfare in the event of a German invasion of Great Britain.
3. Colville, Jock, *The Fringes of Power: Downing Street Diaries 1939–1943*, p. 152.
4. Martel, Gordon (ed.), *The Origins of the Second World War Reconsidered: A. J. P. Taylor and the Historians*, p. 67.
5. Airborne Assault Museum, this article, updated by Tony Hibbert in 2009, is reproduced on the Paradata website with kind permission of Max Arthur – author of *Men of the Red Beret*; www.paradata.org.uk/article/extended-biography-tony-hibbert.
6. TNA WO 193/27, 'Creation of a Parachute Corps', from General Staff MO1 to MO7, 4 June 1940.
7. Prime Minister to General Ismay, 22 June 1940. https://www.paradata.org.uk/article/churchills-letter.
8. TNA, CAB 65/7/76, War Cabinet Conclusions WM (40) 181, 25 June 1940, quoted in Timothy Neil Jenkins, *The Evolution of British Airborne Warfare: A Technological Perspective*, p. 63.
9. Harry Tomlin interview, Imperial War Museum, www.iwm.org.uk/collections/item/object/80016074.
10. Deane-Drummond, Anthony, *Arrows of Fortune*, p. 3.
11. Downing, Taylor, *Night Raid: The True Story of the First Victorious British Para Raid of WWII*, p. 57.
12. Quoted in Steers, Howard J., 'Raiding The Continent: The Origins of British Special Service Forces', p. 89.
13. Hearn, Peter, *Flying Rebel*, p. 114.
14. Following Jackson's move from command of 11 SAS Battalion, he returned to his parent service, the Royal Tank Regiment. In the *London Gazette* dated 28 January 1949 there is the following entry: 'R.T.R. Major

C. I. A. Jackson (serial number 23822) is dismissed the service by sentence of General Court Martial, 20th October 1948.'

15. Though the inventor's name was 'Irvin' his company and subsequent parachute were named 'Irving', reputedly after a secretary mistakenly added the letter 'g' to correspondence and nobody bothered to correct it thereafter.

16. Hearn, *Flying Rebel*, p. 115.

17. The 264 Squadron Defiant, piloted by Flying Officer E. G. Barwell, was forced to ditch on 30 May after engaging German fighters over Dunkirk. As the aircraft went down Williams climbed out of the turret before they hit the Channel and was thrown clear. Barwell was briefly trapped inside the cockpit as the Defiant sank but managed to free himself and struggle to the surface where he found Williams unconscious, supporting him until they were picked up by the Royal Navy.

18. Max Arthur, *Lost Voices of The Royal Air Force*. Harry Ward was later awarded the Air Force Cross for 'flying though not in active operations against the enemy' on 11 June 1942 and posted to the staff of the Army's 1st Airborne Division. Ward finished the war as a squadron leader at the headquarters of 38 Group at Netheravon. He died on 24 July 2000, aged ninety-seven.

19. Deane-Drummond, Anthony, *Return Ticket*, p. 10.

20. Unpublished wartime memoir of Flight Lieutenant Denis Hornsey, DFC, held in the Department of Documents, Imperial War Museum, London.

21. Ettore Zavattoni was among those Italian internees destined for prison in Canada aboard the SS *Arandora Star* when it was torpedoed by *U47* on 2 July 1940; Zavattoni was one of the 805 people killed in the sinking. The popular and perennially effervescent Loreto Santarelli was interned until eventual release on medical grounds. Despite resistance from some staff, he was re-employed at the Savoy but had been physically broken by his period behind bars and died of a heart attack on 11 October 1944.

22. www.sis.gov.uk/our-history.html.

23. In August 1941, SO3 was merged with SO2, and eventually SO1 would be split off entirely and become the independent Political Warfare Executive.

24. Dalton published a diary-like account of his time with Italian forces in 1919 entitled *With British Guns in Italy*, dedicated to 'the high cause of Anglo-Italian friendship and understanding'.

25. Dalton, Hugh, *The Second World War Diary of Hugh Dalton, 1939–1943*, p. 128.

26. Moore, B., and K. Fedorowich,, *The British Empire and its Italian Prisoners of War, 1940–1947*, p. 107.

Chapter Two: **Training**

1. Harold Nelson Tomlin interview, Imperial War Museum, www.iwm.org. uk/collections/item/object/80016074.
2. National Archives, 'Cabinet Office: Minister of Defence Secretariat Records', CAB 120/262, Minute to Churchill by Admiral Keyes, 27 July 1940.
3. RAF Air Staff Note, 'Present Situation in Respect of the Development of Parachute Training', Appendices to Enclosure 5, 12 August 1940.
4. 'Lord Lovat talks about Commando training', Moray Firth Radio; www. ambaile.org.uk.
5. Harry Tomlin interview.
6. Lander would later take command of 21st Independent Company (Pathfinders) and be killed in action during the fighting for Primosole Bridge, Sicily, during Operation Husky on 13 July 1943, aged forty-seven.
7. Wings were given royal approval by the King on 20 December 1940, awarded four days later at the Central Landing Establishment. Finally, on 27 December, the official authorisation came in Army Council Instruction 1589. Prior to this, qualified military parachutists wore the GQ parachute pin badge. Information courtesy of Sam Stead, Airborne Museum.
8. Deane-Drummond, Anthony, *Return Ticket*, p. 8.
9. 'No Car for a Prince', www.paradata.org.uk/article/no-car-prince; reproduced from *Pegasus Journal*, Vol. 1, No. 4, January 1947.
10. 'A "Tiger's" Account of the First Paratroop Operation and its Consequences', by 2564415 Sergeant P. Clements, *The Green Tiger, The Records of The Leicestershire Regiment*, Vol. 22, No. 6, May 1944, pp. 100–2.

Chapter Three: **The Target**

1. Grassini, Laura, 'Water resources management and territorial development: Technological changes in Apulia during the post-unification period', pp. 95–6.
2. General Ismay to Prime Minister, 8 January 1941, 'Operation COLOSSUS in Italy', PREM 3/100.
3. 'Operation Instruction No. 1, Operation Colossus, 25 January 1941', National Archives, WO 193/798.
4. Harry Tomlin interview.
5. Lt.-Col. J. F. Rock, 'The Italian Parachute Raid', *Royal Engineers Journal*, June 1942.
6. This is the most accepted list of the personnel attached as reserves although 'Operation Order 1' dated 25 January lists the reserves as a total of four men: 2nd Lieutenant Davies, Lance-Corporal Allen (2003936), Lance-Corporal G. Jones (1875896) and Private Coult.

(4975689), all 'subject to accommodation in aircraft being available. O.C. C.L.E. may authorise the sending of reserves.' Operation Instruction No. 1, Operation Colossus, 25 January 1941; '"Colossus": destruction of bridge in South Italy by paratroops from Malta', National Archives WO 193/798.

7. Major Tony Hibbert's Account of early days with No 2 Commando and 11 SAS Battalion. https://www.paradata.org.uk/article/major-tony-hibberts-account-early-days-no-2-commando-and-11-sas-battalion.

8. National Archives, DEFE 2/152.

9. Roche would later rise to squadron leader and relinquish his commission in 1954.

10. National Archives, DEFE 2/152.

11. Gino Antonio Lucovich died suddenly of pneumonia in 1920.

12. Deane-Drummond, *Return Ticket*, p. 9.

13. Sub-Lieutenant Peter John Hoad was on attachment to the RAF from HMS *Daedalus* – one of the primary shore airfields of the Fleet Air Arm – having been made a sub-lieutenant for special duties on 15 June 1940. He took part in several long-distance raids over Germany and Italy as an observer aboard a Whitley of 78 Squadron and was involved in a crash landing towards the end of 1940. Not long after his part in Operation Colossus was completed, Hoad was killed at the age of twenty-two, along with all of his crew. On 27 March 1941 while Hoad acted as observer aboard Whitley Z6470, which was taking part in a raid on Düsseldorf, the bomber was intercepted and shot down by a Bf 110 night-fighter captained by Oberfeldwebel Gerhard Herzog of Nachtjagdgeschwader 1.

14. Hornsey, Denis, '"Here Today – Bomb Tomorrow", Private Papers of Flight Lieutenant D. G. Hornsey, DFC', Imperial War Museum.

15. www.102ceylonsquadron.co.uk/memWallyLashbrookOperationColossus.html.

16. Guncotton – nitrocellulose, a highly flammable compound formed by nitrating cellulose through exposure to nitric acid – was formed into a white fibrous 'slab'. Despite not being as effective as TNT, it could stand a considerable force or blow before exploding, ensuring safety in transport and making it perfect for paratroop use. To assist the detonator in firing prepared guncotton, a small hole approximately 1½ inches in diameter was left in the centre of each slab into which a primer was fitted, the detonator, in turn, fitting into a hole in the primer.

17. Later the Mk 1 was replaced by the now more familiar all-metal construction Mk 1T.

18. Deane-Drummond, *Return Ticket*, p. 11.

19. Chiefs of Staff Committee: Meeting to be held on Thursday 6th February 1941. Operation 'Colossus'. The War Office, 5 February 1941; National Archives WO 193/798.

Chapter Four: **Malta**

1. Lashbrook, Wally, 'Some Anxious Moments in World War Two', unpublished memoir.
2. Raymond Foxall, *The Guinea Pigs*, p. 47.
3. Hornsey, Denis, 'Here Today – Bomb Tomorrow'.
4. Lashbrook, 'Some Anxious Moments in World War Two'.
5. Deane-Drummond, *Return Ticket*, p. 13
6. www.telegraph.co.uk/news/uknews/1430110/RAFs-wartime-daredevil-finally-laid-to-rest.html.
7. Deane-Drummond, *Return Ticket*, p. 23.
8. Harry Tomlin interview.
9. Email from Tony Chapman, Ralph Chapman's only son, 21 November 2018.

Chapter Five: **The Raid**

1. Lashbrook, *Some Anxious Moments in World War Two*.
2. Lashbrook, *Some Anxious Moments in World War Two*.
3. Deane-Drummond, *Return Ticket*, p. 16.
4. 'A "Tiger's" Account', pp. 100–2.
5. Besagni, Olive, 'The Hill, 1993', *Backhill, Rivista Della Communita' Italiana, London*, p. 13.
6. Deane-Drummond, *Arrows of Fortune*, p. 17.
7. J. F. Rock, 'The Italian Parachute Raid', *Royal Engineers Journal*, June 1942.
8. The Syko code had been broken by the Germans at the beginning of 1940 and read concurrently both by them and their Italian allies since then.
9. Deane-Drummond, *Return Ticket*, p. 19. Captain Lea agreed to sign the certificate, if produced by the Italian, though he could never recall after the war whether he applied his signature to any such piece of paper.

Chapter Six: **Manhunt**

1. 'A "Tiger's" Account'.
2. The return to Mildenhall took a course via Marseilles and Orfordness. At 1000 hours on 18 February Whitley 'J' commanded by Sub-Lieutenant Hoad made a forced landing with undercarriage up in a field near Swanton Morley without any casualties. His gunner, Webb, was subsequently recommended for the DFC on 26 June 1941 for his part in Operation Colossus.
3. www.102ceylonsquadron.co.uk/memWallyLashbrookOperationColossus.html.
4. Deane-Drummond, *Return Ticket*, pp. 24–5.
5. Deane-Drummond, *Return Ticket*, p. 27.
6. Deane-Drummond, *Return Ticket*, p. 29.

7. Deane-Drummond, *Arrows of Fortune*, p. 26. Raymond Foxall's book *The Guinea Pigs* has a different version of the capture of Pritchard's group. I have chosen to go with verifiable eyewitness accounts to piece together the exact events, relying heavily on Deane-Drummond's two memoirs, both similar but with differences in the details. I have found no evidence that the men were attached to a ball and chain, nor that they were assembled before two local dignitaries. That is not to say that these events definitely did not occur, but in the absence of clear proof, I have omitted them and followed Deane-Drummond's timeline of events.

8. Niall Cherry, *Striking Back* p. 91.

9. 'A "Tiger's" Account'.

10. After the end of the Second World War Bellomo was arrested, tried and subsequently shot on 11 September 1945 for alleged 'war crimes' by the British for his involvement in the shooting of two escaping British officers from the prison camp of Torre Tresca. The trial and verdict – which involved questionable testimony that changed during the trial and political machinations by other senior Italian military and government officials keen to obscure their own actions during the war – have been considered dubious at best. Bellomo was the only Italian officer so executed by the Allies.

11. Stefani News Agency, quoted and paraphrased in newspapers worldwide on 15 February 1941.

12. Besagni, Olive, 'The Hill, 1993', p. 13.

13. Harry Tomlin interview.

14. Harry Tomlin interview.

15. Deane-Drummond, *Return Ticket*, p. 38.

16. Harry Tomlin interview.

17. A "Tiger's" Account'.

18. Attachment to letter from Major P. M. Lee, 300 F.S.S., to Captain C. Role No. 1 S.C.I., 8 August 1944.

19. Archivio INSMLI (Istituto Nazionale per la Storia del Movimento di Liberazione in Italia). http://www.ultimelettere.it/?page_id=52&ricerca=89&doc=55.

20. *The Times*, 15 April 1941.

Chapter Seven: **Aftermath**

1. Airborne Assault Museum, www.paradata.org.uk/media/208.

2. 'War Cabinet and Cabinet: Chiefs of Staff Committee: Minutes', National Archives, CAB-79-9-13.

3. Sir Roger Keyes to Winston Churchill, 13 February, NA, Prime Minister's Office: Operational Correspondence and Papers, PREM 3/100.

4. https://www.paradata.org.uk/event/tragino-operation-colossus.

5. *New York Times*, 15 February 1941.

6. Circular No. 298, dated 10 March 1941, from General Commanding MSVN.
7. National Archives DEFE 2/152.
8. This last paragraph carried a handwritten notation next to it, by an unknown author, with the words 'This fact has already been fully revealed by the Press.'
9. Records of the Special Operations Executive: 'Operation Colossus: landing parachutists for sabotage of bridges', HS 6/793.
10. Winston Churchill, *The Second World War*, Vol. III, pp. 597–8.
11. Hearn, *Flying Rebel*, p. 124.
12. Jack Benham was in turn superseded by Squadron Leader Maurice Newnham during July 1941. Benham was killed in action on 28 January 1942 as a wing commander while acting as despatcher aboard Whitley Z6728 of 138 Squadron, lost while engaged in SOE operations over Belgium.
13. Strange later returned to RAF transport concerns and in December 1943 was posted to No. 46 Group as Wing Commander, Operations. He assisted in the planning for Operation Overlord and administered a series of Temporary Staging Posts during the Allied advance into Germany. He retired in 1945, returning to his love of agriculture while also maintaining links to civil aviation. He passed away in 1966 at the age of seventy-five.
14. Harry Tomlin interview.
15. 'Account of Escape of Lieutenant A. J. Deane-Drummond, Royal Corps of Signals (Seconded to 11 SAS Bn.)', MI9/S/P.G. (Italy) 801. Sourced from the website www.paradata.com.
16. 'Account of Escape of Lieutenant A. J. Deane-Drummond'.
17. Steptoe, as a physician, was allowed to move freely about the camp and reportedly helped coordinate prisoners' escape attempts with the result that he was finally placed in solitary confinement until released in a prisoner exchange in 1943. Years later he became a specialist obstetrician and gynaecologist and a pioneer of fertility treatment.
18. Deane-Drummond, *Arrows of Fortune*, p. 48.
19. Ibid., p. 52.
20. Eric Newby, *Love and War in the Apennines*, p. 31. Newby escaped confinement after the Armistice but was recaptured in 1944 and sent to camps in Czechoslovakia and Germany for the rest of the war.
21. www.rafmuseum.org.uk/blog/the-extraordinary-story-of-ralph-henry-lucky.
22. Harry Tomlin interview.
23. 'A "Tiger's" Account'.
24. 'Private Alf Parker', article submitted by his son John Parker; www.pegasusarchive.org/pow/alf_parker.htm.
25. Ibid.
26. Harry Tomlin interview.

27. www.rafmuseum.org.uk/blog/the-extraordinary-story-of-ralph-henry-lucky.

28. Ibid.

Chapter Eight: **The Reckoning**

1. DCO to DMC Air Ministry 28 March 1941, K 13/21.

2. Alessandro Affortunati, *Di morire non mi importa gran cosa: Fortunato Picchi e l'Operazione 'Colossus'*, Comune di Carmignano, Pentalinea, Prato, 2004.

3. Fortunato Picchi alias Peter Dupont, National Archives, DEFE 2/1345.

4. Fortunato Picchi alias Peter Dupont, National Archives, DEFE 2/1345.

5. Once again, Lucky's rank is an interesting conundrum. The citation names him as flight lieutenant, although the *London Gazette* of 5 July 1946 records that Flight Lieutenant (temp) Ralph Lucky, MC, MBE, was only granted the rank of flight lieutenant (war substantive) on 9 June 1946.

6. 'Recommendation for Award for Pritchard, Trevor Allan Gordon. Rank: Captain', National Archives, WO 373/93/19.

7. 'Recommendation for Award for Pritchard, Trevor Allan Gordon. Rank: Major', National Archives WO 373/102/861.

8. www.paradata.org.uk/people/anthony-j-deane-drummond.

9. National Archives, WO 373/63/40. Interestingly, the Special Operations Executive personnel file on George Robert Paterson (HS 9/1152/6) remains confidential and closed until 2020.

10. 'Recommendation for Award for Jowett, Arthur Geoffrey. Rank: Lieutenant', National Archives, WO 373/103.

11. 'Recommendation for Award for Lea, Christopher Gerald. Rank: Captain', National Archives, WO 373/100/559.

12. 'Recommendation for Award for Clements, P. P. Rank: Sergeant', National Archives, WO 373/94/268.

13. 'Recommendation for Award for Watson, Robert Brimer. Rank: Lance-Corporal', National Archives, WO 373/100/801.

14. 'Recommendation for Award for Boulter, Harry. Rank: Lance-Corporal. Service No: 5047114. Regiment: Special Air Service', National Archives, WO 373/96/124.

15. 'Recommendation for Award for Daly, Gerrard Francis Kirkpatrick', National Archives, WO 373/102/389.

Bibliography

Websites

102 (Ceylon) Squadron: http://www.102ceylonsquadron.co.uk
51 Squadron. https://www.51squadron.com/main
Airborne Assault Museum: http://www.paradata.org.uk
Airborne Engineers Association: http://www.airbornesappers.org.uk
Harold Nelson Tomlin interview, Imperial War Museum: http://www.iwm.org.
  uk/collections/item/object/80016074
Livingstone, Nicolas, 'Before Tempsford: Royal Air Force operations for SIS
  and SOE 1940–1942', 2016: https://beforetempsford.org.uk/
Messines, The Worcester Regiment: http://www.worcestershireregiment.com/
  h_messines.php
'Lord Lovat talks about Commando training', 1980, *Moray Firth Radio,
  Ambaile, Highland History and Culture*: http://www.ambaile.org.uk
'No Car For A Prince', *Airborne Assault, Paradata*: www.paradata.org.uk
RAF Museum: https://www.rafmuseum.org.uk
'The Aqueduct', *The Apulian Aqueduct*: www.naplesldm.com/apulaq.php
The Pegasus Archive: http://www.pegasusarchive.org

Articles and Documents

The Green Tiger, The Records of the Leicestershire Regiment
Allan, Stuart, 'Commando Country: Special training centres in the Scottish
  Highlands, 1940–1945', PhD thesis, University of Edinburgh, 2011
Barber, Martyn, *Stonehenge World Heritage Site Landscape Project: Stonehenge
  Aerodrome and the Stonehenge Landscape*, Research Report Series No. 07-
  2014, English Heritage, 2014
Bassett, James A., 'Past Airborne Employment', *Military Affairs*, No. 4, 1948,
  pp. 206–16
Besagni, Olive, 'The Hill, 1993', *Backhill, Rivista Della Communita' Italiana*,
  London
Franzinelli, Mimmo, *Il tribunale del Duce*, Mondadori, 2017

Grassini, Laura, 'Water resources management and territorial development: Technological changes in Apulia during the post-unification period', Bari: Polytechnic University of Bari, 2012, Vol. 11

Hargreaves, Andrew, Patrick Rose, and Matthew C. Ford, *Allied Fighting Effectiveness in North Africa and Italy, 1942–1945*, Brill, 2014

Jenkins, Timothy Neil, *The Evolution of British Airborne Warfare: A Technological Perspective*, Birmingham, University of Birmingham, 2013

Margry, Karel, 'Tragino 1941, Britain's First Paratroop Raid', *After The Battle*, No. 81, London, 1993

Powell, Matthew Lee, 'Army Co-Operation Command and Tactical Air Power Development in Britain 1940–1943', PhD thesis, University of Birmingham, 2013

Rock, Lt.-Col. J. F., 'The Italian Parachute Raid', *Royal Engineers Journal*, June 1942

Sadkovich, James J., 'Understanding Defeat: Reappraising Italy's Role in World War II', *Journal of Contemporary History*, Vol. 24, No. 1., 1989, pp. 27–61

Steers, Howard J. T., 'Raiding The Continent: The Origins of British Special Service Forces', thesis in Military Art and Science, US Army Command and General Staff College, Fort Leavenworth, Kansas, 1980

Books

The Air Force List April 1940, London, HMSO, 1940

Affortunati, Alessandro, *Di morire non mi importa gran cosa; Fortunato Picchi e l'Operazione 'Colossus'*, Prato, Pentalinea Comune di Carmignano, Pentalinea, 2004

Arthur, Max, *Lost Voices of the Royal Air Force*, London, Hodder, 2005

——, *Men of the Red Beret*, Hutchinson, 1990

Bailey, Roderick, *Target: Italy*, London, Faber & Faber, 2014

Cherry, Niall, *Striking Back*, Warwick, Helion, 2009

Churchill, Winston, *The Second World War*: Vol. II, *The Gathering Storm*, Vol. III, *The Grand Alliance*, London, Haughton Mifflin, 1949.

Colville, Jock, *The Fringes of Power: Downing Street Diaries 1939–1943*, London, Hodder & Stoughton, 1985

Dalton, Hugh (ed. Ben Pimlott), *The Second World War Diary of Hugh Dalton, 1940–45*, London, Jonathan Cape, 1986

Deane-Drummond, Anthony, *Return Ticket*, London, Popular Book Club, 1952

——, *Arrows of Fortune*, Barnsley, Leo Cooper, 1992

Downing, Taylor, *Night Raid: The True Story of the First Victorious British Para Raid of WWII*, Hachette, 2013

Foot, M. R. D., *SOE: The Special Operations Executive 1940–46*, London, BBC, 1984

Foxall, Raymond, *The Guinea Pigs*, London, Robert Hale, 1981

Bibliography

Hearn, Peter, *Flying Rebel*, London, HMSO, 1994

Hornsey, Denis, '"Here Today – Bomb Tomorrow", private papers of Flight Lieutenant D. G. Hornsey DFC', unpublished, Imperial War Museum, Documents 4559, 1950

Hutton, Colin, *Official Secret*, London, Crown Publishers, 1961

Kellas, Arthur, *Down To Earth (or another bloody cock-up): A parachute subaltern's story*, Pentland Press, 1990

Lashbrook, Wally, 'Some Anxious Moments in World War Two', unpublished memoir, available on the 102 Squadron website www.102ceylonsquadron. co.uk/memWallyLashbrooknotes.html

Martel, Gordon (ed.), *The Origins of the Second World War Reconsidered: A. J. P. Taylor and the Historians*, London, Routledge, 1999

McDonald, Paul, *Malta's Great Siege & Adrian Warburton DSO DFC*, Barnsley, Pen & Sword Aviation, 2015

Moore, B., and K. Fedorowich, *The British Empire and its Italian Prisoners of War, 1940–1947*, London, Palgrave Macmillan, 2002

Newby, Eric, *Love and War in the Apennines*, London, Hodder & Stoughton, 1971

Pettinelli, Diego, *L'Acquedotto Pugliese*, Bari, Gius. Laterza & Figli, 1939

Saunders, Hilary St George, *The Red Beret: The Story of The Parachute Regiment at War, 1940–1945*, London, Michael Joseph, 1950

Williams, George K., *Biplanes and Bombsights*, Air University Press, Maxwell Air Force Base, Alabama, 1999

Wylie, Neville, *The Politics and Strategy of Clandestine War*, London, Routledge, 2012

Index of X Troop Personnel

Boulter, Harry, 55, 79, 88, 95, 102, 112–13, 115–17, 134, 213–14, 220

Chapman, Ralph, 26, 38, 40, 55, 88–90
Clements, Percy, 45–6, 55, 88, 97, 117, 131–2, 168, 170, 179, 187, 209–11, 220
Crawford, Jock, 56, 88, 117, 216, 221

Daly, Gerrard, 54–5, 58, 79, 88–9, 96, 100, 102, 104, 107–8, 110, 112, 131, 141–6, 151, 182, 192, 214–15, 220
Davidson, R., 51, 56, 88, 215, 221
Deane-Drummond, Anthony, 15, 33, 40–1, 44, 54–5, 63, 72–74, 80, 88, 92–7, 99, 101–3, 105, 106, 108–9, 113–14, 116, 121, 124, 128, 136–7, 146, 158, 168–75, 177–9, 200, 203–5, 208, 220
Dennis, William, 55, 68, 100
Dupont, Pierre (see Picchi, Fortunato)
Durie, Edward, 55, 88, 96, 101, 211, 220

Fletcher, Derry, 45, 55, 88, 117, 215, 220

Grice, J. E., 55, 88, 117, 215, 220

Henderson, Douglas, 56, 88, 113, 121, 125, 127, 215, 220
Humphrey, Ernest, 56, 79, 88, 215, 221

Jones, Doug, 11, 35, 56, 88, 100, 107, 113, 137, 215, 220
Jowett, Arthur, 54–5, 88, 96, 103, 105, 117, 131–2, 146, 179, 207–8, 220
Julian, Philip, 55, 79, 88, 113, 215, 220

Lawley, Arthur, 13–14, 55, 88, 95, 97–100, 113, 121, 124, 170, 179, 187–8, 209, 211, 220
Lea, Christopher, 33, 54–5, 88, 103, 105, 117, 129–31, 146, 169–71, 207–8, 220
Lucky, Ralph, 61–3, 74, 76, 88, 103, 117–18, 131–3, 136, 138, 140, 144–5, 168, 170, 173, 175–7, 189–91, 200–1, 220
Lucovich, Raoul (see Lucky, Ralph)

Maher, Jim, 56, 88, 117, 214, 216, 220

Nastri, Nicola, 56, 88, 99, 113, 123–8, 133, 138–40, 155, 214–15, 221

O'Brien, Peter, 55, 88, 117, 215, 220

Parker, Alf, 56, 88, 182, 186–7, 212, 221

Parker, James, 56, 88, 117, 212–13, 221

Paterson, George, 54–5, 88, 96, 100, 104, 107–9, 117, 129, 134, 175, 177, 190, 192–3, 205–7, 220

Pexton, Harry, 40, 45, 56, 88, 98, 117, 169, 216, 218, 220

Phillips, Owen, 56, 88, 215, 221

Picchi, Fortunato, 28–9, 32, 59–60, 63, 74, 76, 88, 96, 103, 113, 121, 125–8, 133, 135–8, 146–9, 159–61, 195, 197–200, 215, 221

Pritchard, Trevor, 33, 44, 53–7, 71–2, 76, 81, 84, 87–8, 96, 98, 102–4, 108–10, 112–14, 117, 121–31, 133, 136, 140, 146, 150, 167–8, 170, 175, 177, 179, 190–1, 194, 201–3, 220

Pryor, Glyn, 56, 88, 216, 221

Ross, Alan, 56, 88, 108, 117, 215, 221

Samuels, Albert, 56, 215, 221

Shutt, Joe, 45, 55, 88, 215, 220

Struthers, David, 56, 79, 88, 117, 215, 221

Tomlin, Harry, 14–15, 33, 53, 56, 88, 102, 141, 155, 179, 188–9, 220

Tristan, John (*see* Nastri, Nicola)

Walker, John, 55, 65–6, 88, 101, 117, 215, 220

Watson, Robert, 9, 56, 88, 107–9, 117, 169, 212, 221, 228

General Index

Ardley, W.G., 47–8, 50–1, 104, 193

Bari, 48, 50, 130, 156, 158
Bellomo, Nicola, 130, 133
Brindisi, 48, 50, 156, 202
British Army Regiments:
  6th Royal Tank, 21, 166
  Derbyshire, 220
  East Lancashire, 221
  Glider Pilot, 167, 186
  Highland Light Infantry, 55, 220
  Leicestershire, 45, 117, 131,
    209–10, 220, 229
  London, 61
  Monmouthshire, 42
  North Staffordshire, 213, 218, 220
  Nottinghamshire and Derbyshire,
    220
  Parachute, 209, 210
  Royal East Kent, 221
  South Staffordshire, 220
  Worcestershire, 61

Calitri, 1–2, 50, 91, 94–5, 101, 103,
  106, 108, 114–15, 117, 129–34,
  208
Capodichino (Italian airfield), 140,
  144–5, 203
Carter, Hugh, 42
Cleasby-Thompson, Peter, 44–5, 55

Dalton, Hugh, 29–31
Dill, John, 3, 73

Evans, Ralph, 35–6

Foggia, 67, 87, 105–6, 156
Fort Bravetta, 147–8

Gubbins, Colin, 4, 30, 161

Harvey, Leslie, 41–2, 71, 154, 165
Hoad, Peter, 66, 88, 102, 105, 107,
  216
Hornsey, Denis, 27, 66–7, 78
Houghton, James, 66, 102, 216

Ismay, Hastings, 2–3, 11–12, 52,
  153, 162, 164

Jackson, Charles, 21–2, 43, 52–3, 72,
  161–2, 166
Jebb, Gladwyn, 30, 160–1

Keyes, Roger, 13, 31, 34–5, 50–1,
  59–60, 72, 76–7, 146, 154, 162,
  196, 200, 202

Lantieri, Florence, 28, 149, 199
Lashbrook, Wally, 66, 68, 79–80, 88,
  92, 94–5, 118–20
Lindsay, Martin, 16
Luqa (RAF airfield), 79, 81–2, 87, 94,
  105, 118

Meddings, Henry, 66, 216

Norman, Nigel, 20, 42, 64–5, 77–8, 81, 87, 118, 150, 156, 163, 165–6

Picchi, Jacopina, 28, 198–9
Prisoner of War camps:
  Campo 5 (Forte di Gavi), 177, 179, 189, 202, 205, 214
  Campo 17 (Rezzanello), 207
  Campo 27 (San Romano), 175–7, 202, 205
  Campo 54 (Fara Nel Sabina), 213
  Campo 78 (Sulmona), 145, 157, 167–9, 170–1, 173, 180, 181–9, 202–5, 207–9, 212–13, 216, 218
  Campo di Lavoro 102 (Aquila), 169, 212–13, 216
  Oflag VIII-F, 207
  Oflag IX-A/Z, 208
  Oflag XII-B, 216
  Stalag IV-A, 215
  Stalag IV-B, 189, 215
  Stalag IV-D, 215
  Stalag, VII-A, 212, 215
  Stalag VIII-A, 215
  Stalag VIII-B, 215
  Stalag XI-A, 216, 218
  Stalag XI-B, 215, 216
  Stalag XVII, 189
  Stalag (Luft) I, 190, 202
  Stalag (Luft) III, 207, 216
  Stalag 357, 216
Poggioreale (Naples Central Prison), 117, 134–6, 139, 142–3, 145

Quilter, Raymond, 36, 41

RAF Squadrons:
  24 Squadron, 18
  35 Squadron, 216
  51 Squadron, 65–6, 68

69 Squadron, 82, 118
78 Squadron, 27, 66, 68, 216–17, 225
102 Squadron, 231
115 Squadron, 62
138 Squadron, 227
148 Squadron, 81
608 Squadron, 82
617 Squadron, 217
810 Squadron, 177
Ringway (RAF airfield), 9, 16–17, 20–4, 26, 33–7, 40–2, 44, 46, 56, 60–1, 65–6, 68, 71–2, 74–6, 98, 146, 154, 157, 161, 163, 210
Rock, John, 15–16, 20, 22, 24, 27, 34–6, 41–2, 53–4, 104, 146, 161, 166–7

Southam, Frederick, 66, 216
Strange, Louis, 17–20, 22–6, 34–6, 41–2, 44, 61, 155, 157, 161–6

Tait, James, 65–6, 68, 77, 81, 88, 92, 98, 101, 216–17
Taranto, 2, 29, 48, 50, 83, 156, 173, 180, 186
Tatton Park, 26–27, 34, 57–8, 64, 68, 71, 81, 100, 103
Tor Castle (Special Training Centre), 37–9, 162
Triumph, HMS, 73–4, 81, 84, 87, 106, 110, 112, 114, 142, 153–4, 194

Warburton, Adrian, 82–4, 95, 104, 120–1, 153, 194, 217
Webb, Alfred, 66, 79, 216
Williams, Bruce, 23–4, 66, 77, 94–5, 157, 165
Woods, Wilfrid, 74, 84, 153
Wotherspoon, Jack, 66, 88, 106, 153